Red, Blue & Purple America

Red, Blue & Purple America

The Future of Election Demographics

Ruy Teixeira

Editor

BROOKINGS INSTITUTION PRESS

Washington, D.C.

Library of Congress Cataloging-in-Publication data

Red, blue, and purple America : the future of election demographics / Ruy Teixeira, editor.

   p.   cm.

Includes bibliographical references and index.

  Summary: "Analyzes changing patterns of immigration, settlement, demography, family structure, and religion, describing trends and their impacts on 2008 politics and beyond. Lays out implications for public policy and shows how these trends have shaped the Red and Blue divisions and might break apart those blocs in new and surprising ways"—Provided by publisher.

  ISBN 978-0-8157-8316-9 (cloth : alk. paper) — ISBN 978-0-8157-8315-2 (pbk. : alk. paper)

  1. Party affiliation—United States. 2. Demographic transition—United States—Political aspects. 3. Political parties—United States. 4. Elections—United States. 5. Voting—United States. I. Teixeira, Ruy A.

  JK2271.R43 2008

  324.60973—dc22   2008027702

9 8 7 6 5 4 3 2 1

The paper used in this publication meets minimum requirements of the American National Standard for Information Sciences—Permanence of Paper for Printed Library Materials: ANSI Z39.48-1992.

Typeset in Minion

Composition by Circle Graphics
Columbia, Maryland

Printed by R. R. Donnelley
Harrisonburg, Virginia.

Contents

Family, Religion, and Generational Change

Red, Blue & Purple
America

Beyond Polarization?

THE FUTURE OF RED, BLUE, AND PURPLE AMERICA

RUY TEIXEIRA

Change is in the air. This fall we shall see if America takes the extraordinary step of electing its first African American president—an African American, moreover, whose mother was white, whose father was Kenyan, and who spent part of his childhood in Indonesia. The very fact that such an individual could be the nominee of a major political party says a great deal about how much change is occurring in the American electorate and how rapidly.

Although Barack Obama is the most visible sign of this change, many broad social trends underlie the transformation of today's electorate and make a candidate like Obama possible. Some groups, such as Hispanics and Asians, are growing rapidly; others, like the white working class, are in decline. Outer suburbs and exurbs are increasingly important and are a locus of exceptionally fast population growth. Population migration favors some states and regions at the expense of others. Immigration is changing the face of communities far from the coasts, deep in the South, and in America's heartland. Family structure is shifting, as married couple households with children decline and single and alternative households expand. Educational levels continue to rise, and the occupational structure of the country continues to shift away from manufacturing and unskilled work. Women play an increasingly strong role in every facet of the economy and society. A younger generation, whose attitudes are quite different from older generations and whose diversity is unprecedented, is on the rise. At the other end of the age structure, the baby boom generation is transforming the nature of the senior population.

The ranks of highly observant, white Christian evangelical denominations are increasing, but so are the ranks of the secular, the highly nonobservant, and those who practice nontraditional religions.

These trends present the political parties with huge challenges in forging and maintaining majority electoral coalitions and in governing effectively to meet the needs of rapidly changing constituencies. But the phenomenon of demographic and geographic changes reshaping American politics and public policy is nothing new. Indeed, the evolution of American politics and policy since World War II has been intimately bound up with these kinds of change. Right after World War II, for example, the anticipated wave of returning soldiers led to passage of the GI Bill of Rights, which, among other things, paid the costs of higher education for GIs and provided them with low-interest, zero-down-payment home loans. These provisions, in turn, promoted the expansion of the public university system to accommodate the sudden influx of new students and accelerated the suburbanization of metropolitan areas as returning GIs used their loans to buy inexpensive houses in the suburbs. Suburbanization, in turn, promoted the development of the interstate highway system, which led, of course, to even more suburbanization.

The rapid advance of suburbanization in the years after the war was quite extraordinary. Between 1940 and 1950 the suburban share of the population increased from 15 percent to 23 percent, while cities' share was basically unchanging, at around 33 percent. By 1960 suburbs accounted for 31 percent of the total, with cities' share slightly declining, to 32 percent. By 1970 there were, for the first time, more suburban residents (38 percent) than city residents (31 percent), and by the 1990s suburban voters were casting the majority of ballots in national elections.[1]

Another important postwar development is the rise of the baby boom generation—the roughly 76 million Americans born between 1946 and 1964—the largest generation up to that point in American history. Boomers' attitudes toward everything—from the nature of authority, the roles of women and minorities, to, of course, American foreign policy and the Vietnam War—had tremendous effects on American society and politics. Indeed, all the various "movements" of the sixties—civil rights, women's liberation, environmental, gay liberation, antiwar, and so on—drew their shock troops from the ranks of the baby boomers and would have been inconceivable without the energies of that generation. So, too, would the raft of legislation—from the Civil Rights Act and other antidiscrimination statutes to the creation of the Environmental Protection Agency—that grew out of these movements.

Although all of these social movements were and are important, a special note should be made of the women's movement and the structural changes that propelled it. It was not so long ago (1950) that only about a third of adult women were in the workforce. But that figure rose to 38 percent in 1960, 43 percent in 1970, 52 percent in 1980, 58 percent in 1990, and 60 percent in 2000. Among twenty-five-to-thirty-four-year-old women—those who would be expected to leave the workforce after marriage—participation rates went up by an astonishing 42 percentage points between 1950 and 1998 (including a 21 percentage point increase during the 1970s alone).[2] As women entered the labor force, they also moved up within it. In 1970 less than 10 percent of medical students and 4 percent of law students were women.[3] By the early 1990s more than 40 percent of first-year law and medical students were women; today it is about 50 percent.[4] By the end of the twentieth century, 55 percent of all professionals were women.[5]

These structural changes reinforced shifting social norms about the role of women and led to the emergence of the gender gap, as women began to see the Democratic Party as the party most supportive of these changes. In 1964 women began to vote slightly more Democratic than men, and in 1968 and 1972 the trend grew. Then, after subsiding for the 1976 election (when the Republican candidate was the pro-choice, pro–equal rights Gerald Ford), it reappeared in force in 1980. According to the CBS/*New York Times* exit poll, men in 1980 supported Republican Ronald Reagan over Democrat Jimmy Carter by 55 to 36 percent, while women supported Reagan by only 47 to 45 percent. Gender gaps of that magnitude are now commonplace in American politics. In the 2000 presidential race, men supported Republican George Bush by 53 to 42 percent, but women supported Democrat Al Gore by 54 to 43 percent.[6]

Another critical change was dramatically increased levels of educational attainment. Incredible as it may seem today, in 1940 three-quarters of adults twenty-five years old and over were high school dropouts (or never made it as far as high school), and just 5 percent had a four-year college degree or higher. But educational credentials exploded in the postwar period. By 1960 the proportion of adults lacking a high school diploma was down to 59 percent; by 1980 it was less than a third; and by 2005 it was down to only 15 percent. Concomitantly, the proportion with a bachelor's degree or higher rose steadily, reaching 29 percent in 2005. Moreover, those with some college (but not a four-year degree) constituted another 25 percent of the population, making a total of 54 percent who had at least some college education.[7] Quite a change, this move from a country in which the typical adult was a high school dropout (more accurately, never even reached high school) to a country in which the typical adult not only has a high school diploma but some college as well. This shift had tremendous effects on the character and aspirations of voters, especially working-class voters.

Other demographic and geographic changes pushed the country in a very different direction from that of the baby boom–driven movements of the sixties. These changes were identified by Kevin Phillips in his 1969 book, *The Emerging Republican Majority*, and by Richard Scammon and Ben Wattenberg in their 1970 volume, *The Real Majority*. Among these changes were a growing middle class less dependent on unionized, blue-collar jobs; the movement of whites, especially working-class whites, to the suburbs in search of order, security, and living space; and the increasing population of the Sunbelt. These trends fed a reaction both against the excesses of the boomer-led movements and against the failures of the postwar liberal approach to government, which could not seem to cope with the great changes sweeping the nation.

Of course, demographic-geographic changes did not stop with those identified by Phillips and Scammon/Wattenberg. One obvious example: immigration. Since 1970 immigration flows have increased and become heavily dominated by immigrants from Latin America and, secondarily, Asia. By 1990 over a million immigrants a year were entering the country, and by 2000 that figure had increased to 1.5 million, with unauthorized immigrants starting to outnumber authorized immigrants. Since then that number has subsided to around 1.2 million, but countries of origin and high proportions of unauthorized immigrants remain the same.[8]

Immigration has hardly been the only structural trend reshaping American politics in the last several decades. Indeed, behind every political icon lionized by the press (since Scammon and Wattenberg introduced the "Dayton housewife" in their 1970 book) lies some recent demographic or geographic trend whose force is real, if poorly understood. Here are some examples from the last fifteen years of media-driven political discourse:

—Angry white men. This term rose to prominence around the 1994 election, when a Republican tsunami rolled over the U.S. Congress. Like most of these terms, it was never very precisely defined but appeared to refer primarily to blue-collar white men who were moving into the Republican camp. Little noticed in the brouhaha was the fact that blue-collar white men were becoming fewer: only a quarter of even non-college-educated white men had blue-collar jobs or worked in manufacturing.[9] More attention should have been paid to the huge transformations that had moved the bulk of less-skilled white men out of blue-collar occupations and into low-level white-collar and service jobs. If white men were angry and voting Republican, the real story was likely among white men with these jobs, not blue-collar ones.

—Soccer moms. The concept of angry white men gave way in the 1996 election to that of soccer moms. Soccer moms were generally thought of as college-educated suburban women with children who were moving in the Democratic direction. And certainly college-educated women were a growing group newly leaning Democratic (college-educated women tripled as a percentage of women in the years after 1970).[10] But most women in the suburbs were not college educated, and large numbers did not have children. These suburban women were much more important to the 1996 election than well-educated mothers driving their kids to soccer practice.

—Wired workers, office park dads. Both of these terms came into use in the run-up to the 2000 election and were attempts to label groups of voters who were allegedly becoming more conservative by dint of job trends—the increase in occupations involving computers and working in teams (wired workers) and the rise in office jobs for men and the concomitant decline in manufacturing jobs (office park dads). Remarkably fuzzy even by the standards of these catch phrases, the terms quickly fell into disuse due to their inability to explain anything about the 2000 election—or even general attitudes about government. But in their brief lives the terms still managed to muddy the waters considerably about what are, in fact, some very real trends in the occupational structure.

—Exurban voters. The 2002 election, which seemed to signal a sharp turn toward the right in American politics, saw the rise of yet another political icon: the exurban voter, famously encapsulated by commentator David Brooks in an influential *New York Times* op-ed, "For Democrats, Time to Meet the Exurban Voter." In that article Brooks argued that the rise of America's exurbs—those fast-growing counties at the fringes of metropolitan areas populated by legions of conservative white voters—contributed mightily to the GOP's success in that election and would continue to do so in the future, putting the Democrats on the demographic ropes, so to speak. But while the growth of exurbs is real, the true significance of the trend can only be assessed as part of the overall story about America's changing suburbs—a story that includes very important changes taking place in closer-in suburbs, the relatively small size of exurbs compared to other types of suburb, and the tendency of exurbs themselves to become less conservative as their rapid growth brings higher population density and a more cosmopolitan and diverse population. These subtleties were lost in the media hype about this new category of voter.

—White evangelicals. In 2004 it was white evangelicals' turn to be anointed as the voter group that was remaking American politics. This group was widely credited with reelecting George Bush. It was typically asserted that 23 percent of voters were white evangelical Christians, up from 14 percent in 2000, and that these voters overwhelmingly supported Bush. The part about overwhelmingly supporting Bush was correct, but the part about a spike in white evangelical voter turnout was not: the 14 percent figure was based on a very different question asked in the 2000 exit poll about being part of the religious right. Other data indicate that, no, there had not been much change in the proportion of white evangelical voters across the two elections and, indeed, that Bush had gotten bigger increases in support from the moderately observant in 2004 than from the highly observant.[11] Furthermore, the nonobservant and the purely secular voted very heavily against Bush, and there is some evidence that these groups have been growing steadily as a proportion of voters. But again, the complexities of the changing American landscape of religion and religious observance were lost in the media urge to concentrate on one part of that landscape.

—White working-class voters. In the 2008 campaign, white working-class voters have been the group receiving the most attention, starting with their tendency to support Hillary Clinton over Barack Obama in the Democratic nomination contest. This is indeed a large and important group. But confusion abounds about who these voters are, with media accounts frequently referring to them as blue-collar and stressing their connection to America's declining manufacturing sector. But today most white working-class jobs are not blue-collar but are rather in low-level white-collar (technical, sales, clerical) and service occupations. Only about a sixth of the white working class holds manufacturing jobs (even among men, the proportion is still less than a quarter). In fact, the entire goods-producing sector—which includes construction, mining, and agriculture, as well as manufacturing—provides less than three in ten white working-class jobs. This leaves the overwhelming majority—over seven in ten—in the service sector, including government. There are about as many members of the white working-class working in trade alone (especially retail) as there are in all goods-producing jobs.[12]

These examples show that there is certainly an awareness that big changes are reshaping our politics. But they equally demonstrate that there is precious little real understanding of what these changes actually are and how they are likely to reshape the contours of red, blue, and purple America. Instead, the speculative and superficial have completely dominated the serious and analytical. This impoverishes the public conversation and undermines our ability to understand the shifting fault lines of American politics. And worse, superficial analysis reinforces the natural tendencies of both parties to believe that they can accommodate change without really changing; that is, to assume that a changing public—neatly sorted into red, blue, and purple states—can be easily assimilated into current political models. A deeper understanding, one suspects, would be far less comforting.

Based on papers produced for the Brookings-American Enterprise Institute project, The Future of Red, Blue and Purple America, this book aims to provide that deeper understanding through in-depth examination of seven trends reshaping the American electorate. The trends, each covered by a separate chapter in the book, are

—The changing face of suburbia and the growth of exurbia

—The increased political homogeneity of American communities

—The minoritization of America

—The decline of the white working class and the rise of a mass upper-middle class

—The growth of unmarried and alternative households and the decline of traditional values

—The concomitant rise of white evangelical and secular, nonobservant religious populations

—The rise of the millennial generation and the aging of the baby boomers

Here are a few of the many findings from these chapters, selected to highlight the scale and dynamism of the changes transforming the American electorate. In chapter 1, "The New Suburban Politics," the geographers Robert Lang, Thomas Sanchez, and Alan Berube point out that 53 percent of the population now resides in the top fifty metropolitan areas in the country (which roughly correspond to those with a million or more in population). Using commuting patterns, land use and population density, and population growth, the authors classify the counties in these metropolitan areas into five categories: core, inner suburbs, mature suburbs, emerging suburbs, and exurbs. Inner and mature suburbs may be thought of as urbanizing suburbs, while emerging suburbs and exurbs constitute the metropolitan fringe.

The distinction between emerging suburbs and exurbs is an important one. Emerging suburbs may be thought of as halfway between borderline-rural exurbs and fully developed suburbs. It is these counties that political observers generally have in mind when they talk about exurbs, using examples like Loudoun County, Virginia; Douglas County, Colorado; and Warren County, Ohio. But all of these counties are properly classified as emerging suburbs based on their relatively high densities and land use patterns. As a group, emerging suburbs are far more politically consequential than true exurbs, having much larger populations and faster growth rates than their lower-density, farther-out cousins on the metropolitan fringe (think Loudoun County versus Fauquier County in Virginia, for example).

Lang, Sanchez, and Berube find that Democrats dominate core counties and are starting to dominate urbanizing suburbs, while Republicans do well on the metropolitan fringe. More generally, they find a strong relationship between population density and voting behavior: with increasing distances from the urban core and declining density, Democratic voting declines. The authors argue that the political battle line in these large metropolitan areas, therefore, comes down to how far out in the suburbs the dividing line falls between Democratic and Republican dominance. In 2002 and 2004 the dividing line was relatively close in, while in 2006 it was much farther out, with Democrats dominating suburban rings out through mature suburbs and being competitive in emerging suburbs. A battle line that far out in the 2008 election would decisively advantage Democrats.

Lang and his colleagues note that although both components of the metropolitan fringe (emerging suburbs and exurbs) are growing significantly faster than closer-in urbanizing suburbs (inner and mature suburbs), the combined population weight of the metropolitan fringe in these large metro areas is still much smaller than that of urbanizing suburbs (20 percent of these areas, compared to 64 percent for urbanizing suburbs). Moreover, inner suburbs in particular are so populous that despite their relatively slow growth rates, they are actually adding more people to these areas than either exurbs or emerging suburbs. This situation is unlikely to change any time soon.

Indeed, as these areas continue to grow (America will add its next 100 million people by 2037, faster than China will add its next 100 million, with that growth heavily concentrated in large metro areas), the percentage of population gains in the metropolitan fringe is likely to drop significantly due to changing consumer preferences, more singles and childless couples, and greater land use regulation and resource constraints. This means that fewer very-low-density suburbs, of the kind that have been so reliably Republican, are likely to be built. This factor will enhance the political importance of urbanizing suburbs and the policy issues linked to these built-up areas, such as reinvestment in adequate infrastructure and schools. And as the political importance of urbanizing suburbs grows, the GOP will be forced to try to move the political battle line back into urbanizing suburbs, where they will have to engage Democrats on these very same policy issues. Retreating to their political corner, so to speak—the metropolitan fringe—would not appear to be a viable strategy over the long haul.

In chapter 2, "The Big Sort," the political analyst Bill Bishop and the sociologist Robert Cushing argue that Americans have become increasingly likely to live in close proximity to those who look, act, and think like they do. In the very close presidential election of 1976, just 27 percent of voters lived in landslide counties—counties in which the winning presidential candidate had a margin of 20 points or more. That figure rose throughout the 1980s and 1990s, reaching 45 percent in the even closer election of 2000. Even that figure was topped in the 2004 election, when almost half of the country's voters (48 percent) lived in landslide counties. Looked at another way, 60 percent of voters in the 2004 election lived in counties that had not changed their presidential party preference since 1988.

Bishop and Cushing unpack the reasons for this increased political homogeneity. Above all, the driving force is geographic mobility: Americans choose to live near those similar to them. Take people with college degrees. In 1970 these highly educated Americans were evenly distributed across cities, but since then they have tended to concentrate in certain places. In 2000 in sixty-two metro areas less then 17 percent of adults had college degrees, while in thirty-two cities 34 percent or more had college degrees (45 percent of the population of Austin, Texas, for example, had college degrees).

Those with college degrees tend to concentrate in Democratic-leaning areas. Adults in landslide Democratic counties in 2000, for example, were 29 percent college educated, while just 20 percent had that level of education in landslide Republican counties. The foreign-born too tend to settle in Democratic counties: landslide Democratic counties were 21 percent foreign-born in 2000, compared to only 5 percent in Republican landslide counties.

White voters, on the other hand, have migrated to Republican counties. Back in 1970 today's Democratic and Republican landslide counties each contained about a quarter of the nation's white population. By 2000, however, Democratic landslide counties contained just 18 percent of the nation's white population, while 30 percent resided in the Republican landslide counties.

More generally, Bishop and Cushing find that people who migrate from a Republican-leaning county are two and a half times more likely to move to another Republican-leaning county than to move to a Democratic-leaning one. In Colorado people moving from out of state into the Democratic-trending Denver suburbs are three times as likely to be from Democratic-leaning counties as are people moving from out of state into heavily Republican counties along the Kansas, Oklahoma, and Nebraska borders.

Bishop and Cushing expect this sorting process to continue, with consequent growth and reinforcement of communities of interest. In their view, this will promote something we are already seeing quite a lot of: lopsided congressional districts and, more generally, a politics focused on mobilizing parties' landslide communities along with microtargeting designed to pick off parties' supporters that reside in "enemy" territory. The way to undercut this tendency, the authors believe, is for issues that cut across current communities of interest to become salient. This outcome may depend on political parties moving beyond many of the culturally tinged issues that currently divide communities—or on the rise of a younger generation that simply sees these issues as less important.

In chapter 3, "Race, Immigration, and America's Changing Electorate," the demographer William Frey takes a detailed look at the shifting race-ethnic composition of the electorate. He notes that growth in the minority population accounts for more than four-fifths of U.S. population growth in this decade. Hispanics and Asians were up by nearly a third in just the first six years of the decade, while blacks increased by 10 percent and non-Hispanic whites by just 2 percent. These trends mean that by 2016 the white share of the population will be down to 62 percent.

Frey cautions, however, that the impact of these trends on the eligible electorate is blunted for Hispanics and Asians—the immigrant minorities—by the fact that so many in these populations tend to be under eighteen years old or not citizens. This creates a translation gap between demographic strength and voting strength. Only about five in ten Asians and four in ten Hispanics are actually eligible to vote, compared to almost two-thirds of blacks and 77 percent of whites. In addition, Hispanics and Asians who are eligible to vote tend to register and vote at lower rates than do blacks and whites. The end result, according to Frey's estimate, is that for every hundred Hispanics in the United States, only nineteen will vote in the 2008 election; and for every hundred Asians, only twenty-two will vote. The comparable figures for whites and blacks are fifty-two and forty, respectively.

Frey stresses that these race-ethnic changes are not equally distributed across states. This can be seen quite clearly when states are broken out by political leanings: solid red (voted for Bush in 2004 by 10 points or more); slow-growing purple; fast-growing purple; and solid blue (voted for Kerry in 2004 by 10 points or more). Eligible voters in solid blue states are 34 percent minority, while in solid red states they are 26 percent minority. In slow-growing purple states (such as Wisconsin, Ohio, Pennsylvania, Michigan, Minnesota, and Missouri) eligible voters are just 16 percent minority, while in fast-growing purple states (such as Nevada, Colorado, Florida, Virginia, Oregon, and New Mexico) they are 25 percent minority. Moreover, eligible voters grew at a 12 percent clip in the fast-growing purples between 2000 and 2007, with about half of that growth from minority voters.

Frey notes that despite the gap between demographic numbers and voting strength, young, eligible voters are becoming strikingly diverse. In twenty-one states over 30 percent of eighteen-to-twenty-nine-year-old voters are minorities. In California 56 percent of young voters are minorities, compared to 36 percent of all voters. In Texas the analogous figures are 51 and 33 percent; in Arizona they are 42 and 23 percent.

Given current political leanings, these race-ethnic shifts favor Democrats. Blacks, Hispanics, and Asians are all strongly Democratic (89 percent, 69 percent, and 62 percent, respectively, in the 2006 election), and recent polling data suggest that these loyalties are likely to continue into the 2008 election. But Frey emphasizes that these leanings should not be taken for granted over the long haul. Hispanics, in particular, vary substantially in their pro-Democratic leanings by area of the country, and as recently as 2004, 40 percent voted Republican nationwide. Moreover, these race-ethnic shifts are likely to present both parties, not just Republicans, with significant policy and political challenges in the years ahead.

Take the fast-growing purple states mentioned above, where immigration is such a big factor. For Democrats there will be a premium on immigration reform to consolidate their hold on Hispanic voters and to defuse white hostility to immigrants (particularly among low-skilled whites) that could divide the coalitions that Democrats are trying to build in these states. Democrats may also want to emphasize aspirational issues like education and home ownership, which appeal to the younger, more dynamic populations of these states. But even if successful, such an approach could produce problems in slow-growing purple states, which are heavily white, older, and more oriented toward economic security issues like health care and Social Security. Republicans for their part will have to decide whether to soften their currently tough stance on immigration to try to reach the burgeoning Hispanic population in the fast-growing purples or whether to retain that stance and perhaps emphasize economic security issues in a bid to reach voters in the slow-growing purples. Neither set of choices presents the parties with easy options, but they are options that will have to be considered as race-ethnic change continues.

In chapter 4, "The Decline of the White Working Class and the Rise of a Mass Upper-Middle Class," the political scientists Alan Abramowitz and Ruy Teixeira examine the shifting class structure in the United States since World

War II and the way it has shaped—and will continue to shape—American politics. Abramowitz and Teixeira note that while America was once overwhelmingly white working class, it is no longer. Across a wide range of definitions of white working class—by education, by occupation, or by income, broad or narrow—they find a 30–50 percentage point decline in the proportion of American adults in that group. But they are still a formidably large group. By a broad education-based definition (as whites without a four-year college degree), they are still 48 percent of voting-age Americans.

The white working class has also gone through some profound transformations as it has declined. The typical member of the white working class today is not blue-collar and certainly does not work in manufacturing; instead, he or she is likely to work in the service sector in a low-level white-collar or service job. Moreover, two-fifths of the white working class now has some college, and only 14 percent are high school dropouts. And the median income of white working-class families has gone up 150 percent since 1947.

Accompanying the decline and transformation of the white working class has been a significant shift in their political orientation, from pro-Democratic in most respects to pro-Republican, especially on the presidential level. By the 1968–72 period, just 35 percent of the white working class (once the bulwark of the Democrats' New Deal coalition) was voting Democratic, a number that was repeated in the 1980–84 period. Bill Clinton, however, did manage to carry this group's vote by a slender 1 point margin in 1992 and 1996 (though he averaged only 41 percent white working-class support across the two elections, as many of these voters preferred Ross Perot to the Democrats). Al Gore and John Kerry were not able to duplicate Clinton's success: they lost the white working class by 17 and 23 percentage points, respectively, pulling an average of just 39 percent support from this group.

Abramowitz and Teixeira argue that white working-class defection from the Democrats can be attributed to both a cultural reaction against the social movements of the sixties (especially around race) and an economic reaction to post-1973 trends of slow growth, declining wages, and stagnating living standards—trends that stand in stark contrast to the white working class's experience in the 1946–73 period. These voters came to doubt that the Democrats had their concerns and values at heart or that the government programs that Democrats proposed were in their interest. Abramowitz and Teixeira point out that this disaffection with the Democrats not only played out on the presidential level but manifested itself in a long-term decline in Democratic party identification among white working-class voters. They also note that the decline in party identification among these voters was concentrated among those who self-identify as conservatives and that it cannot be explained simply by hot-button issues like abortion, which appear to have had more effect on white voters of higher socioeconomic status.

Looking at the 2008 electoral landscape, Abramowitz and Teixeira observe that ten of the twelve states with the closest vote outcomes in the last two presidential elections have proportions of white working-class voters well above the national average: Iowa (70 percent), Wisconsin (64), Oregon (64), Ohio (60), New Hampshire (60), Michigan (59), Minnesota (58), Missouri (58), Pennsylvania (56), and Nevada (56). They point out that Democrats need not win the white working class to be successful in 2008 but that they do need to avoid a Kerry-style loss. They estimate that a deficit of around 10–12 points nationally would be adequate for a solid popular vote victory, with deficits slightly below that necessary to carry the highly competitive states just listed.

On a more long-range basis, they believe that the changing white working class is more accurately characterized as aspirational, rather than downtrodden. This presents a challenge to Democrats, who have been more inclined toward a simple economic populism that stresses economic security than toward an aspirational populism focused on helping these voters move ahead. For Republicans, electoral victories will depend on increasing supermajorities of the white working-class vote as the white working class shrinks (down to a little over 40 percent of the population by 2020). But this presents a challenge, since the white working class is likely to become more socially liberal as younger cohorts replace older ones and is already showing signs of impatience with reflexively antigovernment approaches to solving their economic problems. The GOP may therefore need to rethink its approach to both social and economic issues if it wishes to maintain the loyalties of these voters.

That need is underscored by another trend explored by Abramowitz and Teixeira: the rise of a mass upper-middle class. In the 2006 election 23 percent of voters reported household incomes of $100,000 or more. By the year 2020 a third of families may have incomes over $100,000; and by 2030, 40 percent could have incomes that high. But this rich trove of potential voters will include a very large segment of professionals, who tend to be liberal on social issues and moderate on economic ones. Reaching these voters will be difficult with the GOP's current mix of social conservatism and antipathy toward government programs. But Democrats, while more simpatico on social issues with these voters, may not find many takers for an uncomplicated populism focused on economic security issues. So, as with decline and change in the white working class, future trends are likely to present both parties with uncomfortable choices to make.

In chapter 5, "Changes in Family Structure, Family Values, and Politics," the sociologist Tom Smith takes a detailed look at how the American family and social values have changed over the last four decades. He points out that marriage, while still a central institution in American society, is far less dominant than it once was. In the early 1970s three-quarters of American adults were married. That proportion declined to 56 percent in the 2000s. The average age of first marriage has gone up over the same time period, from the early twenties to twenty-seven years old for men and twenty-five years old for women; the divorce rate has doubled. Married couples with children now account for fewer than one in four households, a share that has been cut in half since 1960. And the share of children being raised by continuously married couples declined since 1972 from 73 percent to 50 percent, while the proportion being raised by single parents has increased from 5 percent to 16 percent.

Another profound change is the decline of the traditional gender role family, in which the husband works and the wife keeps house. In 1972, 53 percent of all married couples fit that definition; just 26 percent do today. And over the same time period, the proportion of married couples that both work outside the home has risen from 32 to 52 percent. Even among married couples with children, the traditional gender role family has declined, from 60 to 32 percent, while the modern arrangement has increased from 33 to 62 percent.

Accompanying these structural shifts have been substantial changes in attitudes toward sexuality and marriage. About half of adults now say that it is a good idea for couples to live together before they get married, and only about a quarter now believe that premarital sex is always wrong. A little over half now say homosexual sex is always wrong, down from almost three-quarters in 1973. And the proportion disagreeing that homosexual couples should have the right to marry dropped from 73 to 51 percent just over the 1988–2002 time period.

The changes in attitudes toward gender roles are even more dramatic. In 1972, 67 percent approved of a wife working if a husband could support her; by 1998 that figure had risen to 82 percent, after which the General Social Survey (GSS) stopped asking the question because answers were approaching consensus level. In 1977 less than half agreed that a mother who works can be as close to her children as one who does not work, but now two-thirds agree. Also in 1977 only 43 percent disagreed that it is more important for a wife to help her husband's career than to have one herself. Twenty years later, in 1998, 81 percent disagreed (after that year, the GSS stopped asking the question). Similarly, in 1977 a mere 34 percent disagreed that it is best for the man to be the achiever and the woman to take care of home and family; thirty years later that number was up to 65 percent. And over the same time period the number disagreeing that preschool children suffer if the mother works rose from 32 to 59 percent. Finally, just in the 1988–2002 period, those agreeing that both spouses should contribute to household income rose from 49 to 68 percent.

These are momentous changes, and they have been associated with a widening political gap between those in more traditional family structures and those who are not. For example, in 1968 married voters were 6 points more likely to vote Republican than Democratic, while never-married voters were 2 points more likely to vote Democratic than Republican. By 2004 that modest marriage gap had turned into a chasm: married voters were 12 points more likely to vote Republican, while never-married voters were 25 points more likely to vote Democratic (separated voters were even more Democratic—35 points more likely to vote Democratic). Among married voters, those with children were 11 points more likely to vote Republican than those without, while among single voters those with children were 8 points more likely to vote Democratic than those without.

Smith expects this evolution away from traditional family forms and family values to continue in the future (with some exceptions, like approval of extramarital sex and support for abortion rights, where change is not currently evident). This is because the trends away from tradition reinforce one another—nontraditional family forms promote nontraditional values, and vice versa—and because younger cohorts are so much more likely than older cohorts to embrace nontraditional values. As younger cohorts continue to replace older ones, most family values will trend in a nontraditional direction. Smith argues that the political appeal of positions based on traditional values will therefore steadily diminish in the future.

This means, he suggests, that appeals to family values will themselves have to evolve to be effective. There will simply be fewer and fewer voters from traditional families to respond to traditional appeals; more broadly, the family values of the twenty-first century will not be our parents' family values. The parties must recognize this reality and adapt their rhetoric accordingly. Smith also stresses that parties' policies should evolve to fit the needs of twenty-first-century families, especially nontraditional ones, whose weight in the population is large and increasing. Possibilities he mentions include quality, affordable day care, after-school programs for children of working parents, financial and other assistance for single parents, and workplace nondiscrimination policies for those in nontraditional families. Of course, the GOP might prefer to support policies that promote traditional family forms, like promarriage incentives, divorce-avoidance programs, and faith-based initiatives, but the implication of Smith's analysis is that such policies are unlikely to be effective substitutes for policies that address the diverse realities of twenty-first-century families. Elaborating those policies, in fact, will be the task for both parties, as the modern American family continues to evolve.

In chapter 6, "Religion and American Politics," the political scientists John Green and E. J. Dionne trace the changes in religion and religious observance since World War II and analyze their effects on past, present, and future politics. The authors point out that both a secularization trend and an evangelical trend have had large effects on America's religious landscape in the postwar period. Consider secularization: from 1944 to 2004 the percentage of adults reporting no religious affiliation rose steadily, from 5 to 14 percent. By 2024 the authors project that 20 percent of adults will be unaffiliated. As for white evangelical Protestants, the gain has been more modest: rising from 18 to 23 percent of adults over the 1944–2004 period. However, the gain was larger among the observant (attend church weekly or more), who grew from 6 to 14 percent; the less observant declined by 2 percentage points. By 2024 Green and Dionne project that the group overall will gain only slightly—to 25 percent of adults; again, the observant will gain more and the less observant will decline.

But these have hardly been the only changes. In fact, the biggest change has been the decline of white mainline Protestants, down from 44 to 18 percent of adults in the 1944–2004 period (20 points of this decline was among the less observant). And those of "other faiths" (not Catholic or Protestant) have increased from 8 to 19 percent.

Green and Dionne note that levels of observance overall have remained fairly stable over the 1944–2004 period, at least in terms of the broad distinction between the observant and the less observant. The observant group equaled 42 percent of adults in 1944 and 43 percent of adults in 2004: that is, practically no change. But these endpoints conceal a substantial trend toward more observance between 1944 and 1964 (up to 51 percent) and then a substantial trend downward after that (back to 41 percent by 1984).

Changes in the mix of religious affiliations, while large, have been accompanied by other changes that are just as important. This has to do with the rise of a gap in voting between the observant and the less observant, which parallels, and in some respects now overshadows, the traditional gap in voting among those of different religions. For example, in the 2004 election less-observant white Protestants voted Republican over Democratic by 6 points, while their observant counterparts voted more Republican by 14 points. More spectacularly, less-observant Catholics voted Republican over Democratic by 6 points and the observant by 24 points. Less-observant other faiths voted Democratic over Republican by 32 points, while observant members of this group voted Republican over Democratic by 3 points. This pattern extended to white evangelicals: less-observant white evangelicals voted Republican over Democratic by a very strong 44 points, but their observant counterparts topped that with a 64-point margin in favor of the GOP. Comparing 2004 voting patterns with those of 1944, Green and Dionne find declines in Democratic presidential voting of 34 points among observant white evangelicals, 31 points among observant white Catholics, 21 points among observant other faiths, and 8 points among observant white mainline Protestants.

Green and Dionne tie this large attendance gap, which emerged in full force in the 1980s and 1990s, to that era's rise in the political relevance of cultural issues. Before that, cultural issues played less of a role in politics, and the attendance gap was consequently smaller. They speculate, based on recent trends, that an era of culturally based politics (say from 1980 to 2008, when religious values regarding individual and family behaviors were intertwined with political choices) may be coming to an end. Other issues like global warming and economic justice are receiving more attention from the observant even among white evangelicals. And pressing economic and foreign policy issues seem to be overshadowing the culture wars we have gotten so used to. If so, the attendance gap may moderate as we move into an era in which these issues predominate—an era more similar to the 1940s or the 1960s than to the recent past. This shift will present a challenge to both parties as they confront the need to reorganize their coalitions and reach out to the observant (on the Democrats' part) and to the less observant (on the Republicans' part).

In chapter 7, "The Aging of the Boomers and the Rise of the Millennials," the survey researcher Scott Keeter analyzes generational change and its impact on American politics. His chief focus is the millennial generation, who are, according to his definition, those born in 1977 and thereafter. He estimates there are 58 million American adults (ages eighteen to thirty-one) who are members of this generation.

Keeter believes that the millennials are distinctive in several social and demographic ways from preceding generations. They are less likely than earlier generations to have grown up in two-parent families and to have had two married parents and more likely than earlier generations to have had a mother who worked full time outside the home. Keeter notes, however, that despite the fears of many that millennials' relative lack of connection to traditional families would lead to social dysfunction this cohort has actually experienced lower levels of teen pregnancy, flat or declining levels of substance abuse, and lower rates of violent crime.

The millennial generation is also highly diverse. In 1972 almost nine in ten eighteen-to-twenty-four-year-olds were non-Hispanic whites; today, that figure is about six in ten. About 20 percent are Latino, 13 percent are black, and 5 percent are Asian.

Millennials have also been affected by the broad trends that characterize the era they are growing up in. Certainly one such trend is the persistent combination of increasing national wealth with growing inequality and insecurity. But perhaps the most distinctive imprint on this generation has been made by the extremely rapid pace of technological change. This imprint is demonstrated by the cohort's essentially universal use of the Internet and its enthusiastic embrace of communication innovations like instant messaging, text messaging, and social networking sites. This generational difference seems likely to persist as new innovations extend the boundaries of electronic communication and information access.

Millennials so far are exhibiting a distinctive political orientation. Those who have come of age since 1997 (eighteen-to-twenty-nine-year-olds) identify with or lean toward the Democratic Party by 18 points over the GOP. Gen X (born 1965–76) and late boomers (born 1956–64), by contrast, are much more evenly divided, with only a modest advantage for the Democrats. In fact, the only other generation in the electorate that comes close to the orientation of the millennials is the early boomers (born 1946–55), with those born 1951–54 being particularly pro-Democratic. Given the stability of party identification, millennials' pro-Democratic orientation is likely to persist as the generation ages.

Other attitudes, particularly about social issues, are distinctive among millennials. On gay marriage, for example, 58 percent favor allowing gays to marry, compared to 35 percent who are opposed. Among older cohorts, it is the reverse: 60 percent are opposed, and only 31 percent in favor. There is essentially universal acceptance among millennials (94 percent) of interracial dating and marriage and less concern about the economic or cultural impact of immigration. However, the millennial cohort is no more accepting of abortion than older cohorts.

On religion, millennials are less likely to express traditional beliefs about Judgment Day, the importance of prayer, and the existence of God. And they are significantly more likely to be secular—that is, unaffiliated with any religion: 19 percent are unaffiliated, compared to 14 percent of Gen X, 11 percent of early boomers, and 5 percent of older cohorts. Keeter notes that lack of religious affiliation tends to persist across the life course, so high levels of secularism among millennials are likely to continue.

Millennials express far greater support for active government than older cohorts. For example, they overwhelmingly say they prefer a bigger government providing more services to a smaller government providing fewer services, a view not shared by older generations. Keeter believes, however, that this relatively high level of support for active government is an age-related phenomenon and therefore will largely disappear as millennials get older. He also notes that millennials are more likely to favor private Social Security accounts and that they are significantly more pro-business than other age groups.

On foreign and military issues, Keeter points out that millennials were actually somewhat more supportive than the rest of the population of military action in Iraq before the invasion and in the initial phases of the war. Now, however, millennials are more likely to believe that the country did not make the right decision in using military force and that the United States should remove troops as soon as possible—though their differences from older age groups, Keeter stresses, are fairly modest. Millennials are also significantly less likely to think that the best way to achieve peace is through military strength.

Keeter believes the millennial generation shows encouraging signs of civic engagement that compare favorably with earlier generations. In terms of voter turnout, while young voters continue to lag older ones, the turnout gap shrank significantly in recent elections as millennials have come to dominate the ranks of the youth vote. Millennials are also catching up with older cohorts in other forms of electoral engagement. In 2004 young voters were more likely than older voters to try to influence the vote of other people, to attend a campaign event, and to support a candidate by displaying a sticker, button, or sign. Millennials are also participating in civic activities—volunteering, community problem solving, and charitable giving—at rates comparable to older cohorts.

The current political leanings of millennials should be a substantial benefit to the Democrats in the 2008 election, Keeter observes, especially since, judging from this year's primary contests, their turnout could be high. And since Barack Obama, who has generated exceptional excitement among millennials, is the Democratic nominee, the Democrats could benefit even further. Keeter stresses, however, that young voters' turnout will still likely be substantially below that of older voters. And over the longer run, the relatively pro-Republican and conservative late boomers and Gen Xers should be gaining political weight as the early boomers move into retirement. This could provide some counterweight for the GOP to the rise of the millennials.

Keeter is skeptical that the relatively liberal views of millennials on government will provide much of an impetus toward activist government. This is partly because of the life-cycle effect mentioned above and partly because millennials tend to be cynical about the ability of today's politicians in either party to accomplish the tasks government should perform. Other priorities of the millennials—like education, the environment and global warming, and a less force-oriented American role in the world—could have more staying power, though Keeter is not sure millennials' views in these areas hold enough intensity to have much of an impact on politics.

Keeter is more certain that millennials' distinctive views on social and cultural issues will have an impact. An orientation toward tolerance and away from racism, sexism, and nativism will surely have an effect on the political culture, perhaps lessening some of the more acrimonious differences between the parties and facilitating solutions to the immigration problem. He also thinks that the millennials' religious profile could contribute to less polarization, due to the large numbers of unaffiliated and high levels of religious diversity. Millennials also seem fairly uninterested in the standard association of liberal economic views with liberal social views and of conservative economic views with conservative social views. That would undermine a key basis of today's political polarization.

Each of these chapters contains critical lessons for our political parties. Looking across all the chapters, though, several overarching themes stand out. The first is that the days of the culture wars may be numbered. Generational change and changes in family and class structure and religious trends are all likely to reduce the salience of these issues over time and, consequently, the political premium to be gained by emphasizing these issues.

The second is that a set of issues is coming to the fore that both parties will have to engage. The needs of urbanizing suburbs for investment in education and infrastructure seem likely to become increasingly important. The central role of immigration in population growth, including in some of the most politically contested states, indicates that the urgency of reforming the current system (or nonsystem) will rise. The growth of nontraditional families should increase the salience of issues like quality day care and after-school programs. And changes in the race-ethnic and class structure are likely to increase the demand for programs that promote upward mobility (access to college and advanced training, affordable homeownership) and that remedy obstacles to upward mobility (lack of access to health care, poor or no retirement options).

Together, these changes are likely to mean that both parties will need to substantially retool their political approaches. Democrats will have to actively cultivate the set of the issues just mentioned if they hope to retain the loyalties of a group of emerging constituencies that have been favoring them (such as Hispanics, millennials, nontraditional families, and urbanizing suburbs). And they will need to update their economic populism to focus on opportunity and aspirations, not just security, if they hope to attain adequate support levels among the dwindling, but still important, white working class. Republicans, for their part, will need to rely less on cultural conflicts and, instead, directly engage Democrats on the same set of issues to build support in urbanizing suburbs, in nontraditional families, among Hispanics and youth, in the professional class, and so on. Otherwise, they will be forced to pile up ever-larger supermajorities among the white working class, a difficult task, since that group of voters is displaying less interest in what the Republicans currently have on offer.

It is difficult to look at these changes and the political pressures they will put on the parties and believe that politics will continue to be as polarized and gridlocked as it is today. The electoral logic of moving to the center—the new center—of this emerging American electorate will simply be too relentless for the parties to ignore. This is likely to overwhelm, in the end, the various factors like media hype, ideological elites, partisan redistricting, and cultural sorting that are said to keep our parties in a contentious, unproductive equilibrium. Demography may not be destiny, but it is awfully hard to ignore.

Notes

1. Frank Hobbs and Nicole Stoops, "Demographic Trends in the 20th Century" (U.S. Census Bureau, 2002).

2. Data on women's labor force participation from Howard N. Fullerton Jr., "Labor Force Participation: 75 Years of Change, 1950–98 and 1998–2025," *Monthly Labor Review,* December 1999, pp. 3–12.

3. Claudia Goldin and Lawrence Katz, "On the Pill: Changing the Course of Women's Education," *Milken Institute Review,* 2nd quarter (2001): 12–21.

4. Alvin P. Sanoff, "Competing Forces," *Prism,* October 2005 (www.prism-magazine.org/oct05/feature_competing.cfm).

5. U.S. Bureau of the Census, "Occupations: 2000," Census 2000 Brief (U.S. Census Bureau, 2003).

6. Author's analysis of 2000 Voter News Service national exit poll.

7. Data for 1940–2000 from U.S. Census Bureau, *Educational Attainment of the Population 25 Years and Over: 1940 to 2000;* data for 2005 from Current Population Survey, "Educational Attainment," historical table A-1 (www.census.gov/population/socdemo/education/cps2006/tabA-1.xls).

8. Data in this paragraph from Jeffery S. Passel and Roberto Suro, "Rise, Peak, and Decline: Trends in US Immigration, 1992–2004" (Washington: Pew Hispanic Center, 2005).

9. Ruy Teixeira and Joel Rogers, *America's Forgotten Majority: Why the White Working Class Still Matters* (New York: Basic Books, 2000).

10. From author's analysis of census educational attainment data.

11. Data in paragraph from author's analysis of 2000 Voters News Service and 2004 national exit polls.

12. Teixeira and Rogers, *America's Forgotten Majority.*

Geography

one

The New Suburban Politics
A COUNTY-BASED ANALYSIS OF
METROPOLITAN VOTING TRENDS SINCE 2000

ROBERT E. LANG, THOMAS W. SANCHEZ, AND ALAN BERUBE

This chapter looks at voting patterns in the American suburbs in the national elections of 2000, 2002, 2004, and 2006. Understanding these patterns is critical to understanding future elections, because the suburbs are now quasi urban and home to over half of the U.S. population.[1] Although it was once reasonably assumed that Republican voters predominated in the suburbs, these areas are now highly contested electorally.

Voting Patterns

The American suburbs have grown remarkably large and complex in the last several decades.[2] Yet the word *suburb* still provokes sneers among some scholars as a place where middle-class people without taste reside. One critic demonizes suburbs by referring to them as the "geography of nowhere."[3] But many suburbs have greater racial and age diversity than their core cities.[4] Likewise, their share of typical urban dwellers (such as singles) continues to grow, now accounting for a larger percentage of households than families with children.[5] The suburbs in all big metropolitan areas—except New York and Chicago—contain more office space than their central business districts.[6] Suburbs essentially have all of the elements that make a place urban, but their

The authors wish to thank Katrin Anacker and Rebecca Sohmer for their help in preparing this chapter.

physical arrangements sustain the popular depiction of suburbia as home to middle-class and wealthy white people.[7]

Robert Fishman, in describing the "rise and fall of suburbia," suggests that suburbs are no longer necessarily the antidote to the city that they were designed to be.[8] As office buildings and other features once thought to define cities spilled outside of the city's borders, the suburbs transcended the monolithic, bedroom communities they started out as. Brian Mikelbank uses multivariate analysis to categorize 3,567 incorporated suburbs into ten types.[9] Using similar statistical methods, Myron Orfield identifies six types of suburb. Peter Taylor and Robert Lang catalogue fifty new terms for suburban places, most of which blend city and suburban imagery.[10] Suburbs sprawl in so many complicated ways that they need a field guide, according to Dolores Hayden.[11] Some authors even use the term *postsuburban*.[12] Given their complexity, it is easy to see why the suburbs are so easily misread.

Misconceptions about suburbia carry over into politics. The simple split between Democratic-dominated cities and Republican-dominated suburbs no longer easily applies. Some early observers understood that inner suburbs had grown so urban in composition that they could now form strategic alliances with central cities.[13] A more recent analysis calls large urbanizing suburbs "boomburbs" and concludes that these places are not easily characterized as favoring either Democrats or Republicans.[14] Another study finds that differences in suburban population densities produce vastly different outcomes in national elections: that is, that density equals Democrats.[15]

Suburbs in the next ring—that between the inner suburbs built after World War II and the still booming communities on the fringe—are the new swing districts in national politics.[16] They are not firmly in either political party's camp. Most of these places were reliably Republican just a generation ago, but a change in their character corresponds with a general political shift. As inner suburbs became more urban, new suburbs and exurbs emerged at the edge of the metropolis. These places have become the next-generation Republican suburbs.[17] In past elections, Republicans lost votes near the center of the region but gained votes at the fringe.

Since the 2000 elections some have commented on the changing nature of the suburban vote.[18] This was especially true of the 2004 presidential election, in which a big story was that voters in the exurbs helped reelect George W. Bush as president.[19] One report shows that much of the GOP's gain came from a combination of the exurban and micropolitan vote.[20] In 2006 Democrats gained majorities in the U.S. House and Senate. A preliminary analysis of the vote shows that Democrats made strong gains across all suburbs.[21] The *New*

York Times columnist David Brooks also correctly predicted the difficulty that Republicans would have in the suburbs heading into the 2006 midterm elections.[22]

Many cities have lost so much population that large Democratic voter margins in urban areas may fail to influence a state's electoral votes or help much in Senate races. For example, in 2004 Democrat John Kerry won all of Ohio's principal cities by impressive margins, but these places now represent a small proportion of the state's total voters. Kerry lost Ohio, which also cost him the White House.[23] It is hard to imagine winning Ohio's cities and yet losing the state in 1964, or even 1984. Likewise, the suburbs have changed. Many once reliably Republican suburbs, such as Fairfax County, Virginia, favored a Democratic presidential candidate in the 2004 election—for the first time in forty years.[24] Fairfax County continued this trend in 2005 and 2006 by strongly supporting Timothy Kaine (D) for governor and James Webb (D) for the Senate with more than 60 percent of the vote.[25] Even the stalwart Republican Orange County, California, may be becoming a Democratic county. In 1996 Congressman Robert Dornan (R) lost his seat in the Forty-Seventh District to Democratic challenger Loretta Sanchez, an election that also demonstrates the power of Orange County's emerging minority vote. In 2005 Orange County became a majority-minority county, a signal that its Republican-leaning days may be numbered.[26]

An analysis that compares the 2000 and 2004 presidential elections shows that many older, once-Republican suburbs trended toward the Democrats.[27] Kerry actually gained a larger share of the vote in older, denser, and more diverse suburbs in 2004 than Al Gore did in 2000, despite the fact that Gore won the U.S. popular vote while Kerry lost to George W. Bush by a 4 percentage-point margin. Thus even as Democratic votes declined at the national level, Kerry made gains in some suburbs. Many metropolitan swing districts in both 2000 and 2004 were located in mature suburbs, or places that had mostly finished adding new population. Republicans, by contrast, made big gains at the metropolitan fringe by increasing their share of votes in the exurbs.

Classifying Metropolitan Areas

The metropolitan classification system used in this chapter describes the 416 counties in the nation's fifty metropolitan areas with populations of at least 1 million in 2006 and that collectively contained a little over half of the nation's population.[28] It relies on Census Bureau data regarding commuting patterns, land use, and growth. Although counties are hardly the perfect unit of analysis for distinguishing urban, suburban, and exurban areas, a county-based classification system offers a much richer array of data—on demographics, economics, attitudes, and voting behavior—than a system using cities, towns, or neighborhoods.

The classification system assigns a county type to each of the 416 counties, using the county's dominant form of development. The defining character of Fairfax County, Virginia, for example, is a 1970s-era, mixed single and multi-family residential area with retail businesses and office space (more than the city of Washington, D.C.).[29] Therefore Fairfax County is categorized as a mature suburb. To classify each county in the study, we examined three characteristics: commuting patterns, land use and density, and population growth.

Suburban and exurban counties are distinguished by the degree to which their workers commute into the metropolitan area's primary central city (or cities) and immediately surrounding areas. This degree of connectedness signals the geographic and economic proximity of outlying counties to the urban core. Commuting also is the census's main measure for establishing which counties belong in a metropolitan area. To assess the strength of this commuting relationship, we identified the county (or counties) containing the largest city (or cities) in each of the fifty largest metropolitan areas and used county-to-county worker flow data from the 2000 census to track the share of workers from each county commuting to those central locations.[30]

Density of population and housing also distinguishes suburbs and exurbs from one another. Older urban and inner suburban counties are denser and largely built out, with little room for new development. Population in newer suburban counties is urbanized to some degree (living at higher densities), but housing tends to be more spread out overall. In exurbs, few or no people live in densely developed areas.

Suburban areas also grow at vastly different rates depending on their baseline population and on whether they lie in the path of development. These growth distinctions signal the newness of their populations and, potentially, important differences in their underlying profiles. To control for differences in regional expansion rates, population growth was analyzed with respect to the overall rate for the metropolitan statistical area in which each county is located. Classification using commuting patterns, population and housing density, and population growth shows that each of the 416 counties in the fifty largest metropolitan areas falls into one of five types: core, inner suburb, mature suburb, emerging suburb, and exurb.[31]

—In a core county at least half of workers commute to (or remain in) the county or counties containing the major urban center in the metropolitan area. Core counties also had at least 1,000 housing units per square mile in 2000. Core counties are in general densely populated central cities, where in many cases the city and county are coincident. Counties that contain a large city together with a sizable ring of suburbs, such as Franklin, Ohio (home to Columbus), tend not to qualify because of their lower housing densities. Examples of core counties are Baltimore City, Maryland; Suffolk County, Massachusetts; Cook County, Illinois; and San Francisco County, California.

—In an inner-suburban county at least half of workers commute to the county or counties containing the major urban center, and at least 90 percent of the population lives in urban areas. These counties retain a strong attachment to the core and are densely populated, though they may contain significant swaths of undeveloped (and undevelopable) land. Several, such as Mecklenburg, North Carolina (home to Charlotte), are characterized by large central cities that, through annexation, grabbed the first, and many times the second and third, rings of suburbanization. Examples of inner-suburban counties are Travis County, Texas; Miami-Dade County, Florida; Hartford County, Connecticut; and Shelby County, Tennessee.

—In a mature-suburban county at least 75 percent of the population lives in an urban area, and population growth between 2000 and 2006 was not more than 1.5 times that of its metropolitan area (*or* less than the national average over that time—6.1 percent). These counties are also fairly urban and are of sufficient size or age that they are not booming in population anymore. They represent the midpoint of the American metropolis, having grown much faster through the mid-to-late twentieth century than they are growing today. Many, such as Fairfax County, Virginia, and San Mateo County, California, contain large secondary cities that feature higher-end neighborhoods and large concentrations of jobs. Examples of mature-suburban counties are Gwinnett County, Georgia; Lake County, Ohio; Westchester County, New York; and Orange County, California.

—In an emerging-suburban county at least 25 percent of the population lives in an urban area, and at least 5 percent of workers commute to the county or counties containing the major urban center in the metropolitan area. These counties have some degree of urbanization, are generally growing faster than the mature suburbs, and retain at least a modest commuting tie to the core part of the metropolitan area. These counties have experienced most of their development in the last two to three decades. As their commuting ties suggest, they are bedroom communities for the urban core, but they are also seeing the growth of local commerce. Examples of emerging-suburban counties are Loudoun County, Virginia; Delaware County, Ohio; Douglas County, Colorado; and Washington County, Rhode Island.

—In an exurban county less than 25 percent of the population lives in an urban area or less than 5 percent of workers commute to the major urban county or counties. Exurban counties are the most distant from the center of the metropolitan area, with little commuting to the core and a mostly spread-out population. Large-scale suburbanization is just beginning to take hold in these counties; as a result, they may also be the places most affected by overbuilding in the context of the current housing downturn. Examples of exurban counties are Strafford County, New Hampshire; Spencer County, Kentucky; Isanti County, Minnesota; and Yamhill County, Oregon.

Analyzing the Data

In 2006, 161 million people (or over half of the U.S. population) lived in the top fifty metropolitan areas (table 1-1). The biggest share, or over 56 million people, resided in inner-suburban counties. Mature-suburban counties followed, with over 47 million residents. Exurban counties had by far the smallest population, with less than 10 million people. About half the residents in these metropolitan areas lived in core and inner-suburban counties, and 90 percent lived in urban areas where population density met or exceeded 1,000 people per square mile.

Table 1-1. Characteristics of the Five County Types

County type	Number of counties	Total population 2006	Percent urban 2000	Median population 2006	Median population density 2006[a]	Percent white 2006	Percent population growth 2000–06
Core	25	25,890,586	100.0	631,366	7,722.3	45.9	−1.3
Inner suburb	36	56,173,091	97.3	1,011,101	1,382.5	58.8	4.6
Mature suburb	84	47,156,796	95.5	495,648	1,333.1	71.1	3.6
Emerging suburb	103	22,345,838	66.6	170,260	354.2	84.6	17.4
Exurb	168	9,701,053	0.0	36,975	80.6	88.5	9.7
Total/ median	416	161,267,364	63.8	130,994	460.2	79.5	8.6

Source: Census 2000; Census Bureau Population Estimates Program.
a. Population density is per square mile.

The overall population growth rate of these metropolitan areas slightly exceeded that for the United States as a whole. Growth rates for the first six years of this decade show that the biggest gains occurred in the less densely settled suburbs. Emerging-suburban counties led the way, with a median growth rate exceeding 17 percent. Exurban counties also boomed but at a considerably slower rate, showing a far smaller absolute gain than emerging-suburban counties. Exurban counties also registered more modest absolute gains than the much bigger inner-suburban counties, which outpaced all other county types in their total population gains.

That inner-suburban counties are adding more residents than emerging-suburban counties is a point often lost in the discussion about places that are gaining political strength. The focus tends to be exclusively on rates of growth rather than on absolute change.[32] Note also that due to the demographic composition of inner-suburban counties—that is, number of adults-only households—their voting strength is even greater than their population gains alone suggest.

The 2000 and 2004 Presidential Vote

In 2000 Democratic candidate Al Gore won the popular vote by over a half million ballots but lost the Electoral College vote and the presidency. Gore ran especially strong in the top fifty metropolitan areas, especially in core, inner-suburban, and mature-suburban counties (table 1-2). George W. Bush, the Republican candidate, won clear victories in emerging-suburban and exurban counties. Bush also ran strong in nonmetropolitan counties, micropolitan areas, and smaller metropolitan areas.[33]

In 2004 Bush won both the popular vote and the Electoral College vote. The Democratic candidate, John Kerry, improved on Gore's 2000 performance in core and inner-suburban counties (which contain over half of all big

Table 1-2. Democratic Presidential Vote, Five County Types, 2000 and 2004

Percent

County type	2000	2004	Change, 2000–04
Core	66.8	68.2	1.4
Inner suburb	53.3	54.9	1.6
Mature suburb	57.7	52.7	−5.0
Emerging suburb	46.4	40.0	−6.4
Exurb	40.9	38.3	−2.6
Median	55.1	53.0	−2.1

Source: Authors' calculations.

metropolitan area voters). Yet Kerry underperformed in mature-suburban and emerging-suburban counties, so that the Democrat's share of the metropolitan vote slid by 2 percentage points. Kerry did much worse in the low-density areas but better in counties with more than 2,500 people per square mile. This is consistent with the general finding that Democrats have been steadily gaining in suburbs with higher population densities.

Ohio's results in the 2004 election provide a good example of how shifting suburban voting patterns played out at the state level. Kerry targeted seventeen of the state's eighty-eight counties, leaving out many emerging-suburban and exurban counties. The Bush campaign, meanwhile, focused its efforts on these very places. The Kerry team simply did not grasp how much risk there was in losing the metropolitan edge by very large margins.[34] In national elections, Democrats need a large share of the vote in the top fifty metropolitan areas to offset probable big losses in small towns and rural areas. The Republican path to victory assumes a major turnout of small town voters and big wins at the metropolitan edge. Democratic hopes lie in reducing their losses in emerging-suburban and exurban counties and in claiming big victories in core and inner-suburban counties.

The 2002 and 2006 U.S. House Vote

The 2002 midterm election for the House of Representatives was a disaster for Democrats. Republicans nationalized the race and turned it into a referendum on which party could keep the county safe from terrorists in a post-9/11 world. Democrats barely won the inner-suburban and mature-suburban counties and lost the emerging-suburban and exurban counties by large margins (table 1-3). Only the strong vote in the core counties kept Democrats from losing the top fifty metropolitan areas outright. If Republicans can bat-

Table 1-3. Democratic House Vote, Five County Types, 2002 and 2006
Percent

County type	2002	2006	Change, 2002–06
Core	73.0	74.6	1.6
Inner suburb	50.8	55.5	4.7
Mature suburb	50.1	54.5	4.4
Emerging suburb	37.3	43.6	6.3
Exurb	32.9	41.8	8.9
Median	50.6	54.8	4.2

Source: Authors' calculations.

tle Democrats to a draw in the nation's largest regions, their vote in rural areas, smaller metropolitan areas, and micropolitan areas will provide the GOP a margin of victory in national elections.

The contrasts between the 2002 and 2006 midterm results are striking, however. Democrats regained their footing in the metropolitan vote in 2006. This suggests that the "metropolitan edge" is volatile. The data also show that Republicans must win the distant suburbs by very large margins if they are to win Congress and the White House.

The biggest shift in votes between 2002 and 2006 occurred in emerging-suburban and exurban counties. In 2006 Democrats saw a gain of almost 9 percentage points in exurban counties over the 2002 returns: in 2002 less than a third of these voters cast their ballots for Democratic candidates for the U.S. House of Representatives. This figure jumped to nearly 42 percent by 2006. Emerging-suburban counties also saw a large jump in Democratic votes in 2006. These shifts, combined with significant gains in inner-suburban and mature-suburban counties, helped Democrats reach nearly 55 percent of the total vote cast in 2006 in the most populous metropolitan areas. The bump in the suburban vote helped Democrats regain the U.S. House of Representatives for the first time since 1994. In sum, Democrats improved their performance in all types of suburban counties in the 2006 midterm election. Were they to hold these gains in 2008, the party would have a good chance at keeping Congress and regaining the White House.

Perhaps the most surprising outcome in the 2006 midterm election is how well Democratic congressional candidates fared in the more distant suburbs. After John Kerry's loss in the 2004 presidential election, the columnist David Brooks quipped that, "for Democrats, it was time to meet the exurban voter."[35] Brooks was correct in his assertion that voters at the metropolitan edge turned away from Democrats in 2004. However, Democrats sharply reversed this trend in 2006 and are perhaps now better acquainted with these voters.

National Elections, 2000–06

Several patterns are evident in the results of the four national elections between 2000 and 2006. The first is that Democrats—even in down years—win the nation's biggest metropolitan areas. It also appears that mature-suburban counties are swing areas. Democrats won these places in all four elections—but just barely in two cases. Most mature-suburban counties were almost equally divided between the two parties. Inner-suburban counties, by contrast, appear more solid for Democrats. The party came close to losing these counties only once: in 2002. In 2004 Kerry actually made gains over

Gore's 2000 vote among inner-suburban county voters, while losing ground in mature-suburb counties.

Emerging-suburban and exurban counties clearly remain in the Republican camp. Democrats failed to win these counties in any national elections since 2000. But Republicans cannot afford to let Democrats gain ground in these areas as they did in 2006. The nation's biggest metropolitan areas are outpacing the nation in population growth.[36] If Republicans do not remain at least competitive here (the GOP lost this vote in all four elections studied— but nearly tied once), they will have to make up for the losses in other places if they are to remain viable.

A regression analysis of balloting that combines county types and the 2004 election results (percentage voting for Kerry) explains over 80 percent of the statistical variation in the 2004 Kerry county-level vote. In more urban counties, John Kerry received a higher proportion of the vote. In the so-called red state of Texas, for example, Kerry matched Bush's vote in the center of the metropolis but lost by large margins at the fringe. Conversely, in the so-called blue state of Connecticut, Kerry won big at the core and held even at the edge. In both red and blue states, the general pattern remains the same: a metropolitan political gradient in which the core tilts to Democrats and the exurbs to Republicans. Between these extremes the vote slides along a continuum, coming to a midpoint in mature-suburban counties.

The New Suburban Politics

In the 1992 presidential race a Democratic strategist famously posted a mantra on the wall of Bill Clinton's campaign headquarters: "It's the economy, stupid." The idea was not to lose focus on what really drove politics that year—a lingering recession. In a similar vein one could imagine that a slogan based on voting patterns correlated with the county classification system used in this chapter might read: It's the density, stupid.

The urban intensity of metropolitan space partly forecasts the opportunities for both Democrats and Republicans. Density is a proxy variable that represents a cluster of factors that predict voter behavior. High population density and a large percentage of population living in urban areas correlate strongly with racial and ethnic diversity. Democrats tend to do better in districts with a greater minority population. In addition, densely built environments feature a different mix of housing types than environments with low density. There are more multifamily and rental units, which in turn attract households of singles and of married couples without children. *USA Today* published an analysis that shows that "Republicans control 49 of the 50 districts with the highest rates of married people [while] Democrats represent all 50 districts that have the highest rates of adults who have never married."[37] Thus density per se does not cause people to vote Democratic but instead produces a built environment that tends to attract Democratic-leaning voters and a demographic mix that includes a high percentage of minority voters. By contrast, married couples with children are often drawn to the metropolitan edge, where large single-family homes offer more space to growing households.[38] White voters are also overrepresented in low-density fringe counties.

Republicans already grasp this metropolitan reality, as demonstrated by their effective 2004 presidential campaign strategy that targeted the outer suburbs.[39] The Bush strategists correctly predicted that an appeal to "family values" in these places would lift both turnout and the Republican margin of victory in exurban and emerging-suburban counties.[40]

There clearly are voting patterns that divide the nation by settlement type.[41] One of the most demonstrable of these patterns is the split between city and country. According to conventional thinking, cities vote blue (Democratic) and rural areas vote red (Republican). One online journal describes this voting pattern from the Democratic perspective as "the urban archipelago."[42] Perhaps this is a more precise characterization of red and blue differences than a genuine moral divide. Urban areas in red states often tilt toward Democrats. For example, although Bush won Dallas County, Texas, it was only by 1 percentage point. In 2006 this county—an inner-suburban county—went strongly for Democrats.

Bush won low-density places, which is why so much of the nation's space appears Republican red on county maps showing voting patterns. In fact, Republicans have dominated low-density areas for years. The journalist Paul Overberg generated an unpublished red and blue county map for the 1996 Clinton versus Dole election. Visually, the nation is a giant field of red, even though Clinton won decisively. Without zooming in on big population centers, the map would lead one to believe that Dole must have been victorious.

In the battle over George Bush's legitimacy as the winner of the 2000 contested election, Republicans pointed to the county map as proof that more of America wanted Bush over Gore. Yet Gore supporters note that the Democratic candidate won the popular vote by over half a million and that, besides, land does not vote—people vote. To better interpret the 2004 returns, social scientists devised new ways to graphically depict the vote. These efforts include proportional maps and a density map that shows the Democrats' concentrated strengths at the coasts as giant swathes hemming in the vast interior.[43]

Republican presidential candidates dominate two kinds of quasi-urban space: the metropolitan edge and micropolitan areas. An analysis of the 2000 vote in forty-seven fast-growing exurban counties shows that Bush won forty-three of these places.[44] A similar analysis finds that in 2004 Bush won ninety-seven of the hundred fastest growing counties, holding a 1.7 million vote edge.[45] In 2000 Bush took ninety-four of these places, but his margin of victory in them barely topped 1 million votes.[46] An analysis of the micropolitan vote for the 2004 presidential election shows that Bush won about six in ten voters in these small-town areas.[47]

By contrast, both Kerry and Gore won the densest parts of the United States, including the Pacific coast, Great Lakes metropolitan areas, and the northeast corridor from Boston to Washington. Since the 2002 midterm defeat, Democrats have been gaining strength in older suburbs, even in many red states.

In 2005 the Virginia Democratic gubernatorial candidate Timothy Kaine sought to narrow the Republican advantage with so-called values voters at the metropolitan edge by running as a social moderate and addressing quality-of-life issues in northern Virginia's sprawling suburbs.[48] The strategy worked, and Kaine even succeeded in winning such emerging-suburban counties as Loudoun and Prince William.[49] Kaine's victory also shows that centrist Democratic candidates who offer practical solutions to problems such as transportation and education can reach voters in exurban and emerging-suburban counties. The political analyst Ruy Teixeira, writing about the "battle for the exurbs," specifically comments on Kaine's wins in Loudoun and Prince William Counties, noting that "exurban voters are tax-sensitive and concerned about government waste, but not ideologically anti-government. They tend to be religious and family-oriented, but socially moderate in comparison to rural residents. . . . And they worry as much or more about public education as they do about moral values."[50]

In 2006 Democratic Senate candidate James Webb followed the same strategy, including an explicit appeal to suburban voters in Northern Virginia, and won a narrow victory over the Republican George Allen. Allen clearly created an opening for Webb with the now infamous "macaca" comment, but Webb still had to beat a Republican incumbent in a conservative state.[51] Webb's camp focused on sweeping the inner-suburban counties of Arlington and Alexandria and the mature-suburban county of Fairfax and breaking even in the emerging-suburban counties of Loudoun and Prince William. The bet was that a wide margin of victory in the suburban north would offset the vote in the rest of Virginia, the same pattern that helped elect Kaine.

The 2006 Democratic suburban wave also helped in Missouri's close Senate race, in which Democratic challenger Claire McCaskill beat Republican incumbent James Talent. The shift in suburban St. Louis and Kansas City, as seen in the U.S. House of Representatives vote, helped increase McCaskill's metropolitan totals and countered her losses in rural Missouri. Republicans also suffered at the metropolitan edge, as Democrats ran more centrist candidates and made calculated appeals on bread-and-butter issues that appeal to swing voters. Thus it appears that in 2006 the suburbs helped elect a Democratic majority to both the Senate and the House—a reversal of fortune when compared with 2002 and 2004.

The Republicans' 2006 suburban problem was especially acute in the Northeast. Consider the three suburban seats that the Democrats picked up in Pennsylvania alone. One seat in suburban Pittsburgh—the Fourth District—was lost, as were two in suburban Philadelphia—the Seventh and Eighth Districts. Democrats won virtually all inner-suburban and mature-suburban counties surrounding northeastern cities.

One of the primary findings of our research, then, is the relationship between density and voting behavior: with increasing distance from the urban core and, therefore, declining density, Democratic voting declines. Voting in large metropolitan areas, then, is very much about how far out into the suburbs the dividing line falls between Democratic and Republican dominance. In 2002 it was closer in and in 2006 it was farther out; by then Democrats dominated mature-suburban counties and were competitive in emerging-suburban counties. Of particular interest is how this line can shift. Further research could illuminate the demographic trends that could put emerging-suburban counties, in particular, into play.[52] Politically competitive emerging-suburban counties could decisively advantage Democrats.

Finally, although we argue that density itself does not draw people to Democratic candidates, there are some types of politics that may be tied to urban environments. For example, while it is very unlikely that the experience of place will shift people's basic values on such critical issues as abortion, it is possible that living in an urbanized suburban setting may shift support on such issues as investment in rapid transit. Mayors in virtually all of the "boomburbs" interviewed in a 2007 study self-identify as Republicans, yet almost to a person these leaders sought a much larger investment in such traditionally public works projects as light rail.[53] In the same year that George Bush was reelected president, transit initiatives passed in the majority of metropolitan areas where they were on the ballot, including such Sunbelt cities as Phoenix and Denver. As urban America gains on small towns and rural areas in the coming decades, it is likely that the politics of public investment may shift.

Looking Ahead: The 2008 Election and Beyond

The recent congressional and presidential elections point to a new suburban politics, which reflects a changing metropolitan structure. It is likely that new density-based political strategies will factor into the 2008 presidential race. The metropolitan political battle line is not between city and suburbs but instead lies in the transition area between mature-suburban and emerging-suburban counties. The Republicans count on strongly winning rural areas and then sweeping much of suburbia. The Democrats start at the core and work outward. The further the Democrats can push into the suburbs—and in the 2006 midterm election they practically ran the board—the greater the likelihood that they will prevail.

One big divide between the suburbs is newness, which often correlates with lower density.[54] The outer suburbs are products of the last two decades. But much of older suburbia dates to the post–World War II era. On a superficial level these two areas may seem similar—perhaps old sprawl versus new sprawl. Yet as the county classifications used in this study show, these places are now very different. A key concern for the old sprawl areas is that some communities have started to experience a decline similar to the decline of central cities.[55] Policies that manage this change and provide reinvestment opportunities in upgrading aging infrastructure are favored by many of these voters.[56] Many voters at the metropolitan edge want policies that slow growth so that local services can catch up with demand.[57] Both political parties can play to these politics. The next several elections may be determined by which party does a better job of addressing the new suburban politics.

There is already a sense that the 2008 election may come down to a battle over the suburban vote.[58] But each election is in some ways unique. There are structural forces that help shape the outcome, such as a pattern that favors Democrats at the metropolitan center and Republicans at the periphery. Yet— especially in presidential elections—the qualities of the candidates also factor significantly in how the structural dynamics play out. For instance, a Republican moderate such as Arizona Senator John McCain may perform much better than would be predicted based on party affiliation alone in swing districts such as mature suburban counties. Likewise Democratic Senator Barack Obama from Illinois may do very well in the same exurban counties that gave John Kerry such a difficult time because of Obama's appeal for post-partisan politics. Still, it is unlikely McCain would ever carry core counties or Obama exurban counties, and thus metropolitan voting patterns remain an important lens through which to view the possibilities regarding the presidential race.

What do the findings presented in this chapter mean beyond 2008? We expect that projected metropolitan population growth and urban expansion will continue to impact the political landscape. Looking forward a decade or two, suburbia as we know it and metropolitan areas in general are likely to go through dramatic changes. In the past four decades a large share of metropolitan development occurred at the fringe.[59] But as the nation adds its next 100 million people by 2037 (a rate faster than in China), the share of this gain accommodated in ever-more distant suburbs is likely to drop significantly. The reasons are a combination of shifting consumer preferences, changing household composition with big increases of singles and childless couples, greater land-use regulation and preservation efforts, and perhaps even environmental and resource constraints such as global warming and energy shortages. The bottom line is that fewer very-low-density suburbs, of the kind that have been so reliably Republican in historic voting patterns, are likely to be built. In addition, the minority populations in all types of suburb will also grow, another sign of trouble for Republicans based on their current demographic strengths.

The prediction of greater density and diversity in metropolitan America would seem to favor the Democrats. However, both major political parties are likely to adapt their messages to reflect the new metropolitan reality. The American metropolis is so dynamic that it is a moving target. So many millions of people are added to the mix in each decade that it is hard to make predictions as to the future politics of these places. Neither political party can afford to maintain static strategies for winning big metropolitan areas. The candidates and campaigns that closely follow and understand shifts in voting patterns will gain a critical advantage over opponents who fail to factor in the new metropolitan politics.

Appendix 1A. Metropolitan Statistical Areas, County Type, and Counties

Atlanta–Sandy Springs–Marietta, GA
  —Inner suburbs: De Kalb, Fulton
  —Mature suburbs: Cobb, Clayton, Douglas, Fayette, Gwinnett, Rockdale
  —Emerging suburbs: Cherokee, Coweta, Forsyth, Henry, Newton, Paulding, Spalding

—Exurbs: Barrow, Bartow, Butts, Carroll, Dawson, Haralson, Heard, Jasper, Lamar, Meriwether, Pickens, Pike, Walton

Austin–Round Rock, TX
—Inner suburb: Travis
—Emerging suburb: Williamson
—Exurbs: Bastrop, Caldwell, Hays

Baltimore-Towson, MD
—Core: Baltimore City
—Mature suburbs: Anne Arundel, Baltimore County
—Emerging suburbs: Carroll, Harford, Howard
—Exurb: Queen Anne's

Birmingham-Hoover, AL
—Mature suburb: Jefferson
—Emerging suburb: Shelby
—Exurbs: Bibb, Blount, Chilton, St. Clair, Walker

Boston-Cambridge-Quincy, MA-NH
—Core: Suffolk
—Mature suburbs: Essex, Middlesex, Norfolk, Plymouth
—Exurbs: Rockingham, Strafford

Buffalo–Niagara Falls, NY
—Mature suburb: Erie
—Emerging suburb: Niagara

Charlotte-Gastonia-Concord, NC-SC
—Inner suburb: Mecklenburg
—Emerging suburbs: Cabarrus, Gaston, Union, York
—Exurb: Anson

Chicago-Naperville-Joliet, IL-IN-WI
—Core: Cook
—Mature suburbs: Du Page, Lake (Indiana)
—Emerging suburbs: Kane, Kendall, Lake (Illinois), McHenry, Porter, Will
—Exurbs: De Kalb, Grundy, Jasper, Kenosha, Newton

Cincinnati-Middletown, OH-KY-IN
—Inner suburb: Hamilton
—Mature suburbs: Butler, Campbell, Kenton
—Emerging suburbs: Boone, Clermont, Warren
—Exurbs: Bracken, Brown, Dearborn, Franklin, Gallatin, Grant, Ohio, Pendleton

Cleveland-Elyria-Mentor, OH
—Core: Cuyahoga

—Mature suburbs: Lake, Lorain
—Emerging suburb: Medina
—Exurb: Geauga
Columbus, OH
   —Inner suburb: Franklin
   —Emerging suburbs: Delaware, Fairfield, Licking
   —Exurbs: Madison, Morrow, Pickaway, Union
Dallas–Fort Worth–Arlington, TX
   —Inner suburbs: Dallas, Tarrant
   —Emerging suburbs: Collin, Denton, Rockwall
   —Exurbs: Delta, Ellis, Hunt, Johnson, Kaufman, Parker, Wise
Denver-Aurora, CO
   —Core: Denver
   —Mature suburbs: Arapahoe, Jefferson
   —Emerging suburbs: Adams, Douglas
   —Exurbs: Clear Creek, Elbert, Gilpin, Park
Detroit-Warren-Livonia, MI
   —Core: Wayne
   —Mature suburbs: Macomb, Oakland
   —Emerging suburb: Livingston
   —Exurbs: Lapeer, St. Clair
Hartford–West Hartford–East Hartford, CT
   —Inner suburb: Hartford
   —Emerging suburbs: Middlesex, Tolland
Houston–Baytown–Sugar Land, TX
   —Inner suburb: Harris
   —Mature suburb: Galveston
   —Emerging suburbs: Brazoria, Fort Bend, Montgomery
   —Exurbs: Austin, Chambers, Liberty, San Jacinto, Waller
Indianapolis, IN
   —Inner suburb: Marion
   —Emerging suburbs: Hamilton, Hancock, Hendricks, Johnson, Morgan
   —Exurbs: Boone, Brown, Putnam, Shelby
Jacksonville, FL
   —Inner suburb: Duval
   —Emerging suburbs: Clay, St. John's
   —Exurbs: Baker, Nassau
Kansas City, MO-KS
   —Inner suburb: Jackson

—Mature suburb: Wyandotte

—Emerging suburbs: Cass, Clay, Johnson, Platte

—Exurbs: Bates, Caldwell, Clinton, Franklin, Lafayette, Leavenworth, Linn, Miami, Ray

Las Vegas–Paradise, NV

—Inner suburb: Clark

Los Angeles–Long Beach–Santa Ana, CA

—Inner suburb: Los Angeles

—Mature suburb: Orange

Louisville, KY-IN

—Inner suburb: Jefferson

—Mature suburb: Floyd

—Emerging suburbs: Bullitt, Clark, Oldham

—Exurbs: Harrison, Henry, Meade, Nelson, Shelby, Spencer, Trimble, Washington

Memphis, TN-MS-AR

—Inner suburb: Shelby

—Emerging suburbs: Crittenden, De Soto

—Exurbs: Fayette, Marshall, Tate, Tipton, Tunica

Miami–Fort Lauderdale–Miami Beach, FL

—Inner suburb: Miami-Dade

—Mature suburbs: Broward, Palm Beach

Milwaukee–Waukesha–West Allis, WI

—Core: Milwaukee

—Mature suburb: Waukesha

—Emerging suburb: Ozaukee

—Exurb: Washington

Minneapolis–St. Paul–Bloomington, MN-WI

—Core: Ramsey

—Inner suburb: Hennepin

—Mature suburbs: Anoka, Dakota

—Emerging suburbs: Carver, Scott, Washington

—Exurbs: Chisago, Isanti, Pierce, Sherburne, St. Croix, Wright

Nashville-Davidson-Murfreesboro, TN

—Inner suburb: Davidson

—Emerging suburbs: Robertson, Rutherford, Sumner, Williamson, Wilson

—Exurbs: Cannon, Cheatham, Dickson, Hickman, Macon, Smith, Trousdale

New Orleans–Metairie–Kenner, LA
  —Core: Orleans
  —Mature suburbs: Jefferson, St. Bernard
  —Emerging suburbs: Plaquemines, St. Tammany
  —Exurbs: St. Charles, St. John the Baptist
New York–Northern New Jersey–Long Island, NY-NJ-PA
  —Core: Bronx, Hudson, Kings, New York, Queens, Richmond
  —Mature suburbs: Bergen, Essex, Middlesex, Monmouth, Morris, Nassau,
    Passaic, Rockland, Suffolk, Union, Westchester
  —Emerging suburbs: Putnam, Somerset
  —Exurbs: Hunterdon, Ocean, Pike, Sussex
Oklahoma City, OK
  —Inner suburb: Oklahoma
  —Mature suburb: Cleveland
  —Emerging suburb: Canadian
  —Exurbs: Grady, Lincoln, Logan, McClain
Orlando, FL
  —Inner suburb: Orange
  —Mature suburb: Seminole
  —Emerging suburbs: Lake, Osceola
Philadelphia-Camden-Wilmington, PA-NJ-DE-MD
  —Core: Philadelphia
  —Mature suburbs: Bucks, Camden, Delaware, Montgomery, New Castle
  —Emerging suburbs: Burlington, Gloucester
  —Exurbs: Cecil, Chester, Salem
Phoenix-Mesa-Scottsdale, AZ
  —Inner suburb: Maricopa
  —Exurb: Pinal
Pittsburgh, PA
  —Inner suburb: Allegheny
  —Emerging suburbs: Beaver, Fayette, Washington, Westmoreland
  —Exurb: Armstrong, Butler
Portland-Vancouver-Beaverton, OR-WA
  —Inner suburb: Multnomah
  —Mature suburb: Washington
  —Emerging suburbs: Clackamas, Clark
  —Exurbs: Columbia, Skamania, Yamhill
Providence–New Bedford–Fall River, RI-MA
  —Inner suburb: Providence

—Mature suburbs: Bristol, Kent, Newport
—Emerging suburb: Washington
Richmond, VA
   —Core: Richmond City
   —Mature suburbs: Colonial Heights, Henrico, Hopewell, Petersburg
   —Emerging suburbs: Chesterfield, Dinwiddie, Hanover, Prince George
   —Exurbs: Amelia, Caroline, Charles City, Cumberland, Goochland, King
     William, King and Queen, Louisa, New Kent, Powhatan, Sussex
Riverside–San Bernardino–Ontario, CA
   —Mature suburbs: Riverside, San Bernardino
Rochester, NY
   —Inner suburb: Monroe
   —Exurbs: Livingstone, Ontario, Orleans, Wayne
Sacramento–Arden-Arcade–Roseville, CA
   —Inner suburb: Sacramento
   —Emerging suburbs: Placer, Yolo
   —Exurb: El Dorado
Salt Lake City, UT
   —Inner suburb: Salt Lake
   —Exurbs: Summit, Tooele
San Antonio, TX
   —Inner suburb: Bexar
   —Exurbs: Atascosa, Bandera, Comal, Guadalupe, Kendall, Medina, Wilson
San Diego–Carlsbad–San Marcos, CA
   —Inner suburb: San Diego
San Francisco–Oakland–Fremont, CA
   —Core: San Francisco
   —Inner suburb: Alameda
   —Mature suburbs: Marin, San Mateo
   —Emerging suburb: Contra Costa
San Jose–Sunnyvale–Santa Clara, CA
   —Inner suburb: Santa Clara
   —Exurb: San Benito
Seattle-Tacoma-Bellevue, WA
   —Inner suburb: King
   —Mature suburbs: Pierce, Snohomish
St. Louis, MO-IL
   —Core: St. Louis City
   —Mature suburbs: Madison, St. Clair, St. Louis

—Emerging suburbs: Jefferson, Monroe, St. Charles

—Exurbs: Bond, Calhoun, Clinton, Crawford, Franklin, Jersey, Lincoln, Macoupin, Warren, Washington

Tampa–St. Petersburg–Clearwater, FL

—Core: Pinellas

—Inner suburb: Hillsborough

—Emerging suburbs: Hernando, Pasco

Virginia Beach–Norfolk–Newport News, VA-NC

—Core: Newport News, Norfolk

—Inner suburb: Virginia Beach

—Mature suburbs: Hampton, Poquoson City, Portsmouth, Williamsburg

—Emerging suburbs: Chesapeake, Gloucester, James City, York

—Exurbs: Currituck, Isle of Wight, Mathews, Suffolk, Surry Washington-Arlington-Alexandria, DC-VA-MD-WV

—Core: Alexandria, Arlington, Washington

—Mature suburbs: Fairfax, Fairfax City, Falls Church, Fredericksburg, Manassas City, Manassas Park City, Montgomery, Prince George's

—Emerging suburbs: Charles, Loudoun, Prince William, Spotsylvania, Stafford

—Exurbs: Calvert, Clarke, Fauquier, Frederick, Jefferson, Warren

Notes

1. Robert E. Lang, Edward J. Blakely, and Meghan Z. Gough, "Keys to the New Metropolis: America's Big, Fast-Growing Suburban Counties," *Journal of the American Planning Association* 71 (2005): 381–91.

2. Robert E. Lang and Jennifer LeFurgy, *Boomburbs: The Rise of America's Accidental Cities* (Brookings, 2007).

3. James Howard Kunstler, *The Geography of Nowhere: The Rise and Decline of America's Man-Made Landscape* (New York: Free Press, 1993).

4. William H. Frey, *Boomers and Seniors in the Suburbs: Aging Patterns in Census 2000,* Living Cities Census Series (Brookings, 2003); William H. Frey, "Melting Pot Suburbs: A Study of Suburban Diversity," in *Redefining Urban and Suburban America: Evidence from Census 2000,* edited by Bruce Katz and Robert E. Lang (Brookings, 2003).

5. William H. Frey and Alan Berube, "City Families and Suburban Singles: An Emerging Household Story," in *Redefining Urban and Suburban America: Evidence from Census 2000,* edited by Bruce Katz and Robert E. Lang (Brookings, 2003).

6. Thirty-seven percent of office space in major metropolitan areas is located in central business district. See Robert E. Lang, *Edgeless Cities: Exploring the Elusive*

Metropolis (Brookings, 2003). The remainder is in secondary downtowns, suburbs, and exurbs. See also Robert E. Lang, Thomas W. Sanchez, and Asli Ceylan Oner, "Beyond Edgeless Cities: A New Classification System for Suburban Business Districts," *Urban Geography*, forthcoming.

7. Robert E. Lang and Meghan Z. Gough, "Growth Counties: Home to America's New Suburban Metropolis," in *Redefining Urban and Suburban America: Evidence from Census 2000*, vol. 3, edited by Alan Berube, Bruce Katz, and Robert E. Lang (Brookings, 2006).

8. Robert Fishman, "America's New City: Megalopolis Unbound," *Wilson Quarterly* 14 (1990): 24–45; Robert Fishman, *Bourgeois Utopias: The Rise and Fall of Suburbia* (New York: Basic Books, 1987).

9. B. A. Mikelbank, "A Typology of Suburban Places," *Housing Policy Debate* 15 (2004): 935–64. Mikelbank covers only incorporated places. Also see Robert E. Lang and Dawn Dhavale, *Reluctant Cities: Exploring Big, Unincorporated, Census-Designated Places*, Census Note Series 03:01 (Alexandria: Metropolitan Institute at Virginia Tech, 2003).

10. Myron Orfield, *American Metropolitics* (Brookings, 2002); Peter J. Taylor and Robert E. Lang, "The Shock of the New: 100 Concepts Describing Recent Urban Change," *Environment and Planning* 37 (2004): 951–58.

11. Dolores Hayden, *A Field Guide to Sprawl* (New York: W. W. Norton, 2004).

12. Robert Kling and others, *Postsuburban California: The Transformation of Orange County since World War II* (University of California Press, 1991); Jon Teaford, *Post-Suburbia: Government and Politics in the Edge Cities* (Johns Hopkins University Press, 1997).

13. Myron Orfield, *Metropolitics: A Regional Agenda for Community and Stability* (Brookings, 1997); Orfield, *American Metropolitics*.

14. Lang and LeFurgy, *Boomburbs*.

15. Robert E. Lang and Thomas W. Sanchez, *The New Metro Politics: Interpreting Recent Presidential Elections Using a County-Based Regional Typology*, Election Report 06:01 (Alexandria: Metropolitan Institute at Virginia Tech, 2006).

16. Lang and LeFurgy, *Boomburbs;* Lang and Sanchez, *The New Metro Politics*.

17. Lang and Sanchez, *The New Metro Politics*.

18. David Mark, "The Battle over the Suburban, Exurban Vote," *Politico,* December 4, 2007, p. 1.

19. Matt Bai, "Who Lost Ohio?" *New York Times Magazine,* November 21, 2004, pp. 67–74; David Brooks, "For Democrats, Time to Meet the Exurban Voter," *New York Times,* November 10, 2004, p. E9; Ron Brownstein, "Red-State Seats Tricky Fruit to Pluck," *Los Angeles Times,* October 30, 2004, p. A1; Gregory L. Giroux, "A Line in the Suburban Sand," *CQ Weekly,* June 27, 2005, p. 1714.

20. Robert E. Lang, Dawn Dhavale, and Kristin Haworth, *Micro Politics: The 2004 Presidential Vote in Small-Town America*, Census Note Series 04:03 (Alexandria: Metropolitan Institute at Virginia Tech, 2004). Micropolitan areas are a new census

category (2003); they contain from 10,000 to 50,000 people in a core area. See William H. Frey and others, "Tracking Metropolitan America into the 21st Century: A Field Guide to the New Metropolitan and Micropolitan Definitions," in *Redefining Urban and Suburban America: Evidence from Census 2000,* vol. 3, edited by Alan Berube, Bruce Katz, and Robert E. Lang (Brookings, 2006).

21. Jill Lawrence, "Democratic Gains in the Suburbs Spell Trouble for the GOP," *USA Today,* November 26, 2006, p. A1.

22. David Brooks, "Thinning the Herd," *New York Times,* October 22, 2006, p. A22.

23. Lang, Dhavale, and Haworth, *Micro Politics.*

24. Ibid.

25. Robert E. Lang and Dawn Dhavale, *The 2005 Governor's Race: A Geographic Analysis of the "Four Virginias,"* election brief (Alexandria: Metropolitan Institute at Virginia Tech, 2005); Lang and Sanchez, *The New Metro Politics.*

26. Lang, Blakely, and Gough, "Keys to the New Metropolis."

27. Lang and Sanchez, *The New Metro Politics.*

28. Ibid.; Alan Berube and others, *Finding Exurbia: America's Fast-Growing Communities at the Metropolitan Fringe,* Living Cities Census Series (Brookings, 2006). For a listing of the 416 counties, see appendix to this chapter.

29. Lang, Sanchez, and Oner, "Beyond Edgeless Cities."

30. In forty-two of the fifty metropolitan areas, one county was identified as containing the employment core. Metropolitan Atlanta includes both Fulton and DeKalb Counties; Dallas–Fort Worth includes both Dallas and Tarrant Counties; Minneapolis–St. Paul includes both Hennepin and Ramsey Counties; New York includes all five New York City boroughs plus Hudson County, N.J.; San Francisco includes San Francisco and Alameda Counties; Tampa–St. Petersburg includes Pinellas and Hillsborough Counties; Virginia Beach includes the independent cities of Virginia Beach, Norfolk, and Newport News; and Washington includes Washington, D.C., and Arlington and Alexandria, Va.

31. Overall, 292 of the 416 (70 percent) county assignments made under this typology match those in Lang and Sanchez, *The New Metro Politics.* The greatest discrepancies occur between the assignment of inner and mature suburbs, with this typology assigning mature status to suburban counties that are designated inner suburbs in Lang and Sanchez's typology (like Prince George's and Baltimore, Maryland; Essex, New Jersey; and DuPage, Illinois). Conversely, in the Sunbelt, counties like San Diego, California; Duval and Orange, Florida; Mecklenburg, North Carolina; and Tarrant and Travis, Texas, are assigned inner suburban status here, although in the earlier typology they were identified as mature suburbs. The typology from Berube and others, *Finding Exurbia,* does not provide a complete basis for comparison, but of the 168 exurban counties identified in the new method, 125 (74 percent) were considered exurban under the earlier method.

32. See Brownstein, "Red-State Seats."

33. Lang, Dhavale, and Haworth, *Micro Politics.*

34. Kerry's campaign pollster, Mark Mellman, when asked why the Democrats performed so poorly, answered, "Nobody has been willing to spend the time and money to figure out why." Ronald Brownstein and Richard Rainey, "GOP Plants Flag on New Voting Frontier," *Los Angeles Times*, November 22, 2004, p. 1; quotation p. 12.

35. Brooks, "For Democrats, Time to Meet the Exurban Voter."

36. Arthur C. Nelson and Robert E. Lang, "The Next 100 Million: Reshaping of America's Built Environment," *Planning*, January 2007, pp. 4–6.

37. Dennis Cauchon, "Marriage Gap Could Sway Elections," *USA Today*, September 27, 2006, p. A1.

38. Although there may also be some slight ecological impacts of living at higher densities, the likelihood is that these impacts do not require people to change their basic values. For example, a conservative living in a city may support increased funding for transit, while a conservative living in an exurb may reject such spending.

39. Bai, "Who Lost Ohio?"; Fritz Wenzel, "Bush Rallies in Key Ohio Areas, Energized Base at Critical Time," *Toledo Blade*, November 4, 2004, p. A1.

40. Paul Farhi and James V. Grimaldi, "GOP Won with Accent on Rural and Traditional," *Washington Post*, November 4, 2004, p. A1.

41. This relationship has been true from the nation's beginnings. Wilbur Zelinsky, *The Cultural Geography of the United States* (Englewood Cliffs, N.J.: Prentice-Hall, 1973).

42. "The Urban Archipelago," *The Stranger*, November 11–17, 2004 (thestranger. com).

43. Philip A. Kennicott, "Election Map Makers, Exercising Some Latitude," *Washington Post*, November 13, 2004, p. C1.

44. Lang and Gough, "Growth Counties."

45. These are the 100 fastest growing counties based on percentage change from 2000 to 2003. Brownstein and Rainey, "GOP Plants Flag on New Voting Frontier."

46. Ibid.

47. Lang, Dhavale, and Haworth, *Micro Politics*.

48. Lang and Dhavale, *The 2005 Governor's Race*.

49. These fast-growing counties are also changing demographically, which may also account for the Democrats' gains. Rosalind S. Helderman, "Newcomers Push Outer Suburbs Left," *Washington Post*, November 10, 2005, p. B1.

50. Ruy Teixeira, "The Battle for the Exurbs," *New York Times*, November 15, 2005, p. A21.

51. During a campaign stop in rural southwest Virginia in 2006, Republican Senate candidate George Allen twice used the word "macaca" to refer to an Indian American student who was filming the event for the opposing Webb campaign. According to the *Washington Post*, the term is considered a racial slur against African immigrants in some European cultures. Tim Craig and Michael D. Shear, "Allen Quip Provokes Outrage, Apology: Name Insults Webb Volunteer," *Washington Post*, August 15, 2006, p. A1.

52. Ruy Teixeira, *The Next Frontier: A New Study of Exurbia* (Washington: New Politics Institute, 2006; www.newpolitics.net/sites/ndn-newpol.civicactions.net/files/npi%20exurbia%20full%20report.pdf).

53. Lang and LeFurgy, *Boomburbs.*

54. Robert E. Lang, James W. Hughes, and Karen A. Danielsen, "Targeting the Suburban Urbanites: Marketing Central City Housing," *Housing Policy Debate* 8 (1997): 437–70; Lang, Blakely, and Gough, "Keys to the New Metropolis."

55. Lang and LeFurgy, *Boomburbs.*

56. Orfield, *American Metropolitics;* Orfield, *Metropolitics.*

57. William Fischel, *The Homevoter Hypothesis: How Home Values Influence Local Government* (Harvard University Press, 2001).

58. Mark, "The Battle over the Suburban, Exurban Vote."

59. Robert E. Lang and Arthur C. Nelson, "America 2040: The Rise of the Megapolitans," *Planning,* January 2007, pp. 7–12.

two

The Big Sort

MIGRATION, COMMUNITY, AND POLITICS
IN THE UNITED STATES OF "THOSE PEOPLE"

BILL BISHOP AND ROBERT CUSHING

The 2004 election was cause for a countrywide case of cognitive dissonance. The election was one of the closest in history, nationally, with only a few percentage points difference between George W. Bush and John Kerry. In individual counties, however, the election was not close at all. In six of ten counties the margin for one party or the other was 20 percentage points or more.[1] Almost half of American voters lived in a county where the local margin was a landslide, in a national election that teetered on a handful of votes in a single state.

Competitive Elections, Landslide Counties

The last five elections have been closer than in any comparable period in the last century. At the same time, an increasing number of counties have developed overwhelming, and stable, local majorities. This was not the way elections were decided immediately after World War II. From 1948 to 1976 the vote jumped around, but in close elections Republicans and Democrats became more evenly mixed, especially so in the 1976 contest (table 2-1). After 1976 the trend was for Republicans and Democrats to grow geographically segregated. In the electoral blowouts of 1964, 1972, and 1984, close to six of ten voters lived in landslide counties (those won by 20 percentage points or more).

During the 1976 contest between President Gerald Ford and Jimmy Carter, Americans were likely to live, work, or worship with many people who

Table 2-1. Voters in Landslide Counties, Competitive and Noncompetitive Elections, 1948–2004

Percent

Year	Voters (type of election)[a]	National victory margin
1948	35.8 (competitive)	4.7
1952	39.9 (noncompetitive)	10.9
1956	46.6 (noncompetitive)	15.5
1960	32.9 (competitive)	0.2
1964	63.5 (noncompetitive)	22.7
1968	37.2 (competitive)	0.8
1972	59.0 (noncompetitive)	23.6
1976	26.8 (competitive)	2.1
1980	41.8 (noncompetitive)	10.6
1984	55.0 (noncompetitive)	18.3
1988	41.7 (competitive)	7.8
1992	37.7 (competitive)	6.9
1996	42.1 (competitive)	9.5
2000	45.3 (competitive)	0.5
2004	48.3 (competitive)	2.5

Source: http://uselectionatlas.org/.

a. Competitive elections are those with less than a 10 percentage point margin; noncompetitive elections are those with more than a 10 percentage point margin. Landslide counties have more than a 20 percentage point margin.

supported a different political party. Just over 26 percent of the nation's voters lived in a landslide county. Then the country began segregating. In 1992 about 38 percent of American voters lived in landslide counties. By 2000 that number had risen to 45 percent. There was a difference between elections before 1976 and after. In the polarizing, and close, 1968 election between Richard Nixon and Hubert Humphrey, about 38 percent of voters lived in landslide counties. The share of voters in landslide counties in the last five competitive presidential elections has been higher than in the 1968 election. (Competitive elections are those won with less than a 10 percentage point margin.) Beginning in 1992 the percentage of people living in landslide counties began an upward progression. And by 2004, in one of the closest presidential contests in history, about 48 percent of voters lived in counties in which the election was not close at all.

Since 2000 there has been disagreement over whether rank-and-file citizens have deep cultural and ideological differences. Or is polarization only the province of political elites? A favorite argument against the notion that Americans are polarized is that division is the product of an imaginative and conflict-happy press corps that spends too much time with Washington partisans and not enough afternoons, as one critic wrote, "hanging out at big box stores, supermarket chains or auto parts stores talking to normal people."[2]

The geographic polarization that has developed in the last several decades, however, would appear to lend some backing to those who say Americans are more polarized. After all, Americans have had unprecedented physical and economic mobility. But these freedoms seem only to have increased, not lessened, a new kind of political isolation. On the other hand, Americans have been geographically segmented in their politics before—during the Civil War, for example. The fact that American counties have become more politically uniform over the past two decades could be inconsequential or not.[3]

Our purpose here is not to join the battle over whether America is divided or not. We are more interested in the phenomenon of a growing number of landslide counties in competitive elections. There is no disagreement that counties have become more politically homogeneous; the disagreement is over what this phenomenon means. In isolation, the clustering of like-minded voters in the majority of American counties may not matter. The phenomenon, however, is not isolated. There is, instead, a remarkable confluence of social, political, and economic trends—which began in the 1970s and continued on through 2004—that have tended to cause like-minded people to cluster and to exclude others who are different.

The neighborhood has not been the only social setting that became more homogeneous in the last quarter of the twentieth century. So have churches, as the moderate middle of American Protestantism began to lose members in the mid-1960s. "Overwhelmingly, people said the people they met in church were extremely homogeneous with them politically," says the University of Pennsylvania political scientist Diana Mutz.[4] Civic organizations, too, that once crossed boundaries of class, occupation, and politics have dissolved and have been replaced by organizations of advocacy. Marketers found Americans dividing into ever-smaller homogeneous groups. "Individuals will congregate in wandering, venturesome image tribes, held together by their pursuit of common ideas, common icons, common entertainment—linked, in other words, by nothing more than a sense of belonging," predicted two prominent marketers in the early 1990s.[5] New products and new advertising strategies have been shaped with these image tribes in mind, and the newest buzz term in the trade was tribal marketing.

As with these other endeavors, politics has also grown more segmented over the past thirty years. The political divisions we take for granted today did not exist in the early 1970s. Women then voted like men. How often a person went to church did not have political meaning. In 1976 there was not a rural-urban split. The average number of voters in Democratic counties in 1976 was slightly smaller than in Republican counties, but by 2004 the average size of a county voting for John Kerry was five times that of a county that supported George W. Bush. This was not simply a function of a switch in allegiances in the rural South. Rural Crook County and urban Multnomah County (Portland), both in Oregon, differed by only 2 percentage points in the 1976 presidential election. By 2004 the difference between the counties was 42 percentage points. Split-ticket voting began to decline in the late 1970s.[6] Party affiliation began to strengthen.[7] Voters became more partisan, and at the same time both individual income inequality and regional economic inequality grew. Communities were growing more politically homogeneous, and the whole of society was changing.

Discovering the Big Sort

Our initial research had nothing to do with politics. We were curious why a small group of cities, Austin among them, was growing so fast and so rich. Bill Bishop was working at the Austin (Texas) *American-Statesman* at the time, and Bob Cushing had recently retired from the sociology department at the University of Texas. In 2002 we began working with a consortium of researchers, sharing theories and data.[8] What we found was that certain technology-rich and innovative cities were benefiting from a special kind of migration. There have always been patterns to migration and development, of course. White Appalachians took the "hillbilly highway" north to booming Cleveland and Detroit after World War II. These were migrations in response to economic hardship and opportunity. The movements we saw from 1970 to 2000 were different. The flows were selective, and they varied by personal characteristics, not broad demographic descriptions. And the places that people were moving to had little to do with the state they were in and most to do with the places themselves.

The country was sorting, or at least that is how we talked about it in our research group conference calls. In the 1990s, for example, 40 percent of the country's more than 300 metropolitan areas lost white population. Whites were not moving from inner cities to suburbs, though. They were abandoning entire regions in favor of others. Blacks moved to one group of cities and whites to others. Young people left rural America and older manufacturing cities for places like Austin, Texas, and Portland, Oregon.

People with college degrees, for example, were "remarkably evenly distributed" among American cities in 1970.[9] But by 1980 a decidedly un-American trend had developed. The economic landscape stopped flattening and grew "spiky."[10] In the last thirty years of the twentieth century, education levels surged. In 1970, 11 percent of the population had at least a college degree. That figure increased to 16 percent in 1980, nearly 19 percent in 1990, and 27 percent in 2004. But as the national totals of college-educated people grew, the differences in this measure among cities was astounding. The percentage of adults with a college education increased in Austin from 17 percent in 1970 to 45 percent in 2004. In Cleveland, however, the change was only from 4 percent to 14 percent. Not only was Cleveland behind, but it was falling further behind. Schooling attracted schooling, as people with degrees moved to live among others with the same levels of education. By 2000 in sixty-two metropolitan areas less than 17 percent of adults had college degrees, and in thirty-two areas more than 34 percent had degrees.[11] The differences were even more dramatic among the young. More than 45 percent of the twenty-five-to-thirty-four-year-olds in Raleigh-Durham, North Carolina, had a college degree in 2000; that figure was only 16 percent in Las Vegas. Segregation by education was particularly apparent in rural areas. By 2000 the percentage of young adults with a college degree in rural areas was only half that of the average city.

Education had always predicted city growth, but beginning in the 1970s that relationship strengthened.[12] The cities that grew the fastest and were the richest were those in which people with college degrees congregated. (Fast-growing Las Vegas is an obvious exception.) As people sorted themselves into particular cities based on their education, the cities became segregated by income, too. Average wages in a city, which were converging in the 1970s, grew more unequal throughout the 1990s. The per capita income of the ten metropolitan areas with the best-educated residents rose nearly 2 percent a year in the 1990s. The per capita income of the ten cities with the least educated population grew less than 1 percent a year.[13]

This was the "big sort" of the 1990s. Every action produced a self-reinforcing reaction: educated people congregated, creating regional wage disparities, which attracted more educated people to these richer regions. Educated people produced more patented ideas, and so the inequality in patent production increased among cities, which further increased the disparity in income. By 2000 "striking variation in average wages" was found across economic regions.[14] America shattered. Prescription drug abuse mired southeastern Kentucky in a hellish kind of civic dysfunction, while Seattle thrived.

In 2002 twenty-one metropolitan areas produced more patents and technological production per capita than the national average.[15] As expected, these areas had higher incomes and faster growth than cities with fewer patents or technology production. Young people went to these cities, and so did people with college degrees. These cities were certainly different economically and demographically, but were they different socially?

In 2000 Robert Putnam commissioned a survey of 30,000 people living in forty American communities. Putnam is the author of *Bowling Alone,* the book documenting the decline in civic organizations and life in the United States.[16] His 2000 survey was designed to measure the nation's civic well-being, so he asked people if they went to church, voted, volunteered, donated to charities, belonged to clubs, or attended discussion groups. Communities varied widely on their stocks of social capital. We looked at the survey results from the perspective of high-tech communities, and what we found was that cities in which people produced both patents and technology had entirely different social structures from those with more traditional economies. Bismarck, North Dakota; Birmingham, Alabama; and Baton Rouge, Louisiana all were brimming with many forms of social capital, but they produced few new marketable ideas and little technology. San Diego, Los Angeles, Atlanta, and Silicon Valley all had bottom-of-the-barrel levels of social connections but high rates of innovation and growth—and high incomes. These cities scored high on only two of Putnam's eleven gauges of social well-being: their residents registered a higher degree of interracial trust and were more inclined to engage in "protest politics." They voted less than those in more traditional cities but signed more petitions and joined more demonstrations and boycotts.

Did high-tech cities really have different social structures than manufacturing towns?[17] To find out, we compared—on a range of social capital measures—the 21 high-tech cities with the 138 cities with the least technology and the fewest patents. The cities were different:

—People in high-tech cities (compared to low-tech cities) were more interested in other cultures and places, more likely to "try anything once," more likely to engage in individualistic activities, more optimistic, and more interested in politics. Although volunteerism in these cities was increasing, it was less than in low-tech cities. Church attendance, community projects, and club membership were all decreasing.

—People in low-tech cities (compared to high-tech cities) were more likely to attend church, to be involved in community projects, to volunteer, and to be supportive of traditional authority. They were more family oriented, had more feelings of isolation and economic vulnerability, were more sedentary, and had more social activities with other people.

These two groups of cities seemed to be developing in radically different ways, moving along diverging trajectories. There were obvious distinctions in the basic ways people were going about their lives, and these social distinctions seemed to have economic consequences.[18] But were these differences also political? The survey asked people if they thought of themselves as liberal or conservative: people in high-tech cities were slightly more liberal than the nation as a whole before 1990, but since then they had become decidedly more liberal. Before 1990 people living in low-tech cities described themselves as slightly more liberal than the national average, but after 1990 an increasing number labeled their politics as conservative. Before 1990 people in high-tech cities were at the national average in terms of party identification. After 1990 these cities were Democratic strongholds. Manufacturing cities and rural areas moved in the reverse direction, growing more Republican. Not only were there differences, but those differences were increasing.

The same pattern appeared in presidential votes. We divided metropolitan areas into five groups, with descending levels of high technology and patents, and then compared how these groups of cities voted since 1980. In the earliest election, all of the groups voted much the same. The twenty-one high-tech regions were slightly more Democratic than the nation as a whole. Suburban cities adjacent to these high-tech areas (Galveston outside of Houston; Orange County outside of L.A.; Boulder outside of Denver) were slightly more Republican than the national average. But in 1980 the vote in all these areas approximated how the nation voted as a whole.

As time passed, though, voting patterns diverged. The high-tech group tilted increasingly Democratic, and in 2000 these cities voted for Al Gore, the Democratic nominee, at levels 17 percent above the national average. (Take out the Texas high-tech cities of Austin, Dallas, and Houston, and the remaining eighteen high-tech cities voted Democratic at a rate 21 percent above the national average.) Gore won the twenty-one high-tech cities and their adjacent metropolitan areas by 5.3 million votes. Bush made up this deficit (almost) in low-tech cities and rural America. The pattern reappeared in 2004, when John Kerry outpolled George W. Bush by more than 5 million votes in high-tech cities, in an election that the Republican won by more than 3 million votes.

These differences in regional well-being had life-and-death consequences. As the returns to knowledge increased and the educated migrated to a select group of cities, the economy of rural areas stagnated. With few local jobs or educational opportunities, rural young people increasingly joined the military; as a result, rural residents have died at disproportionate rates in Afghanistan and Iraq. By the end of October 2007 the death rates in Iraq for rural America were 50 percent higher than that for urban America. In prosperous cities, young people had other opportunities. In smaller towns, there was only the military recruiter. The death rates for Kokomo, Indiana, and Bismarck, North Dakota, were twelve times that for San Francisco.[19]

Digging Deeper: Three Tests of the Big Sort

Opposites do not attract. Psychologists know that people seek out others like themselves for marriage and friendship. That the same phenomenon could be taking place between people and communities is not all that surprising to social psychologists. "Mobility enables the sociological equivalent of 'assortative mating.' "[20]

The economist Charles Tiebout theorized in 1956 that people would pick and choose among communities to find a desirable array of local services at an acceptable level of taxes.[21] People in Portland love their libraries and would be willing to pay taxes to keep them; people who prefer low taxes to libraries would not move to Portland. There would be millions of such "elections," as people cast their votes with moving vans and apartment leases. According to Tiebout, the sorting would mostly be based on economics, as people sought their own balance between services provided and taxes charged. But he also imagined people making their decisions about where to live based on who would be their neighbors. In a footnote to his classic article, the economist allowed, "Not only is the consumer-voter concerned with economic patterns, but he desires, for example, to associate with 'nice' people." Whether for low taxes or the right kind of neighbors, people would cast their ballots for a community with their feet.

There is no poll or survey that could tell us whether the country has undergone a massive Tiebout migration based on lifestyle, culture, and politics. Places did become more politically homogeneous, particularly over the last five elections, but nobody asked people their political leanings and then tracked them as they moved.[22] Although "party identification and most other social identities are highly stable over time," it could also be that places were becoming more politically homogeneous because people were changing their party allegiances once they moved.[23] So we devised three tests to determine if the big sort was, in part, bringing together politically like-minded people.

Test One: Does Like Attract Like?

If counties have been collecting overwhelming numbers from one party or the other, majorities within counties should grow. The power of assortative migration would attract more Democrats to Democratic counties and more Republicans to Republican counties. Counties would tip toward one party, and then they would keep tipping as they attracted more like-minded inhabitants. Some counties (346, to be exact) have voted for the same party in every presidential election between 1948 and 2004. In each election after 1948 more counties picked a side and stuck with it through the 2004 contest. Fifty-four tipped in 1952; 536 tipped in 1968. (Goodbye Democratic South!)

Before counties tipped, they were on average quite competitive politically. The difference between Republican and Democratic candidates over the years was just 2–3 percentage points in untipped counties. But here is the interesting part about the tipping phenomenon: once a county tipped, the vote spread kept growing. The average vote spread in presidential elections among tipped counties was an overwhelming 20 percentage points in most elections. This was particularly true for Republican counties, which saw the margins for Republican presidential candidates increase over time.

The numbers of people living in tipped counties have grown quite large. One half of U.S. voters live in counties that have remained unchanged in their presidential preference since 1980; 60 percent live in counties that have not changed since 1988; and nearly 73 percent live in counties that have not changed since 1992. In Orange and Los Angeles Counties, local majorities have been growing in recent years, a phenomenon found in most U.S. communities (figures 2-1, 2-2).

Could the tipping phenomenon be a function of migration? We found that Republican counties tended to become more politically concentrated than

Figure 2-1. Voters in Orange County, California, by Party, Presidential Elections 1948–2004

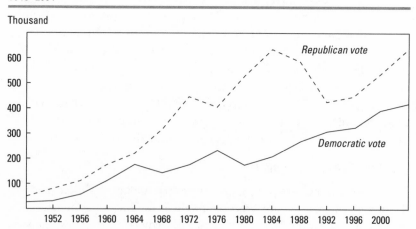

Source: http://uselectionatlas.org/.

Figure 2-2. Voters in Los Angeles County, California, by Party, Presidential Elections 1948–2004

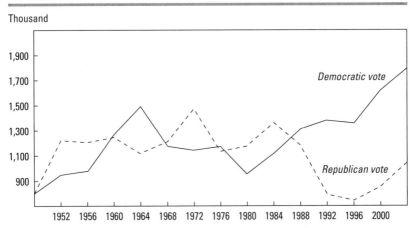

Source: http://uselectionatlas.org/.

Democratic counties. This happened, in part it appears, because people migrating from Republican counties were attracted to other Republican counties to an unusual degree. Between 1995 and 2000, for example, 79 percent of the people who left Republican counties settled in counties that would not only vote Republican in 2004 but that were also likely to be Republican landslide counties. We do not know how individuals voted, but we do know that when people left counties that would vote Republican in 2004, they were two and a half times more likely to move to other counties that would vote Republican than would vote Democratic. (Democrats, on the other hand, migrated to both Republican and Democratic counties.)

Between 1976 and 2004, the gap between the parties increased in 2,085 counties; only 1,026 counties (33 percent) grew more competitive. California is the stereotypical blue (Democratic) state. But within California, seventeen counties grew more Democratic after 1976, and thirty became more reliably Republican. Only eleven (19 percent) became more competitive.

Test Two: Does Geography Matter?

Is it just our imagination or is Lubbock, Texas, really a very different place from Cambridge, Massachusetts? Or more generally, are there significant differences in the lifestyles and beliefs of people living in solidly Republican and solidly Democratic counties? To find out, we compiled evidence from polls conducted by the Pew Research Center from 1996 through 2004 and analyzed the results by how the counties voted in the 2004 election.[24] We compared strong Republican counties (where Bush won by 10 percentage points or more) with strong Democratic counties (where Kerry won by at least 10 percentage points). We found the following three facts about marriage, income, and religion:

—In strongly partisan Republican counties 57 percent of the people were married. In strongly Democratic counties, 47 percent of the people were married.

—In Republican counties 21 percent of the people earned more than $75,000 a year. In Democratic counties, 29 percent earned that.

—In Republican counties 46 percent of the people said that they went to church at least once a week, and half described themselves as evangelicals. In Democratic counties, only 34 percent of the people went to church at least once a week, and 32 percent were evangelicals.

People of the same demographic type (union members, evangelicals, women) differed in their political beliefs based on where they lived. Less than half of the evangelicals living in Kerry-supportive counties supported the Iraq War. In heavily Republican counties, however, this same group supported the war three to one. Labor union members were against the war in Democratic counties but for it in Republican counties. (The gap was nearly 30 percentage points.) Women were against the war in Democratic counties and for it in Republican counties (by a difference of 23 points.)

Scott Keeter at the Pew Research Center did his own calculations with the 2004 data.[25] Keeter looked at landslide counties and found differences on a range of opinions and ways of life. For example, 48 percent of the people living in Democratic landslide counties felt "strongly" that homosexuality "is a way of life that should be accepted by society." Only 21 percent of the people in Republican landslide counties agreed. In Republican landslide counties, 49 percent believed "strongly" that homosexuality should be "discouraged by society," compared to 27 percent in Democratic landslide counties. The two Americas, separated by county lines, disagreed significantly on the war in Iraq, the USA PATRIOT Act, and the use of military force in carrying out foreign policy. And, of course, in Republican strongholds half the people had guns in their homes; in Democratic areas, only 19 percent did.

Test Three: The Hindsight Experiment

If people really have been sorting themselves into two groups over the past three decades, then we ought to be able to look back and see some corresponding demographic trends. We ought to be able to take advantage of the fact that hindsight is 20/20 and find the shifts in population that correspond to the balkanized communities we live in today.

To use our 20/20 vision, we divided the nation's counties into four groups based on the results from the 2004 election. One group was made up of landslide Democratic counties (those with a more than 20 percentage point advantage for Kerry and with a population of 63 million in 2006); the second group was made up of competitive Democratic counties (those for Kerry by less than 20 percentage points and with a population of 68 million); third were landslide Republican counties (more than 20 percentage points for Bush; 84 million people); and fourth, competitive Republican counties (under 20 percentage points for Bush; 87 million people). We examined these groups retrospectively, tracking them through time to see if and how their demographic composition changed. We knew where these counties ended up in the highly polarized 2004 election. We wanted to understand how they got there—and whether the counties in one group had anything more in common than how they voted for president in November 2004.

Here is the first calculation, a measurement that shows the vote between 1948 and 2004 for both landslide counties and competitive counties (figure 2-3). This measure displays the deviation in the vote in each party from the national average: above zero means the county group voted more Republican than the nation as a whole; below zero means the county group voted more Democratic. Before 1976 counties of both majorities jumped around. Beginning in 1980, though, they began to diverge, and they kept separating

Figure 2-3. County Voting Patterns, by Party and Election Competitiveness, 1948–2004

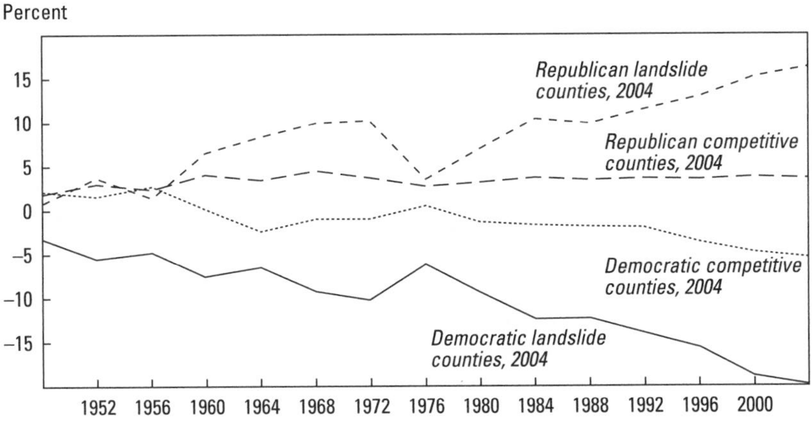

Source: http://uselectionatlas.org/.

Figure 2-4. College Graduates in County Population, by Party and Election Competitiveness, 1970, 1980, 1990, 2000

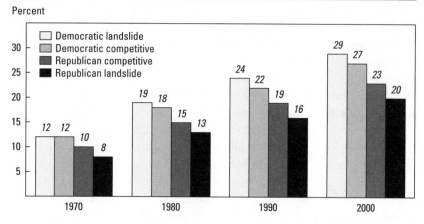

Source: http://uselectionatlas.org and U.S. Census.

for the next quarter century. The division so evident in the 2000 and 2004 elections had been in the making for decades.

Get used to the pattern. It appeared over and again as we evaluated other demographic measures. The distribution of people with bachelor's degrees or higher, for example, shows that landslide Democratic counties have been gain-

Figure 2-5. Churchgoers in County Population, by Party and Election Competitiveness, 1952, 1971, 1980, 1990, 2000

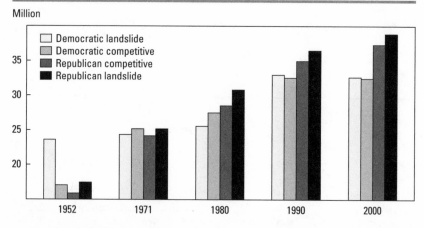

Source: http://uselectionatlas.org; Glenmary Research Center, *Religious Congregations and Membership in the United States* (Cincinnati, 2000).

Figure 2-6. Foreign-Born in County Population, by Party and Election Competitiveness, 1970, 1980, 1990, 2000

Percent

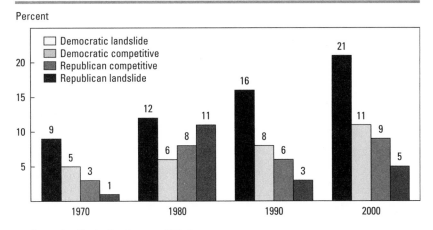

Source: http://uselectionatlas.org and U.S. Census.

ing on this measure (figure 2-4). Republican counties, on the other hand, gained the most in church members. Democratic counties, in fact, lost churchgoers (figure 2-5). All county groups gained foreign-born residents, but by 2000, 21 percent of the population in Democratic landslide counties was foreign-born, compared to just 5 percent in Republican landslide counties (figure 2-6).

In 1970 each of the four county groups was home to about a quarter of the nation's white population. (Republican landslide counties actually had a slightly smaller percentage of the total white population than did Democratic landslide counties.) Over the next thirty years, however, whites became more concentrated in Republican counties (figure 2-7). And Democratic counties, especially Democratic landslide counties, lost shares of white population. By the time of the 2000 census, only 18 percent of the nation's white population lived in Democratic landslide counties, while 30 percent of the white population lived in counties that provided Republicans with landslide margins in 2004. The real white flight of the past two generations has been whites moving to communities that were becoming staunchly Republican.

Everywhere we looked we found differences in migration patterns that related to the vote. One final example: we tracked the average per capita incomes of people moving into and out of our four county groups. Those moving from out of state into Republican landslide counties in 2003 had average per capita yearly earnings of $22,939. Those moving from out of state into Democratic landslide counties had average per capita yearly earnings of $30,492.

Figure 2-7. Whites in County Population, by Party and Election Competitiveness, 1970, 1980, 1990, 2000

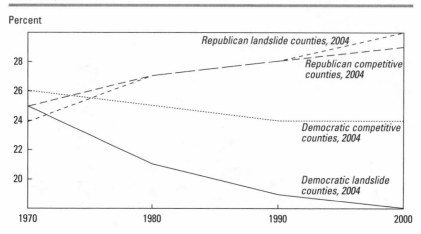

Percent

Source: http://uselectionatlas.org and U.S. Census.

People were sorting by race and place of birth, by income and education, by belief, race, and religion. The numbers of people moving were large, about 4 percent of the population each year moves from one county to another. And the consequence of this shuffling, separation, and segmentation was an increasing political homogeneity in communities. That we could see, too. Before the 1970s about half of all voters lived in counties won by their political opponents. After 1976 that percentage steadily dropped, sinking to less than 40 percent in 2004. This was especially evident in Republican counties. In the first seven elections after World War II, about half of all Democratic voters lived in Republican counties. After 1976 this percentage dropped. By 2004 only 34 percent of Democratic voters lived in Republican counties.

The Big Sort in Action: The Case of the Colorado Twist

Traditionally Republican Colorado has become increasingly Democratic over the years. In 2004 John Kerry cut Bush's margin of victory there to half of what it had been in 2000. A Democrat won the U.S. Senate seat in 2004, and the party swept both houses of the state legislature. Democrat Bill Ritter won the governor's race in 2006 based in large part on his promotion of alternative energy. Ron Brownstein of the *Los Angeles Times,* writing in 2006, found that the language of politics in the state had shifted.[26] People were more concerned with government services than with low taxes or abortion.

"The whole rhetoric has changed in the past four or five years," a Democrat in Denver told Brownstein.

Colorado has become more Democratic overall, but not all of Colorado. Some parts of the state are just as Republican as they have been at any time in the past half-century. Over the past two decades, however, people from other states have flowed into Colorado. When we tracked these migrants, we learned that the Colorado counties with the highest inflows of people from other states were also the counties in which support for Democratic presidential candidates has been growing. The counties least affected by migration from other states had actually grown slightly more Republican since the 1980s. In addition, these politically opposite parts of Colorado were attracting people from entirely different places. The people moving to the fast-growing counties around Denver were three times more likely to have come from blue counties outside Colorado than the people moving to the slower-growing (and heavily Republican) counties along the Kansas, Oklahoma, and Nebraska borders. The county that sent the most people to Colorado between 1981 and 2004 was deeply Democratic Los Angeles County, California.

Migration is helping to turn Colorado purple, but since the big sort works at the community level—and although the state as a whole grew more politically mixed—the divisions between Republican and Democratic areas within the state widened. Colorado's story is of a statewide narrowing of the gap between the parties but also of expanding cultural and political divisions within the state. In that sense, Colorado is a microcosm of the nation, where government is being called on to meet the demands of communities that have less and less in common. It is a chore made harder by the peculiar psychology of like-minded groups.

The Social Psychology of a Landslide; or, What *Was* the Matter with Ohio?

Just as there are no data that directly link the politics of people who move to the increasing partisanship of counties, there are no data that reveal whether individuals in these like-minded communities are growing more extreme in their thinking. In fact, one of the criticisms of our stories in the *Austin American-Statesman* was that even in communities with large partisan majorities there are still plenty of people there with opposite opinions.[27] Even the most partisan county is diverse politically.

It is not the purpose of this essay to delve into the psychology of groups. But it is worth noting that years of political research have found that communities with landslide majorities have a different kind of politics than those with mixed outcomes. The anecdotal evidence is easy to find. The chair of the local Democratic Party in a strong Republican county in the Texas hill country told us about the time his group prepared a float for the annual July 4 parade through the center of town. "We got it all decorated," Gillespie County's George Keller recalled, "but nobody wanted to ride." Nobody wanted to risk the stigma of being identified as a Democrat in an overwhelmingly Republican area. "Thank goodness we got rained out," Keller said of the orphaned float. A Republican county commissioner living in a Democratic precinct in Austin moved to a more Republican address after his car was egged one night. "You really do recognize when you aren't in step with the community you live in," he told us. Another political minority talked of remaining silent in book groups when the conversation turned to politics. A woman told a *New York Times* reporter she moved to a Dallas exurb instead of to Austin because, "Politically, I feel a lot more at home here."

Over the last fifty years political scientists have found that large political majorities do have strong effects over those in the minority. They squelch dissent and embolden majorities. The political scientist Warren Miller used survey data to examine the 1952 presidential vote (Eisenhower versus Stevenson) in counties with overwhelming party majorities.[28] He found that the presence of large partisan majorities had the effect of dampening turnout among citizens in the political minority. Rather than buck the majority and risk social sanction, citizens in the minority simply stayed away from the polls. Minority parties suffered in lopsided counties, while majority parties increased their turnout—a self-reinforcing social mechanism that Miller feared could damage the country's two-party system.

A nearly even mix of Republicans and Democrats increases voter turnout, according to the Notre Dame political scientist David Campbell.[29] People are more interested in the election in this situation and are motivated to campaign for their candidates. In landslide counties, however, there is an entirely different social dynamic. Political minorities in heavily majority counties not only avoid the voting booth but also withdraw from all forms of public life. Campbell has found that political minorities in communities with large majorities are even less likely to volunteer for civic causes. People in the majority do vote in large numbers, but not because they feel that their vote is important to the outcome. Instead, they simply want to support the community, to show allegiance to the majority. A vote becomes more an affirmation of the group than an expression of a civic opinion. "In places where people share opinions you are more likely to find tighter norms," Campbell told us. "And that's because, to put it bluntly, in these communities people can enforce norms. So if you haven't voted, you feel a little bit ashamed."[30] Or as James Gimpel, J. Celeste Lay, and Jason Schuknecht write, "The political segregation and partisan balkanization of neighborhoods promotes a polarization of viewpoints that is intolerant of internal dissent among adherents of a particular party."[31]

The overwhelming attention given to political celebrity—and political conspiracy—in our time has obscured the politics of place. After all, if people simply respond to the faults, successes, and leadership of political elites, then increasingly homogeneous neighborhoods do not matter. But politically like-minded regions practice a different kind of politics than do places with a greater mix of allegiances. A person's politics are affected by that person's neighbors. Here's one example:

In the early 1960s the political scientist John Fenton wondered why working-class voters in Ohio supported Republicans, a political act that was against their economic interests.[32] Fenton explained this phenomenon by looking at the shape of the state's neighborhoods. Upper-class voters lived in tightly knit, geographically compact communities. Physical proximity made it easier for them to maintain political cohesion and to vote as an ideological herd. In Ohio's large number of midsize cities, however, there was no corresponding critical mass of workers. Working-class voters were dispersed. "In Ohio you had a fairly even distribution of these working-class voters across the state," explained University of Maryland's James Gimpel, the scholar today who has done the most work on the political effects of migration.[33] "And because they lived among farmers and clerks and ditch diggers, they were not as inclined to vote so monolithically." In nearby Michigan, Gimpel said, working-class voters lived close to one another, and their geographic proximity powered their ideological and political intensity.

In Ohio, however, workers were spread out, and the effect of this diffusion, John Fenton wrote more than thirty years ago, was profound:

> The postman did not talk the same language as his accountant neighbor, and the accountant was in a different world from the skilled workman at Timken Roller Bearing who lived across the street. Thus, conversation between them usually took the form of monosyllabic grunts about the weather. . . . The disunity of unions and the Democratic party in Ohio was a faithful reflection of the social disorganization of their members.[34]

Thomas Frank, in 2004, bemoaned the failure of Great Plains residents to vote in their economic interests and asked, in the title of his book, what's the matter with Kansas?[35] Frank's answer is that manipulative Republicans, who offered intelligent design rather than a living wage, had duped the working-class voters of his home state. And thin-blooded liberals, who had gotten above their populist upraising, had abandoned Democratic principles. John Fenton asked a similar question forty years earlier: what's the matter with Ohio? He arrived at an explanation that did not depend on either gullibility or duplicity. Fenton found that the way people lived, and the communities they lived in, had shaped their political lives.

Communities shape our political thinking, too. Years of social psychological experiments have shown that like-minded groups over time become more extreme in the way they are like-minded. It is true for fraternity boys, French students, and federal appeals court judges. In 2005 several professors conducted an experiment to see if the mere discussion of political issues in like-minded groups would result in increased polarization.[36] They recruited sixty-three Colorado citizens, ages twenty to seventy-five, half from Boulder and half from Colorado Springs, for an experiment in the effects of political discussion on a homogeneous group.

In 2004, 67 percent of the people in Boulder County voted for John Kerry, and 67 percent of the people in El Paso County (Colorado Springs) voted for George Bush. The authors picked liberals from Boulder and conservatives from Colorado Springs and then measured the individual opinions of these citizens about three issues: global warming, gay marriage, and affirmative action. True to form, the Boulder citizens were initially more liberal on these three issues than participants from Colorado Springs. The authors then divided the citizens from the two cities into batches of six, making ten groups, five from each city. The groups were then asked to discuss these three issues, to deliberate, and then to come to a consensus on the same questions each participant had been asked about individually.

The effects of deliberation are not encouraging for those who look to rational community discussion as an antidote to polarization. The ten groups discussed the three issues and came to a consensus in twenty-five of thirty discussions. In nineteen of these twenty-five, however, the consensus of the group was more extreme than the prediscussion opinions of the individuals had been. Boulder residents came to agreements on the three issues that were more liberal than the answers they had given as individuals. Colorado Springs citizens, once in their like-minded groups, grew more conservative.[37] Before the discussion, "there was considerable overlap between many individuals in the two different cities. After deliberation, the overlap was much smaller."[38] Peoples' initial beliefs had been amplified by exposure to like-minded others. They had grown more polarized after only two hours of discussion. As in hundreds of other group polarization experiments, each like-minded collection of people became more extreme after discussion. Moreover, the differences within the groups narrowed. Discussion did not spark free thinking. Instead, each homogeneous community concluded its deliberations in greater conformity. People who were already like-minded grew more alike after discussing politics with their neighbors even as, within the group, they grew more extreme.

Of course, at times we meet and talk with those having differing political opinions. But less often than we might think. In a comparison of citizens from twelve countries, Americans were the least likely to discuss politics with someone holding a different view.[39] Americans who are poor and nonwhite are more likely than the rich and the white to be exposed to political disagreement. Citizens with the most diverse political discussion mates are those who have not graduated from high school. Those with the most homogeneous political circles have suffered through graduate school.

And how does this play out in our like-minded churches, our homogeneous clubs, and our one-class neighborhoods? Well, do we really need a pollster or a political scientist to tell us? Just look around.

The United States of "Those People"

The effect of growing local majorities is doubled-edged: local majorities use their powers to address every conceivable issue or problem and to enact the will of their like-minded constituencies in local law and regulation in what has been an explosion of federalism. On the national level, congressional members come to Washington with unassailable majorities; as a result, the number of moderates in Congress (both House and Senate) has been declining for the past three decades. Both phenomena are the result of the big sort. The undeniable homogenization of congressional districts does not appear to be a function of redistricting. It is, instead, a product of communities growing more like-minded over time.[40] The federal system and more than a few state legislatures have been slowed to the speed of cold syrup, as a Congress balkanized by a politically lopsided geography has lost the means and the will to deal with issues that demand trust and compromise.

We expect these trends to continue, because we expect the sorting to continue. What we are describing, after all, is not a whim or the result of some particularly manipulative political strategist. The sorting of people into communities of interest is a perfectly natural phenomenon: given the choice, people choose to live around others like themselves. That is not likely to change. This does not mean that communities will remain aligned just-so with political parties. Eventually, issues or events will arise that will create cross-cutting relationships where, today, few exist. Old coalitions will be replaced by new ones, and the map's colors will change. Eventually.

That has not happened yet. In the early part of the 2008 primary season, presidential candidates hopscotched among the states where they found particularly strong tribal affinities. It is not surprising that Senator Barack Obama would find an enthusiastic crowd in technology-rich Boise, a city that has more in common with Austin than any other Idaho city. Similarly, Obama won hip and turquoise Taos but lost to Senator Hillary Clinton by 20 percentage points just a county or two over. Governor Mike Huckabee found particular success in the exurbs, communities rich in large churches. The campaign has revealed splits within parties, but there have not been any new alignments between parties. White evangelicals are not drifting away from the Republican Party (despite stories about the evangelical crackup). Republicans and Democrats still have different views on almost every issue. (The gap between Republican and Democratic opinion on progress in the Iraq War increased throughout 2007, according to the Pew Research Center.)[41] A poll conducted for the Norman Lear Center at the University of Southern California in 2007 found that "When it comes to TV networks, it's quite likely that if conservatives like it, liberals hate it. And vice versa."[42] In New Hampshire pollsters found "the swing voter is vanishing," according to the *Washington Post,* as increasing percentages of voters favored one party or the other.[43] And sure enough, in New Hampshire exit polls, 69 percent of Republican voters wanted a candidate as conservative as—or more conservative than—George W. Bush. Meanwhile, 65 percent of Democrats were "angry" with the president, with another 28 percent merely "dissatisfied but not angry." This is not a likely recipe for the end of political conflict.

The general election this year is looking a lot like 2004, when the Bush campaign realized that, in fact, the swing voter had vanished and that money would be better spent on turnout than on persuasion. This time, however, both parties will have the latest data that will allow them to target likely voters in even the most hostile communities. Parties will conduct campaigns in communities where their opponents have landslide majorities, but it will not be a frontal assault. Targeting allows parties to pluck out the lonely Democrat in a cul-de-sac of Republicans or the misplaced McCain supporter in my neighborhood in Austin. All of the campaign strategies developed over the last few years—from refinements in canvassing to target marketing to the use of social networks in delivering a candidate's message—are aimed at reassuring people who have protected themselves from discordant opinion.

There is certainly a heartfelt desire among voters for the partisanship to end. But it is hard to know exactly what this means. The University of Nebraska political scientist Elizabeth Theiss-Morse describes part of the widespread frustration with politics and politicians. She has conducted focus groups in Omaha and found people confused by the consensus they experience in their neighborhoods versus the conflict they see at large in the nation: "People said many times, 'Eighty percent of us agree. We all want the same thing. . . . It's those 20 percent who are just a bunch of extremists out there.' It didn't matter what their political views were. They really saw it as us against this fringe. The American people versus them, the fringe." And yes, the fringe was associated with a place. Often the good Nebraskans would conclude in frustration, "Those people in California are really weird." In the national focus group of this presidential year, we see a lot of people calling for an end to partisanship and sense that all of us are confounded by "those people" with the weird political beliefs. We see far less indication that groups separated by the economy, education, and culture are finding a sudden common cause in national politics.

And while there is general agreement that politicians should compromise more, most Americans feel like it is the other side that should give in. A January 2007 poll conducted by the Pew Research Center found, according to its title, broad support for political compromise in Washington.[44] But Pew found that "the problem with questions of political compromise is that peoples' answers will always be relative—compromise is fine when it is the other side that is doing the compromising." So 77 percent of Republicans believe that Democratic leaders should work with President Bush, 78 percent of Democrats believe that Republican leaders should work with Democratic leaders, and 42 percent of Democrats say their own leaders should work with the president. Politicians are still rewarded more for their ideological steadfastness rather than for their willingness to find accommodation. They will be rewarded for compromising when cross-cutting issues break through the rigid boundaries of what each party considers permissible political thought.

The generational appeal of Barack Obama reveals what will certainly change the politics of partisanship and geographic segmentation. We found in our research among the young—and especially those in what has come to be called the emerging church—a reluctance to adopt a black and white attitude about politics. "What bothers us is, when we look at it, the issues seem way more gray," one young minister in Louisville, Kentucky, told us. "When it comes to politics, they seem extremely gray, and extremely complicated." The minister speaks for his generation, according to J. Walker Smith, president of the marketing firm Yankelovich Partners.[45] The members of the next generation are seeing politics and political conflict in a different way. We will have to wait to find out if their neighborhood choices will follow their vision.

Notes

1. In all the calculations here, third-party votes are excluded. Including third parties changes the numbers discussed here but does not alter the trends.

2. Morris P. Fiorina, with Samuel J. Abrams and Jeremy C. Pope, *Culture War? The Myth of a Polarized America*, 2d ed. (New York: Pearson Longman, 2006), pp. 21–22.

3. See Philip Klinkner, "Red and Blue Scare: The Continuing Diversity of the American Political Landscape," *Forum* 2004 (forum.com); and Edward Glaeser and Bryce Ward, "The Myth and Realities of American Political Geography," Discussion Paper 2100 (Harvard Institute of Economic Research, 2006). Klinkner had three primary objections to the first part of what became a ten-part series in the *Austin American-Statesman* in 2004 (www.statesman.com/metrostate/content/special reports/greatdivide/index.html). First, he said our math was wrong. On this he was mistaken: he failed to see that we included only Democratic and Republican votes in our calculations. Now we all agree on the results. Second, Klinkner found the results in line with historical trends and therefore unremarkable. But we believe increases in the "segregation index" of about 50 percent over thirty years, given the mobility of our times, to be remarkable enough to be worth exploring. Finally, Klinkner wrote that even if a large number of counties were becoming more politically homogeneous, there is still political diversity in every U.S. community. But a large amount of political science and social psychological research has consistently discovered that heavy political majorities affect the culture and politics of communities.

4. See Diana C. Mutz and Jeffrey J. Mondak, "The Workplace as a Context for Cross-Cutting Political Discourse," *Journal of Politics* 68 (2006): 141–46.

5. Don Peppers and Martha Rogers, *The One-to-One Future: Building Relationships One Customer at a Time* (New York: Currency/Doubleday, 1993), quotations on pp. 174 and 386–87.

6. David C. Kimball, "A Decline in Ticket Splitting and the Increasing Salience of Party Labels," in *Models of Voting in Presidential Elections: The 2000 Elections,* edited by Herbert F. Weisber and Clyde Wilcox (Stanford: Stanford Law and Politics, 2004).

7. Larry M. Bartels, "Partisanship and Voting Behavior, 1952–1996," *American Journal of Political Science* 44 (2000): 35–51.

8. We held regular phone conferences with Richard Florida and Kevin Stolarick, then at Carnegie Mellon University; Gary Gates, then at the Urban Institute; Terry Nichols Clark, at the University of Chicago; and Joe Cortright, a Portland, Oregon, economist. Richard Florida was writing *The Rise of the Creative Class* at the time. Gary Gates was doing research on the distribution of gays and lesbians in the United States. Terry Clark was collecting string for his book *The City as Entertainment Machine*. And Joe Cortright was beginning research on the movement of young people, which would appear in his report "The Young and Restless in a Knowledge Economy."

9. Edward L. Glaeser and Christopher R. Berry, "The Divergence of Human Capital Levels across Cities," Discussion Paper 2091 (Harvard Institute of Economic Research, 2005).

10. Richard Florida, "The World Is Spiky," *Atlantic,* October 2005, pp. 59–51.

11. This and the following information from Glaeser and Berry, "The Divergence of Human Capital," p.11.

12. Joe Cortright, "The Young and Restless in a Knowledge Economy" (Chicago: CEOs for Cities, 2005).

13. Glaeser and Berry, "The Divergence of Human Capital," pp. 2–11.

14. Michael E. Porter, "The Economic Performance of Regions," *Regional Studies* 37 (2003): 550–51.

15. They are San Diego, Chicago, Los Angeles, Philadelphia, San Jose, Phoenix, Denver, Boston, New York, Seattle, San Francisco, Albuquerque, Washington, Rochester (Minn.), Boise, Portland (Ore.), Raleigh-Durham, Austin, Atlanta, Houston, and Dallas.

16. Robert Putnam, *Bowling Alone: The Collapse and Revival of American Community* (New York: Simon and Schuster, 2000).

17. To measure this difference, we used the DDB Needham Life Style survey, conducted by the advertising firm DDB Worldwide of Chicago.

18. Our explanation for these social differences in cities is the same one employed by Rich Florida and Joe Cortright: loose social structures encourage economies based on ideas and the easy transfer of information. Florida, "The World Is Spiky"; Cortright, "The Young and Restless."

19. See "Iraq War's Small Town Sacrifice," in *The Daily Yonder* (www.dailyyonder.com/iraq-wars-small-town-sacrifice).

20. David Myers, interview with author.

21. Charles Tiebout, "A Pure Theory of Local Expenditures," *Journal of Political Economy* 64 (1956): 416–24; quotation on p. 418.

22. Ian McDonald, while allowing the scarcity of evidence, found that, "in general, the empirical tests shown here imply that new migrants most resemble the non-migrant electorate in their new locations. These results complement the argument that migration has tended to geographically sort electoral preferences, and thus homogenize the preferences of local constituencies." See McDonald, "Voters Like Us: Domestic

Migration and Geographic Sorting in the 2000 U.S. Presidential Election," paper prepared for the annual meeting of the American Political Science Association, Chicago, September 1, 2007.

23. Donald Green, Bradley Palmquist, and Eric Schickler, *Partisan Hearts and Minds: Political Parties and the Social Identities of Voters* (New Haven: Yale University Press, 2002), p. 83. There is more evidence that people will change their minds about clear-cut issues in order to remain in step with their party. See Thomas M. Carsey and Geoffrey C. Layman, "Changing Sides or Changing Minds? Party Identification and Policy Preferences in the American Electorate," *American Journal of Political Science* 50 (2006): 464–77.

24. There were nineteen surveys and more than 31,000 interviews in this collection of Pew Research Center polls.

25. Scott Keeter, analysis provided to author.

26. Ronald Brownstein, "As Democrats Look West, Colorado Budges," *Los Angeles Times,* September 28, 2006, p. A20.

27. "The Great Divide" series appeared in the Austin (Texas) *American-Statesman* in 2004 (www.statesman.com/metrostate/content/specialreports/greatdivide/index. html).

28. Warren Miller, "One-Party Politics and the Voter," *American Political Science Review* 50 (1956): 707–25.

29. David E. Campbell, "What You Do Depends on Where You Are: Community Heterogeneity and Participation," paper prepared for the annual meeting of the Midwest Political Science Association, April 15, 2004; see also David Campbell, *Why We Vote: How Schools and Communities Shape Our Civic Life* (Princeton University Press, 2006).

30. David Campbell, interview with author.

31. James G. Gimpel, J. Celeste Lay, and Jason E. Schuknecht, *Cultivating Democracy: Civic Environments and Political Socialization in America* (Brookings, 2003), p. 120.

32. John Fenton, *Midwest Politics* (New York: Holt, Rinehart, and Winston, 1966).

33. James Gimpel, interview with author. Also see Gimpel, Lay, and Schuknecht, *Cultivating Democracy.*

34. Fenton, *Midwest Politics,* pp. 150–52.

35. Thomas Frank, *What's the Matter with Kansas? How Conservatives Won the Heart of America* (New York: Metropolitan, 2004).

36. David Schkade, Cass R. Sunstein, and Reid Hastie, "What Happened on Deliberation Day?" Olin Working Paper 298 (University of Chicago, Law and Economics, 2006).

37. Ibid. The authors devised a simple ten-point scale (ranging from very strongly agree to very strongly disagree) that participants marked in answering three questions, one each about affirmative action, global warming, and gay marriage. The average difference in the answers given by individuals from Colorado Springs and individuals

from Boulder was 4.59 before deliberation. After deliberation, however, the difference between the groups had grown to 6.24.

38. Ibid., p. 3.

39. Diana C. Mutz, *Hearing the Other Side: Deliberative versus Participatory Democracy* (Cambridge University Press, 2006), p. 31.

40. For evidence that geographic sorting, not gerrymandering, is creating more lopsided congressional districts, see Alan Abramowitz, Brad Alexander, and Matthew Gunning, "Don't Blame Redistricting for Uncompetitive Elections," *PS: Political Science and Politics* 39 (2006): 87–90; Bruce Oppenheimer, "Deep Red and Blue Congressional Districts," in *Congress Reconsidered*, 8th ed., edited by Lawrence C. Dodd and Bruce Oppenheimer (Washington: Congressional Quarterly Press, 2005); Keiko Ono, "Electoral Origins of Partisan Polarization in Congress: Debunking the Myth," *Extensions: A Journal of the Carl Albert Congressional Research and Studies Center* (Fall 2005; www.ou.edu/special/albertctr/extensions/fall2005/Ono.html).

41. "Petraeus' Proposals Draw Public Approval, but Fail to Lift War Support: Increases in Optimism Are Mostly Limited to Republicans," report, Pew Research Center, September 18, 2007 (http://pewresearch.org/pubs/596/petraeus-proposals-draw-public-approval-but-fail-to-lift-war-support).

42. Norman Lear Center/Zogby Survey on Politics and Entertainment: 2007 (www.learcenter.org/html/projects/?&cm=zogby/07).

43. Alec MacGillis, "In N.H., the Swing Voter Is Vanishing," *Washington Post,* December 18, 2007, p. A4.

44. Pew Research Center for the People and the Press, "Broad Support for Political Compromise in Washington," January 22, 2007 (http://people-press.org/reports/display.php3?ReportID=302).

45. J. Walker Smith and Ann Clurman, *Generation Ageless* (New York: HarperCollins, 2007), p. 24.

Race and Class

three
Race, Immigration, and America's Changing Electorate

WILLIAM H. FREY

One of the most profound changes in America's demography this century will be its shifting racial and ethnic makeup. The rise of immigration from Latin America and Asia, the higher fertility rate of some minorities, and the low fertility and aging of America's white population will have substantial impacts on the nation's demographic profile, with important implications for the electorate. The significance of these changes on identity politics, racial coalitions, and reactions to immigration has already been seen in the 2008 presidential sweepstakes. Yet these shifts are only the tip of the iceberg, as Hispanic, Asian, and black Americans make up ever larger shares of the electorate.

This chapter discusses the shifts playing out in 2008, with an eye toward what they will mean in the future.[1] It examines the magnitude of minority population growth and how it differs from that of past election cycles; it also examines the lag that immigrant minorities experience in translating their growth into voting power. It then notes how these groups differ from each other in social and demographic profiles and on political issues, with special emphasis on immigration. How important will these groups be in deciding the

The author wishes to thank Ruy Teixeira and Karlyn Bowman for their advice and assistance in obtaining current survey information. He is also grateful to the University of Michigan Population Studies Center and Institute for Social Research, for providing U.S. Census and additional survey data, and to Cathy Sun of the University of Michigan, for assistance with programming and data preparation.

2008 presidential election? What is their projected impact in key battleground (purple) states? What is their projected impact in less competitive states?

The chapter concludes by taking a longer view of what the nation's changing race-ethnic makeup implies for the future, as race-ethnic minorities become larger portions of the electorate and as their geographic reach becomes wider. At the same time, it emphasizes that, for the present, presidential candidates will need to cope with a racially balkanized electorate: regionally distinct voting blocs that have sometimes conflicting interests, especially in the highly prized purple states.

Minorities Matter

If it were not obvious before, the crucial role that racial and ethnic minorities can play in a presidential election became obvious in 2000, when the results of two racially diverse states, Florida and New Mexico, were determined by 537 and 366 votes, respectively. Since then political operatives' attention began to turn to the significant Hispanic population as a target of opportunity. Indeed, President Bush and his political guru Karl Rove subsequently placed greater emphasis on competing with Democrats for the Hispanic voting bloc. At the same time, left-leaning commentators have viewed their rising numbers as part of a new Democratic majority coalition.[2] The importance of racial and ethnic minority voters is still evolving in American politics, as politicians at all levels grapple with the changes, backlashes, and interest groups associated with these shifts in the population and the electorate.

Indeed, most middle-aged Americans grew up at a time when the primary minority group was African American and was located primarily in the South and in large cities in the North and on the West Coast. Although Hispanics, Asians, and other minorities existed, they were heavily clustered in specific locales. This is now changing dramatically, thanks to the huge immigration of the past two decades. The extent of the implication of immigration for politics may take another two decades to be fully realized.

Since the 2000 census the minority population—all but non-Hispanic whites, or Anglos—accounted for more than four-fifths of the nation's 1 percent per annum growth.[3] For the first eight years of this decade, Hispanics and Asians each increased their populations by nearly a third, and blacks grew by 9 percent, compared with a modest 2 percent for whites. The impact on the nation's race-ethnic profile has been both gradual and noticeable, such that over five presidential elections, 2000–16, the white population share will be reduced from about 70 percent of U.S. residents to nearly 60 percent.

Due to both the clustering and dispersion of this minority growth across the United States, fourteen states (including the District of Columbia) already are below or near 60 percent white. These include majority-minority states like California, Texas, New Mexico, and Hawaii; fast-growing interior states like Arizona and Nevada, which are attracting new Hispanic and Asian minorities; and southern states like Florida and Georgia, which have substantial black populations and are also attracting many more Hispanics.

At the same time, a slew of states in the Upper Midwest, Great Plains, and New England, where the new minority dispersion has yet to take effect, remain predominately white. What these geographical variations imply for future politics is discussed below. But it is important to note that the impact of immigrant minority dispersion, as well as the continued growth and southward migration of the black population, is placing the nation in a demographic flux, with respect to race-ethnic groups, that has not been seen for some time.

While these new racial and ethnic demographic shifts may seem dramatic, their implications for the electorate and for politicians are only at the beginning of what is likely to be a long transformation. One reason for this is the uneven dispersal of new immigrant groups away from traditional gateway regions. A more immediate reason is the slow translation of demographic representation into electoral representation. This is especially the case among such immigrant minorities as Hispanics and Asians, whose representation in the overall population heavily outweighs their representation among eligible voters (a large share of both communities is under voting age, and the adults are less likely to be citizens).

Among whites in the United States, 77 percent are eligible voters; among blacks, about 66 percent are eligible voters (figure 3-1). Only 50 percent of Asians and 39 percent of Hispanic residents are eligible voters. The problem of underrepresentation is further compounded by the fact that Hispanic and Asian citizens exhibit a lower propensity to register and actually vote than do whites and blacks. Registration patterns for the 2004 presidential election show that less than half of all Hispanic and Asian citizens voted, compared to two-thirds of whites and three-fifths of blacks (figure 3-2). Overall, if these patterns hold, for every 100 Hispanics residing in the United States in November 2008, only 19 will vote, and for every 100 Asians, 22 will vote. Comparable numbers of whites and blacks are 52 and 40.

This translation gap can be viewed in a broader context, by comparing the racial profiles of the total population with those of the citizen population and also the actual voting population. While it is true that America's population is more diverse than ever before, such that more than 34 percent are

Figure 3-1. Eligible Voters as Share of Total Population: Whites, Blacks, Hispanics, and Asians

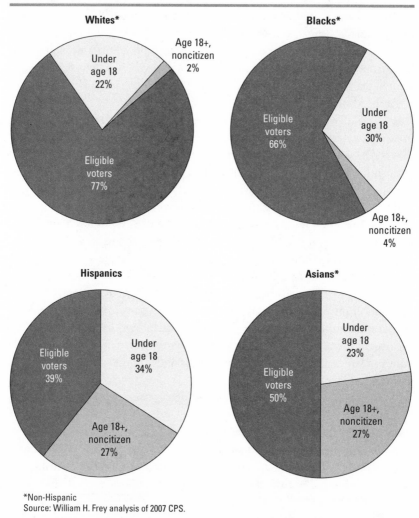

minorities and 15 percent are Hispanic, the citizen population is 74 percent white and only 9 percent Hispanic (figure 3-3). Finally, the expected voting population is the least diverse of all. Almost four out of five voters will be white and only 6 percent will be Hispanic.

The translation gap varies by state. In many immigrant new destination states like Georgia, North Carolina, and Nevada a smaller share of the adult

Figure 3-2. Percent of Eligible Voters, Registered and Voting, Based on 2004 Election Results

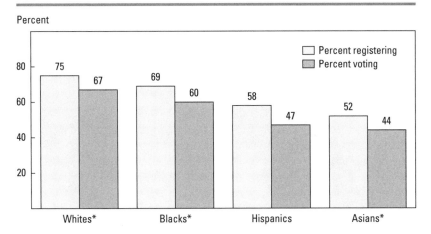

Percent

Whites*   Blacks*   Hispanics   Asians*

*Non-Hispanic
Source: William H. Frey analysis of U.S. Census sources.

immigrant population are citizens, are likely to register to vote, and are likely to vote. This contrasts with historical destination states like New Mexico, which have a higher share of Hispanic citizens likely to register and vote than new destination states do. The shares range from 13 percent in Illinois to 40 percent in New Mexico. In states with fast-growing Hispanic immigrant populations like Arizona, Nevada, and Colorado the Hispanic representation among voters is less than half of its representation in that state's total population.

In comparison to Hispanics, Asian representation is not high except for a few states: Hawaii, California, New Jersey, New York, Washington, and Nevada. As with Hispanics, the Asian translation gap is widest in those states where the Asian presence is newer and more likely to be foreign-born. These states include Virginia, Georgia, Kansas, Colorado, and Nebraska.

To what extent can this translation gap be reduced or eliminated? Part of this problem has to do with the fast growth of the under-eighteen-year-old population. Historical analysis undertaken by the Pew Hispanic Center shows a widening of the gap between the total population of Hispanics and their voter representation; the analysis attributes the gap to the continued growth of the young population due to high rates of immigration, fertility, and non-citizenship.[4] When a larger share of the Hispanic population is native-born, however, the translation gap should decrease.

Figure 3-3. Profiles: Total Population, Eligible Voters, and Likely Voters

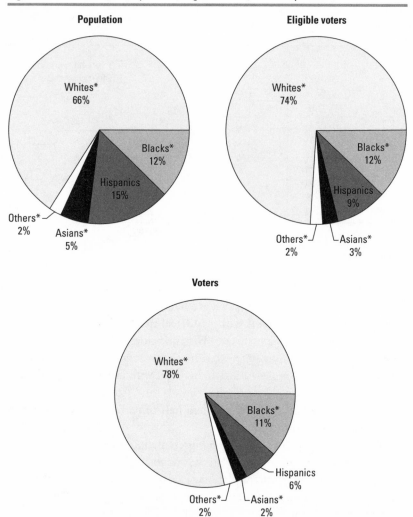

Population

Whites*
66%

Blacks*
12%

Hispanics
15%

Others*
2%

Asians*
5%

Eligible voters

Whites*
74%

Blacks*
12%

Hispanics
9%

Others*
2%

Asians*
3%

Voters

Whites*
78%

Blacks*
11%

Hispanics
6%

Others*
2%

Asians*
2%

*Non-Hispanic
Source: William H. Frey analysis of 2007 CPS.

One way to close the translation gap would be to increase the citizenship rate among permanent residents. In late 2007 the U.S. Citizenship and Immigration Services had a three-year backlog due to the surge of applications during the first part of the year (almost 1 million naturalization applications were pending approval). This surge was caused by several factors, including citizenship campaigns, the charged political climate, and the immigration debate. In addition, many applicants were hoping to avoid a significant increase in the application fee for adult naturalization.

The increased demand for naturalization among legal permanent residents is a positive step toward reducing the translation gap. Equally encouraging is increased voter registration among Hispanic citizens, as evident in the turnout for the 2008 Democratic primaries in most states with large Hispanic populations. Particularly noteworthy is the doubling in California's Hispanic representation, from 16 percent in the 2004 Democratic primary to 29 percent in 2008. To further close the Hispanic and Asian translation gaps, it will be necessary to energize their younger citizens to register and vote.

Identity Politics

The new immigrant minorities represent a break from the recent past in American politics, when the primary minority group was African American with a strong Democratic preference. With the prominence of Hispanics and Asians in all parts of the country, this dynamic is changing. It was already apparent in the 2008 Democratic primaries when Barack Obama, the first nationally viable African American presidential candidate, began to garner black support at the same time that Hillary Clinton got significant support from the Hispanic population. In fact, in some states the white population, and specifically white males, took on the role of swing group. To answer the question whether each minority race-ethnic group represents a distinct voting bloc, it is important to understand how the groups differ in their social and demographic profiles and how they lean in terms of party identification, ideology, and signature issues.

Minority Demographic Profiles

To understand race-ethnic voter blocs, it is first necessary to look at the social and demographic profiles of eligible voters among minority groups and whites (table 3-1).

An attribute of the white eligible-voter population that distinguishes it from the other eligible-voter populations is its age. More dominated by baby boomers than the other groups, over half are over age forty-five and nearly a fifth are over age sixty-five. Compared with the total eligible-voter population, whites are more educated, have higher incomes, are more likely to be married, and are almost universally native-born. But it is their age more than any other attribute that drives their demographic profile.

Table 3-1. Eligible Voters, by Social and Demographic Factors, Race, and Ethnicity
Percent

Group	Total	White[a]	Black[a]	Hispanic	Asian[a]
Age					
18–29	21.3	19.3	25.8	30.4	22.1
30–44	26.4	25.2	29.0	31.0	30.0
45–64	35.1	36.5	32.8	27.6	34.0
65 and over	17.2	19.0	12.3	11.0	13.9
Education					
College graduate	26.7	29.2	16.3	14.3	45.3
Some college	28.5	28.6	29.1	27.8	22.7
High school only	32.1	31.9	36.8	31.4	21.2
Not high school graduate	12.7	10.2	17.9	26.5	10.9
Family income					
More than $100,000	22.6	24.8	11.6	14.8	35.4
Less than $25,000	22.7	20.1	35.9	28.3	16.4
Poverty status					
Poor	9.9	7.6	20.0	14.7	7.6
Marital status: women					
Currently married	53.2	57.3	31.4	48.6	60.3
Never married	22.1	18.1	39.3	28.2	24.7
Divorced, separated, or widowed	24.7	24.5	29.4	23.2	15.0
Marital status: men					
Currently married	58.0	61.4	41.3	50.7	62.3
Never married	28.1	24.7	42.0	36.7	31.5
Divorced, separated, or widowed	13.9	13.9	16.8	12.6	6.2
Nativity					
Foreign-born	6.9	2.7	5.2	25.0	61.4
English proficiency					
Speaks English at home	87.0	95.2	95.7	28.2	28.6
Does not speak English well	1.8	0.5	0.3	11.1	13.7

Source: Author's analysis of U.S. Census sources.
a. Pertains to non-Hispanic members of group.

The Hispanic population is the youngest of the eligible-voter groups: three of ten are under age thirty, and only about a tenth are over age sixty-five. They are also the least educated: over a quarter did not graduate from high school. They are more likely to be in poverty and less likely to be currently married than whites. As immigrant minorities, Hispanics show a low propensity to speak English at home, although only about a tenth of them do not speak English well.

It is nonetheless important to distinguish between Hispanic eligible voters and adults who are not citizens. Census surveys do not identify undocumented residents, but it is fair to say that some segment of noneligible voters is undocumented. Compared with Hispanic eligible voters, noncitizen adults are younger and far less educated. In fact, well over half do not have a high school education, more than a fifth are in poverty, and three of five do not speak English well. This sharp distinction raises the question: To what extent do Hispanic eligible-voter preferences and concerns differ from those of Hispanics who are not able to vote?

The demographic profile for black eligible voters lies somewhere between those of whites and Hispanics on age and education. They have higher rates of poverty and are more likely to be single or divorced than any other group. Eligible voters are more likely to be college graduates and less likely to be high school dropouts than Hispanics. However, their family situation and related poverty levels reflect a unique aspect of the African American profile.

As a group, eligible-voter Asians are by far the most educated, with well over four of ten holding college degrees or higher. They have high incomes and low poverty levels and are more likely than any other group to live with a spouse. Yet fully 60 percent are foreign-born and 13 percent do not speak English well. Because Asian eligible voters are not that distinct from their adult noncitizen counterparts, their interests may well reflect their racial counterparts who are not eligible to vote.

The social and demographic profiles indicate that Hispanics and blacks rank below Asians and whites on dimensions of education and income. As subsequent sections show, these attributes shape each group's party preference to some degree.

Party Preferences

The suggestion that specific minority groups should be thought of as solid voting blocs is certainly open to debate. African Americans have a long history of voting solidly Democratic. In 2004, when their support for the Democratic candidate, John Kerry, dipped to just 88 percent (from 90 percent in 2000), questions were raised about their disaffection for the party. A Pew Research Center analysis of blacks who either identify or lean toward the Democratic Party shows a high and consistent level of black Democratic Party identification annually since 1990.[5] The black groups most strongly identified with the Democratic Party are older, middle income, and have more than a high school education. This strong identification with the Democratic Party is well over 50 percent among blacks in almost all demographic groups. Nonetheless, shifts are apparent. The 2006 General Social Survey question on party identification reveals that younger blacks, aged eighteen through twenty-nine, are almost as likely to identify themselves as independents as Democrats. For blacks aged forty-five and above, however, the ratio of Democrats to independents is three to one.

The Hispanic population has leaned more strongly Democratic than Republican. Yet many Hispanic leaders promote Hispanics as a swing group in order to keep their issues in play for both parties. Some who make this case like to compare the relatively strong (40 percent) support for George W. Bush in 2004 to the 21 percent they gave Robert Dole in 1996. Yet the polling question asked in 1996 understated Hispanic Republican support.[6] Using more reliable identification of Hispanics beginning with post-1998 polls, the Democrat-to-Republican margin among Hispanics was 63 to 37 percent in the 1998 House vote, 62 to 35 percent in the 2000 Gore-Bush presidential election, and 69 to 30 percent in the 2006 House vote. So while Republicans enjoyed a small spike among Hispanics in the 2004 Kerry-Bush election, this appears to have subsided in 2006.

A Pew Research Center analysis of Hispanic party identification over the period 1999–2007 shows relative stability in their registration as Democrats, ranging between 42 and 48 percent. When one counts Democratic leaners as well as those registered with the Democratic Party, one finds a general 55 percent in support for Democrats, with the exception of July 2006, when it dipped to 49 percent. Republican preferences among registrants and leaners ranged between 23 and 28 percent.

Despite the perceived miniswing of Hispanics to Republicans in the 2004 presidential election, their national support for Democrats has been stronger in recent years. Still, it is well known that voting patterns for Hispanics differ across states. In 2004 Hispanic support for George W. Bush was 49 percent in Texas but only 32 percent in California. Yet in the latter state the Republican governor, Arnold Schwarzenegger, garnered almost 40 percent of Hispanic support in the 2006 election.

The Asian vote is probably more unpredictable, in light of the varied Asian populations and their geographical clustering. In terms of presidential support, Asians split parties in the last four elections, voting strongly for Republican candidates in 1992 and 1996 but favoring Al Gore and John Kerry over George Bush by substantial margins (54 to 41 and 58 to 44) in the last two presidential elections. Recent data collected by the Institute of Politics at Harvard University suggest a new Democratic leaning among Asians, led by the younger segment of Asian American voters.[7] Observers of this trend indicate that the Republican preferences of older Asian Americans can be attributed to their pro-business positions and, among Korean and Vietnamese refugees, their anticommunist stances. Yet younger Asian Americans are less swayed by these issues than by the anti–Iraq War and pro-immigration stances of the Democratic Party. Indeed, it has been speculated that the young Asian vote in Virginia helped to defeat the Republican senator, George Allen, after his videotaped disparagement of an American of Asian ancestry in 2006. Responses to a 2006 General Social Survey question on party identification asked of all adults show Asians to be somewhat more strongly identified as Democrats than Hispanics are, though both groups on the whole have a relatively large (50 and 56 percent) independent orientation.

All three minority groups are more heavily Democratic than whites. This is apparent in the 2006 General Social Survey data shown in table 3-2. It is also evident from the presidential results. More whites favored the Republican candidate in each of the last eight cycles, with white Republican support ranging between 52 and 58 percent in elections that did not have major third-party candidates. Of course, there are well-known divisions by gender, class, marital status, and age that are much more dramatic than those apparent with other racial groups. As with blacks, the percentage of whites claiming independent identification is much higher for the under-age-thirty group than for those in older age groups.

This leads to the question: To what degree do race and ethnic groups reflect distinct political identities? The data in table 3-2 permit a comparison. The detailed responses ranging from "strong Democrat" to "strong Republican" show that there are wide ranges within each of these groupings. Yet there is

Table 3-2. Eligible Voters, by Party Identification, Race, and Ethnicity

Percent

Party identification	White[a]	Black[a]	Hispanic[a]	Asian[a]
Strong Democrat	11	39	11	9
Not very strong Democrat	13	25	18	29
Independent, close to Democrat	11	13	11	11
Independent	20	17	39	33
Independent, close to Republican	9	2	6	6
Not very strong Republican	19	3	9	7
Strong Republican	15	1	4	6
Other party, refused to say	2	0	1	0
Total Democrats	24	64	30	38
Total independents	40	32	56	50
Total Republicans	34	4	14	13
N	3,087	550	653	158

Source: Author's analysis of 2006 NORC General Social Survey 2006, persons 18 and over.
a. Pertains to non-Hispanic members of group.

also a strong clustering of responses, the most distinct being that for blacks (almost two of five respondents consider themselves strong Democrats). Hispanics and Asians range mostly between independents and strong Democrats. In contrast, whites span a much larger spectrum, though with very few non-leaning independents.

This same survey queried these groups on political ideology and shows some similar tendencies over a broad spectrum of responses. Blacks are clearly the most liberal: fully one-third classify themselves as liberal or slightly liberal. Hispanics and Asians are much more balanced on political ideology than they are on party affiliation. In fact, it is the white group that seems to be most out of balance, showing almost four of ten members in the conservative or slightly conservative category. Nonetheless, the modal category for all groups is moderate, suggesting that although there is a strong party identification associated with each minority group, the range of views within a party tends to be fairly wide.

2008 Election Issues

What do these patterns mean for the forthcoming election? A hint was given in a survey of likely voters by Peter D. Hart Research Associates in January 2008 asking them to describe their overall point of view in terms of political parties (as opposed to actual registration). The survey reveals distinct race-ethnic preferences among blacks, Hispanics, and whites. Not unexpectedly, blacks show a strong tendency to lean or be Democratic as opposed to lean or be Republican (71 to 7 percent). The disparity for Hispanics is also quite strong (65 to 15 percent). Both of these differ from the preferences of whites, which are more evenhanded but favor Republicans over Democrats (42 to 37 percent).

These early 2008 likely voters were also asked which issues would be most important to them in the upcoming election. In light of the economic situation when these questions were asked, it is not surprising that the economy and jobs was the first concern for all groups, though a much more primary concern for blacks than Hispanics (table 3-3). For Hispanics, in fact, there was a virtual tie among economic issues, the war in Iraq, and health care, the latter two issues being also important for blacks.

In light of the importance of immigration as a prospective wedge issue in the 2008 campaign, it is significant that illegal immigration was tied for second place, along with health care and the war in Iraq, among white voters; it was fourth among Hispanics and was not among the first five for blacks. The issue of illegal immigration has been used successfully by Republicans, who prof-

Table 3-3. Eligible Voters, Important Election Issues, by Race and Ethnicity

Percent

Group	Election issue	Most important
White (*N* = 1,107)	Economy and jobs	25.5
	Health care	15.3
	Illegal immigration	15.3
	War in Iraq	14.5
	Terrorism and national security	11.9
Black (*N* = 152)	Economy and jobs	35.0
	Health care	22.6
	War in Iraq	19.5
	Energy prices	5.8
	Terrorism and national security	4.6
Hispanic (*N* = 98)	Economy and jobs	25.7
	War in Iraq	25.1
	Health care	22.9
	Illegal immigration	12.1
	Terrorism and national security	6.4
All groups (*N* = 1,407)	Economy and jobs	27.1
	Health care	16.5
	War in Iraq	15.7
	Illegal immigration	13.4
	Terrorism and national security	10.5

Source: Author's analysis of Peter D. Hart Research Associates, Immigration Survey of likely voters, January 7–10, 2008, table 5: Attitudes on Immigration for Voters: Race-Ethnicity, Whites by Education.

fered more punitive and strict immigration measures in the 2006 congressional campaign. Although many of their candidates were not successful, it still appears to be an important issue for whites. In fact, whites stand alone in not placing strongest importance on the economy, health care, and the Iraq War, which were the top issues for 77 percent of black expected voters and 78 percent of Hispanic expected voters. In contrast, after the economy, white concerns were split among a myriad of issues, two of which are illegal immigration and terrorism and national security.

Overall, then, identity politics are evident and quite nuanced. There are strong differences from whites among blacks, Hispanics, and Asians on party preference, which at least for blacks and Hispanics may be attributable to their significantly lower socioeconomic standing. Yet even the highly educated Asian population is more strongly Democratic than Republican, especially among younger members. The economy seems to be the preeminent issue among all groups. The Iraq War and health care, issues that weigh more heavily on lower-income populations, are more important among blacks and Hispanics than among whites.

Immigration as an Issue

In the analysis of likely-voter issues above, whites showed greater concern for "illegal immigration" than either blacks or Hispanics. Nonetheless, both of the latter groups, as well as Asians, have a strong interest in immigration for different reasons. Surveys show that many blacks, especially those with low income and educational attainment, feel that there would be more job opportunities available to them were it not for immigrants.[8] Hispanics, on the other hand, tend to favor the high current levels of immigration and are put off by political punitive measures against undocumented immigrants.[9]

A survey taken by Greenberg Quinlan Rosner Research of a sample of likely voters in November-December 2007 gives a sense of the opinions of likely voters about immigration (see appendix table 3A-1). When asked whether immigration was good or bad for America, more than 50 percent of likely voters from each race-ethnic group regarded immigration as good. Among Hispanics, however, a majority of respondents felt strongly that immigration is good for America. At the other extreme, about 45 percent of blacks felt that immigration is bad. Whites lie somewhere in the middle though typically have a positive view of immigration.

This is not the case for all categories of whites. Earlier studies show that less educated whites feel threatened by immigrants as possible competitors for their jobs. The survey, in fact, shows that such whites have the least favorable view of immigration. Yet white college graduates, many of whom employ immigrants and benefit from their work, show a strongly favorable view of immigration, almost to the same level as Hispanics.

How do these attitudes about immigration translate into support for Democratic or Republican views of the immigration issue? This needs to be seen in the context of the fierce immigration debate of the first half of 2007. A largely Democratic-led group of senators attempted to provide a "comprehensive" immigration reform bill, which would both offer greater enforcement measures directed toward illegal immigration and also provide a "path toward citizenship" for large numbers of undocumented immigrants.[10] Many Republicans also supported this bill, as did President Bush, who has a long-standing interest in overhauling the immigration system. A conservative Republican rebellion occurred against what they saw as amnesty (allowing undocumented residents to obtain citizenship), a rebellion that ultimately defeated the bill.

In December 2007 likely voters were asked if they were more inclined to trust Democrats or Republicans on immigration (see table 3A-2 in the appendix). Not unexpectedly, Hispanics had a much more favorable view than whites of the Democrats' position. Perhaps because of strong African American allegiance with the Democratic Party, blacks' less-than-positive view of immigration, overall, does not translate into a lack of trust in the Democratic Party to deal with immigration. Somewhat surprising is the tendency for less-skilled rather than highly educated whites to trust the Democrats on improving immigration. At the time the survey was taken, Democrats were less inclined to adopt a strictly proenforcement stance.

The issue of whether immigration per se is good or bad appears less a point of contention than the issue of illegal immigration. A survey by Peter D. Hart Research Associates in January 2008 queried respondents on just how big a problem illegal immigration was (see table 3-4). Here again are noticeable race differences but also a broad consensus among all groups that illegal immigration is at least a moderately big problem. The distinction across groups varies, however, on which ethnicities deem it to be a "very big problem." While approximately half of all whites feel this way, this is the case for less than a third of Hispanics and blacks. This strong feeling among whites is especially amplified for those with no more than a high school education: six of ten of this group are quite concerned about illegal immigration. Even among that large segment of whites with only some college, fully half believe that illegal immigration is a very big problem.

The same survey shows that white likely voters, especially low-skilled whites, are most adamant about deporting illegal immigrants and controlling the border, because they believe that immigrants take jobs away from

Table 3-4. Voter Attitudes toward Size of Problem Presented by Illegal Immigration, by Race, Ethnicity, and White Voters' Education

Likely voters responding to question:
How big of a problem do you think illegal immigration is for the country today, if at all?
Response: a very big problem, a moderately big problem, a small problem, or not a problem
Percent

Group	Very big problem	Moderately big problem	Small problem	Not a problem or not sure
White (*N* = 1,107)	50	33	13	3
Black (*N* = 152)	32	37	17	13
Hispanic (*N* = 98)	31	31	19	19
White education				
College graduates (*N* = 384)	38	38	19	5
Some college (*N* = 311)	52	33	12	3
High school or less (*N* = 404)	60	30	9	2

Source: Author's analysis of Peter D. Hart Research Associates, Immigration Survey of Likely Voters, January 7–10, 2008.

American citizens. On the other side of the spectrum are Hispanics, who feel strongly that immigrants who are here illegally should have the opportunity to earn legal status and, further, that these immigrants take jobs that Americans do not want. Among whites, college graduates are closest to these views; blacks typically fall somewhere in between.

Clearly, illegal immigration is a political concern, and there is a specific geography associated with it. Immigration destinations have begun to disperse widely, away from the so-called immigrant magnet states. As a result, views associated with large numbers of immigrants that were often confined to a few states like California, New York, Texas, and Florida have spread to other parts of the country. As evidence of this, all fifty states have enacted immigration-related laws, many of them punitive. These laws focus on verifying the legal status of workers and renters and on withholding medical and social services to illegal immigrants and their families.[11] According to the National Confer-ence of State Legislatures, 1,562 pieces of legislation related to immigrants or immigration were introduced across the states up through November 2007; and 244 of these were passed into law. This is three times the number of immigration bills introduced the previous year.

The dissemination of immigrants into areas that have not traditionally been immigrant magnets can be seen in the attitudes of white voters. States classed as immigrant magnets (for example, California, New York), those classed as nonmagnet fast immigrant-growth states (for example, Georgia, Nebraska), and those classed as nonmagnet modest immigrant-growth states (for example, Ohio, Maine, Montana) are shown on the map in the appendix (map 3A-1). The January 2008 survey results indicate that the white likely voters most likely to see immigration as a problem are located in nonmagnet, fast immigrant-growth states (see appendix, table 3A-3). Well over half of whites in these states saw immigration as a very big problem, compared to 48 percent in immigrant magnet states and in those states that have not seen the immigrant population grow as rapidly. The distinction across these states is especially important for whites who have at most a high school education. Among these likely voters in the high immigrant-growth states, 70 percent feel that illegal immigration is a big problem, compared to 58 percent in the immigrant magnet states. In essence, it is the fast growth of immigrants in areas that have not had a long history of receiving them that seems to raise the greatest concern among whites, and especially less-educated whites.

This is also the case when one compares the attitudes, based on the same survey, about illegal immigration between urban areas and suburban and small town areas. Here again it is the less-educated whites in suburban areas that have the highest negative attitudes about immigration. Suburban areas, to which immigrants are just starting to filter, are where negative attitudes toward immigration are largest.

Overall, then, immigration, especially illegal immigration, appears to be a bigger issue for whites than for blacks and Hispanics. It is more likely to become a wedge issue in parts of the country where the number of immigrants is growing rapidly. Many of these areas are purple, or battleground, states in which whites or Hispanics are significant voting blocs.

Race and America's Political Geography

This chapter thus far has taken a national view of trends, yet because in presidential politics the focus is often on states, it is useful to examine how these trends play out in states and regions that are important politically. Hispanic, black, Asian, and white populations are distributed quite differently across the country, even taking into account the broad dispersal of immigrant minorities to new destinations. Maps 3-1, 3-2, 3-3, and 3-4 provide perspective by showing states in which these groups compose the greatest shares of eligible voters. They also point up where recent minority group dispersal has begun.

For instance, Intermountain West states like Arizona, Nevada, and Colorado now show significant Hispanic shares of their electorate. These states, as well as New Mexico and Florida, are important battlegrounds, where Hispanics can have a significant say in the next election. The Asian eligible-voter population is quite small and has its biggest effect in California and Hawaii. Yet as has been seen in the Nevada 2008 Democratic primary, as well as in local elections in Washington and Virginia, Asian voters can make a difference even when they make up a relatively small segment of the electorate. Blacks have a long history of affecting elections. The recent phenomenon of black middle-class professionals returning to the South may serve to tip elections in this Republican-dominated region toward socially progressive issues, if not toward more Democratic candidacies. The rising black population in Virginia, Tennessee, and North Carolina, for example, may soon serve to uproot long-standing Republican dominance in those states.

Finally, a look at white eligible voters makes plain that broad swaths of states in New England, the Midwest, the Upper Great Plains, and Appalachia are still overwhelmingly white. Population shifts over the last twenty years continue to move whites from the Rust Belt to the Southeast and from the West Coast to the Intermountain West, the same states that are now attracting Hispanics and blacks. Yet because most northern and midwestern states

Map 3-1. Hispanic Share of Eligible Voters

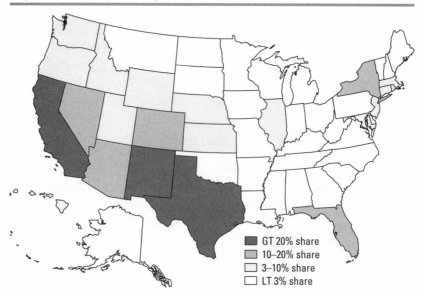

GT 20% share
10–20% share
3–10% share
LT 3% share

Map 3-2. Asian Share of Eligible Voters

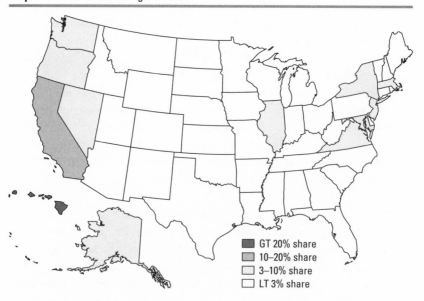

GT 20% share
10–20% share
3–10% share
LT 3% share

Map 3-3. Black Share of Eligible Voters

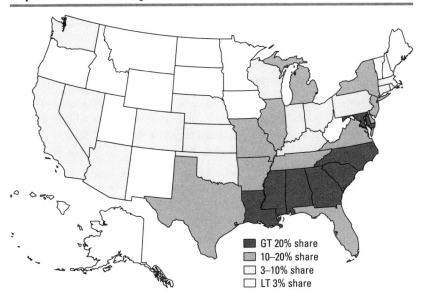

- GT 20% share
- 10–20% share
- 3–10% share
- LT 3% share

Map 3-4. White Share of Eligible Voters

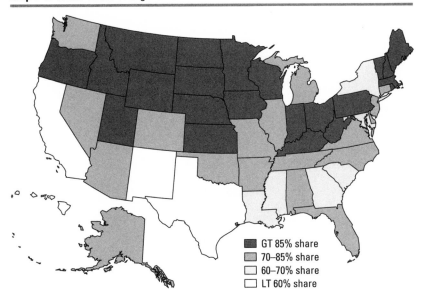

- GT 85% share
- 70–85% share
- 60–70% share
- LT 60% share

do not attract as many new minorities and are sustaining an outmigration of whites, they are left with slow-growing, aging, white populations. In these states voter profiles and issues differ strikingly from those in states with larger minority populations. And the fact that whites tend to be better represented in the voting population than any one minority group gives them an outsized influence, relative to their population, in most state electorates.

Having reviewed these regional racial distributions of eligible voters, it is useful to superimpose on them a map of the states that will be most and least up for grabs in the 2008 presidential election. To do this, I have classed states into four categories based in large measure on the results of the 2004 presidential election (see map 3-5 and table 3-5). These include nine solid blue states (including Washington D.C.) mostly on the coasts, where John Kerry beat George Bush by a greater than 10 percent margin; twenty-one solid red states located mostly in the South, the Great Plains, and the Northern Mountain West, which were won by Bush by more than 10 percent.

Purple states are the battleground states that Bush or Kerry carried by less than 10 percent, plus Arizona, which is now widely viewed as a battleground state. Purple states are divided into two categories: fast growing and slow growing. The nine fast-growing purple states are experiencing turbulent demographic shifts associated with new immigrant minorities as well as fast growth

Map 3-5. Red, Blue, and Purple States

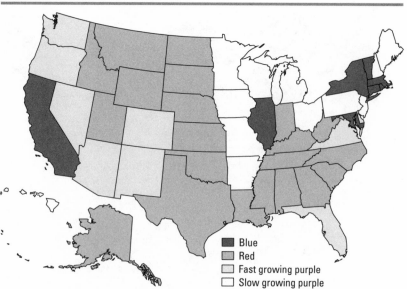

Blue
Red
Fast growing purple
Slow growing purple

Table 3-5. Likely Voters, by Race, Ethnicity, and State

Percent

States by category	Margin 2004		White	Black	Asian	Hispanic
Fast-growing purple states						
New Mexico	0.8	Bush	55.7	2.0	1.1	30.4
Nevada	2.6	Bush	76.2	6.3	4.8	9.7
Oregon	4.2	Kerry	91.2	0.9	2.1	2.1
Colorado	4.7	Bush	87.0	2.3	0.6	8.4
Florida	5.0	Bush	74.7	11.4	1.0	11.9
Washington	7.2	Kerry	87.4	2.1	4.2	2.6
Delaware	7.6	Kerry	79.7	15.7	1.6	2.0
Virginia	8.2	Bush	79.8	15.4	1.6	2.2
Arizona	10.5	Bush	77.1	2.7	1.2	14.3
Slow-growing purple states						
Wisconsin	0.4	Kerry	91.6	4.0	0.6	2.5
Iowa	0.7	Bush	94.4	1.8	1.7	1.5
New Hampshire	1.4	Kerry	96.6	0.2	0.6	1.2
Ohio	2.1	Bush	86.6	10.0	0.4	1.7
Pennsylvania	2.5	Kerry	89.2	7.8	0.5	2.0
Michigan	3.4	Kerry	83.3	12.5	1.0	1.8
Minnesota	3.5	Kerry	93.0	2.7	1.5	1.3
New Jersey	6.7	Kerry	73.1	12.5	5.5	8.3
Missouri	7.2	Bush	85.2	11.3	0.6	1.1
Hawaii	8.7	Kerry	28.5	1.1	48.1	4.4
Maine	9.0	Kerry	96.7	0.4	0.2	0.5
Arkansas	9.8	Bush	84.0	12.7	0.4	1.1
Solid blue states						
California	10.0	Kerry	64.1	7.7	8.4	17.7
Illinois	10.3	Kerry	76.3	15.5	2.0	5.5
Connecticut	10.4	Kerry	85.3	7.1	1.9	5.2
Maryland	13.0	Kerry	68.5	25.4	2.3	2.5
New York	18.3	Kerry	74.0	12.3	3.8	9.1
Vermont	20.1	Kerry	96.9	0.5	0.3	0.4
Rhode Island	20.8	Kerry	90.4	2.8	1.3	4.2
Massachusetts	25.2	Kerry	90.4	3.4	2.8	2.6
District of Columbia	79.8	Kerry	42.5	52.1	1.4	2.9
Solid red states						
North Carolina	12.4	Bush	74.0	21.7	0.9	0.6
West Virginia	12.9	Bush	96.7	2.0	0.3	0.1
Tennessee	14.3	Bush	82.2	15.2	1.2	0.3
Louisiana	14.5	Bush	69.9	27.9	0.3	1.7
Georgia	16.6	Bush	67.2	30.0	0.8	1.4
South Carolina	17.1	Bush	70.5	26.3	0.5	1.6
Mississippi	19.7	Bush	60.1	37.9	0.3	0.4
Kentucky	19.9	Bush	90.9	7.0	0.2	1.0
Montana	20.5	Bush	92.8	0.2	0.2	0.9
Indiana	20.7	Bush	90.2	7.5	0.3	1.3
South Dakota	21.5	Bush	94.0	0.2	0.2	1.8
Texas	22.9	Bush	66.6	12.2	1.9	18.3
Kansas	25.4	Bush	90.0	4.2	0.8	3.0
Alabama	25.6	Bush	71.6	26.2	0.2	0.3
Alaska	25.6	Bush	78.6	2.3	2.6	2.2
North Dakota	27.4	Bush	91.0	0.2	0.3	0.5
Oklahoma	31.1	Bush	77.9	6.1	0.2	1.5
Nebraska	33.2	Bush	92.4	2.6	0.5	2.0
Idaho	38.1	Bush	95.7	0.2	0.2	1.9
Wyoming	39.8	Bush	92.9	0.5	0.1	4.2
Utah	45.5	Bush	91.8	1.0	1.9	3.4

Source: Author's analysis of U.S. Census sources.

of their white middle-class populations. Most of these states are located in the western part of the United States (except for Florida, Virginia, and Delaware). The twelve slow-growing purple states are located in the eastern and central part of the United States and are not experiencing significant demographic change except for recent but small growth in their immigrant or new minority populations. Compared with fast-growing purple states, population shifts in these areas are stagnant, and the communities are characterized by long-term residents.

The racial clustering of the populations in red, blue, and purple states yields distinct race-ethnic signatures of eligible voters in each state category (figure 3-4). Solid blue states, located mostly in the nation's immigrant-magnet urban coastal areas, have the most racially diverse population. This stands in contrast to solid red states, which are generally whiter, though they have large black populations because they include a good number of southern states. However, the main focus here is the distinction between the racial profiles of the fast-growing and the slow-growing purple states. Fast-growing purple states, with their rapidly changing new minority populations, are far more diverse than slow-growing purple states in the racial profiles of their eligible voters.

The eligible-voter population of fast-growing purple states grew by over 12 percent in the seven years after the 2000 election, while that of slow-growing purple states grew only about a third as much. Moreover, race-ethnic minorities—especially Hispanics and Asians—accounted for almost half of this gain, the result of many in-and-out movers in this dynamic part of the country. In contrast, slow-growing purple states are gaining mostly white voters who are newly registered rather than being new residents.

The growth patterns of eligible voters in five fast-growing purple states are depicted in figure 3-5. In Nevada eligible voters grew by 27 percent, with Hispanics, Asians, and blacks contributing more than half of these gains. Similarly, Arizona' eligible voters grew by nearly 20 percent, with two-thirds of that growth contributed by minorities. When these eligible voters are translated into estimated voters, the Hispanic share is far greater than the 2004 Bush margin of victory in New Mexico, Nevada, Colorado, Florida, and Arizona.

The racial dynamic is not the only demographic distinction between fast-growing purple states and slow-growing purple states; it is related to other aging and socioeconomic differences in their respective electorates. These two classes of state can be contrasted on the basis of eligible voters who are minorities, whites over sixty-five years of age, working-age whites with college degrees, and non-college-educated working-age whites (figure 3-6). It makes

Figure 3-4. Eligible Voter Profiles: Red-Blue-Purple State Categories

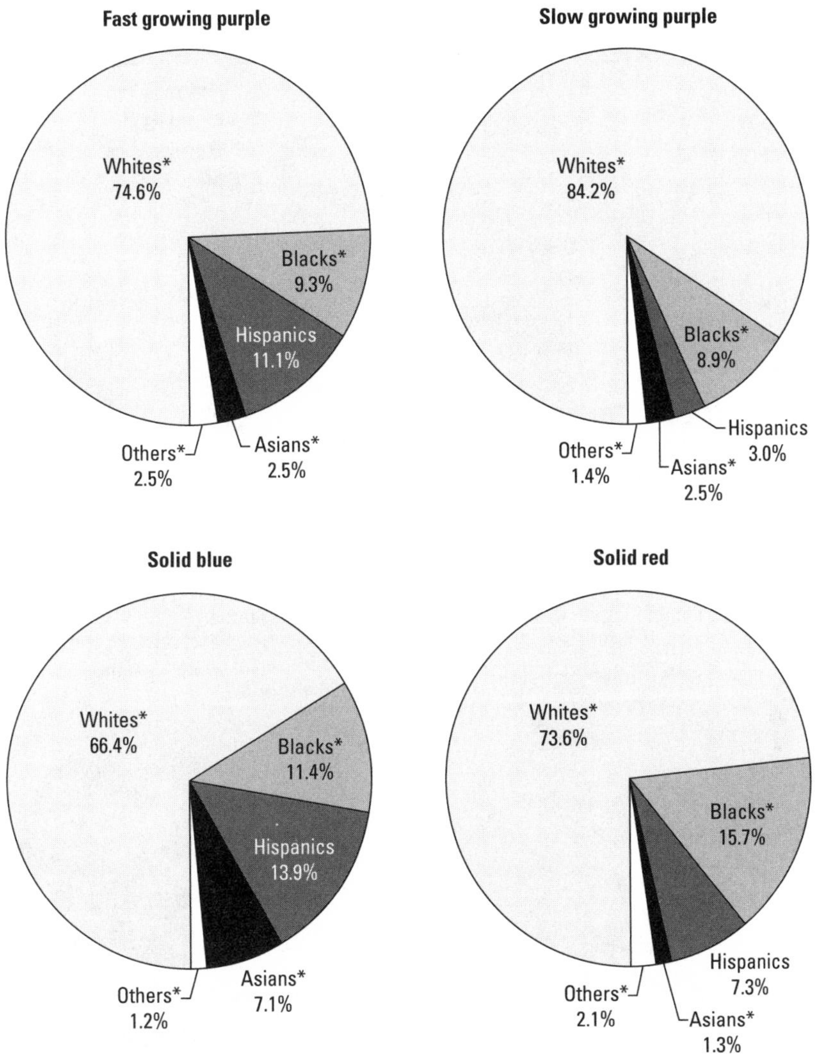

Fast growing purple

Whites*
74.6%

Blacks*
9.3%

Hispanics
11.1%

Others*⌐
2.5%

⌐Asians*
2.5%

Slow growing purple

Whites*
84.2%

Blacks*
8.9%

⌐Hispanics
3.0%

Others*⌐
1.4%

⌐Asians*
2.5%

Solid blue

Whites*
66.4%

Blacks*
11.4%

Hispanics
13.9%

Others*⌐
1.2%

Asians*
7.1%

Solid red

Whites*
73.6%

Blacks*
15.7%

Hispanics
7.3%

Others*⌐
2.1%

⌐Asians*
1.3%

*Non-Hispanic
Source: William H. Frey analysis of 2007 CPS.

Figure 3-5. Growth in Eligible Voters, 2000–07, by Race-Ethnicity: Five Fast Growing Purple States

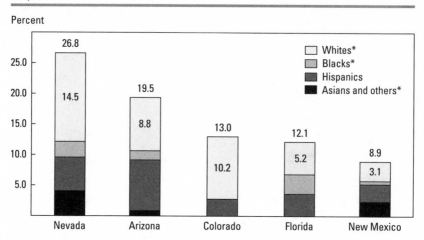

Percent

*Non-Hispanic
Source: William H. Frey analysis of U.S. Census sources.

Figure 3-6. Eligible Voters in Demographic Groups: Purple States

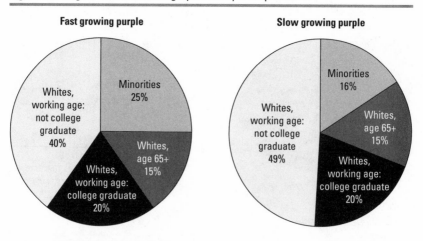

Source: William H. Frey analysis of U.S. Census sources.

plain that fast-growing purple states have a substantially larger minority-electorate share but that slow-growing purple states have the advantage with non-college-educated whites. These comparisons point up the fact that the steady demographic transformation of America's national electorate holds immediate implications for those politically strategic states experiencing dramatic shifts in race-ethnic voter populations.

Implications for the Future

The new race-ethnic mix in the United States is beginning to show an impact on America's political demography and geography. Courting the Hispanic vote in recent elections has paid off for both Republicans and Democrats—in reelecting George Bush in 2004 and in some early 2008 primary victories by Hillary Clinton. With the rise of the first nationally viable African American presidential candidate in 2008, the black population as a constituency has become the focus of attention for both old and new Democratic allies. The importance of the Asian population was brought to light in the Virginia 2006 U.S. Senate election, when Asian American voters took credit for electing Jim Webb in reaction to George Allen's use of the term *macaca* in reference to an Asian American man in the audience.

Yet these are only tip-of-the-iceberg instances of minorities making a difference in particular places and elections. Census projections show that the nation as a whole will be minority white in 2050, which means that states like California, New Mexico, and Texas, whose minority populations are already in the majority, may be models for other parts of the country.

One can get a glimpse of this by looking at the race-ethnic composition of eligible U.S. voters ages eighteen through twenty-nine (figure 3-7). Twenty-one states show minority shares over 30 percent among these young eligible voters, compared with only twelve states for actual voters (of all ages). In California, for example, 56 percent of under-age-thirty eligible voters are minorities, compared with only 36 percent of its total voters. Respective contrasts are 51 versus 33 percent in Texas and 42 versus 23 percent in Arizona. As these young voters move into their thirties and forties they will compose a varied multiethnic electorate. Thus it is not too soon to begin building the groundwork for these new racial and ethnic constituencies and coalitions.

As for the here and now, we are still a balkanized nation in terms of our racial and ethnic makeup. Much attention has correctly been paid to the political dividends that can be reaped in such fast-growing purple states as Nevada,

Figure 3-7. Minority Shares of Eligible Voters, 18 to 29 Years Old[a]

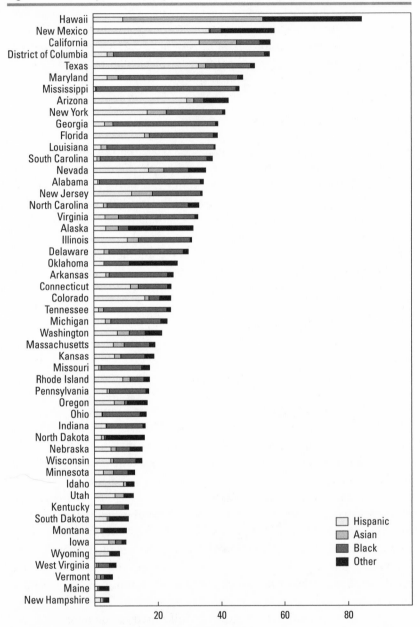

Source: William H. Frey analysis of 2007 Current Population Survey.
a. Based on estimates of population as of March 2007.

New Mexico, and Colorado, whose large Hispanic and other minority populations could very well tip what were Republican Bush states in 2004 into the Democratic presidential column in 2008. Yet in the zeal to focus on these culturally vibrant and demographically changing parts of the country, political analysts should not lose their focus on still powerful, slow-growing purple states like Ohio, Pennsylvania, Michigan, and Missouri. The 2004 presidential election also showed the outsized influence that the aging populations of these states played in the final outcome.

Politicians must tread carefully in this balkanized political geography when addressing issues like immigration and affirmative action. Issues like education and homeownership are of concern to younger voters, while constituencies in slower-growing parts of the country care more about health care and social security. For Democrats, who are traditionally associated with the latter economic security issues, the challenge will be to appeal to fast-growing younger voting blocs in battleground states like Nevada, Arizona, and Colorado. A focus on education reform is certainly important, and the cultural liberalism that is usually associated with the party will also appeal to newly arrived minorities. But to buoy their effectiveness in these battlegrounds states, Democrats may need to appeal to the aspirational attitudes prevalent in these states in ways that differ from the messages that have worked for them in the heartland.

Republicans have shown success in slow-growing purple states in the past. Yet those states' largely white and aging populations want to see greater GOP emphasis on economic security issues that have long been identified with Democrats. And while anti-immigrant messages may find some adherents in these parts of the country, they could backfire for the GOP in the fast-growing battlegrounds, whose changing electorate will respond to more culturally positive messages than have been heard from the party in the recent past. In these states, the Republican Party could also gain support by emphasizing its own aspirational programs.

Indeed, the 2008 election year featured two presidential candidates that reflect the past and future of America's voting population. White, pre–baby boomer John McCain and postethnic, post–baby boomer Barack Obama represent demographic bookends to the broad-based change that America's electorate is going through. The challenge faced by their respective parties, in the near term, will be to appeal to voters in a country that is still balkanized, with states and regions changing in different ways and at different speeds, as part of the continued transformation of our racial demography.

Appendix: Immigration

Map 3A-1. Immigrant Magnet and Growth States

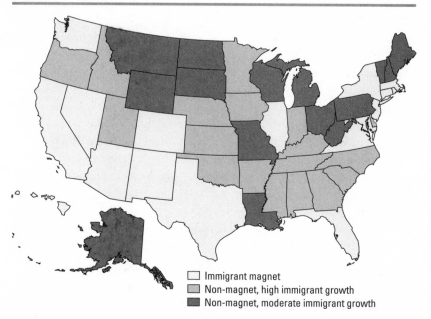

- ☐ Immigrant magnet
- ▨ Non-magnet, high immigrant growth
- ▦ Non-magnet, moderate immigrant growth

Table 3A-1. Voter Attitudes toward Immigration, by Race, Ethnicity, and White Voters' Education

Likely voters responding to question:
Is immigration good for America or is immigration bad for America?

Percent

Group	Good, strong	Good, not strong	Bad, not strong	Bad, strong
White (N = 718)	43	22	10	25
Black (N = 97)	21	34	18	27
Hispanic (N = 80)	58	16	4	22
White education				
College graduate (N = 311)	51	23	9	16
Some college (N = 210)	41	20	12	27
High school or less (N = 196)	32	22	9	37

Source: Author's analysis of Greenberg Quinlan Rosner Research, Democracy Core Survey of Likely Voters, November 29–December 3, 2007.

Table 3A-2. Voter Attitudes toward Illegal Immigration, by Race, Ethnicity, and White Voters' Education

Likely voters responding to statements:
On immigration, I am more inclined to trust the Democrats right now, or
On immigration, I am more inclined to trust the Republicans right now.

Percent

Group	Democrats, strong	Democrats, not strong	Republicans, not strong	Republicans, strong	Neither
White (*N* = 711)	26	15	17	30	12
Black (*N* = 100)	54	14	14	10	8
Hispanic (*N* = 82)	39	28	2	26	4
White voters' education					
College graduate (*N* = 310)	23	18	19	31	10
Some college (*N* =208)	25	13	16	31	15
High school or less (*N* =193)	32	14	14	28	12

Source: Author's analysis of Greenberg Quinlan Rosner Research, Democracy Core Survey of Likely Voters, November 29–December 3, 2007.

Table 3A-3. Voter Attitudes toward Illegal Immigration, by Region and White Voters' Education

(Regional categories are depicted on map 3A-1.)
Likely white voters responding to question:
How big a problem do you think illegal immigration is for the country today?
Response: a very big problem, a moderately big problem, a small problem, or not a problem.

Percent

Group	Immigrant-magnet state	Non-immigrant-magnet state, high immigrant growth	Non-immigrant-magnet state, moderate immigrant growth	Total
White, total				
Very big problem	48	55	48	50
Moderately big problem	33	30	38	33
Small problem	15	13	11	13
Not a problem	2	2	2	2
Not sure	2	1	2	2
White, high school graduate or less				
Very big problem	58	70	53	60
Moderately big problem	26	25	39	30
Small problem	14	3	6	9
Not a problem	1	0	0	0
Not sure	2	2	2	2
White, some college or more				
Very big problem	43	47	43	44
Moderately big problem	37	32	37	35
Small problem	16	18	15	16
Not a problem	2	3	3	3
Not sure	2	0	2	1

Source: Author's analysis of Peter D. Hart Research Associates, Immigration Survey of Likely Voters, January 7–10, 2008.

Notes

1. Statistics in this chapter are the most recent available at the time of this writing. Statistics on total population, eligible voter population, and estimated voter population are drawn from the U.S. Census Bureau's *Current Population Survey 2007* and *American Community Survey 2006;* polling information drawn from the following sources: 2006 General Social Survey (National Opinion Research Corporation); Greenberg Quinlan Rosner Research, Democracy Core survey of likely voters November 29–December 3, 2007; and Peter D. Hart Research Associates, immigration survey of likely voters, January 7–10, 2008. Also, the author has analyzed U.S. Census Bureau estimates and projections by race or ethnicity and has used information from the U.S. Census Bureau, "Voting and Registration in the Election of November 2004," Current Population Report P20-556.

2. John B. Judis and Ruy Teixeira, "Back to the Future: The Reemergence of the Emerging Democratic Majority," *American Prospect,* July–August 2007, pp. 10–18.

3. In this chapter my practice is to collapse the categories of Hispanic ethnicity and race to form single specifications of race-ethnicity; these are Hispanic, non-Hispanic white, non-Hispanic black, non-Hispanic Asian, and non-Hispanic other races. This is consistent with earlier research and polling practices. The term *other races* includes American Indian, Alaskan Native, and "all other races." Hawaiian Natives and other pacific islanders are grouped with the Asian category in the census survey tablulations.

4. Roberto Suro, Richard Fry, and Jeffrey Passel, "Hispanics and the 2004 Election: Population, Electorate, and Voters" (Washington: Pew Hispanic Center, 2005).

5. Pew Research Center, "Optimism about Black Progress Declines" (Washington: 2007).

6. Before 1998 exit polls used a single race question ("Are you white, black, Hispanic/Latino. . . .") to capture Hispanics, as opposed to later polls, which include a race question plus another question on whether the respondent is of Hispanic descent. Because of the differences in the way the question is asked and the fact that more conservative or Republican respondents identified with Hispanic descent than with race, a comparison of pre-1998 Hispanic exit poll figures to 1998 and onward Hispanic exit poll figures understates Republican responses.

7. Ben Adler, "Asian-American Youth Trend Democratic," *Politico,* December 20, 2007 (www.politico.com/news/stories/1207/7503.html.

8. Pew Research Center, "Optimism about Black Progress Declines."

9. See Pew Research Center, "No Consensus on Immigration Problem or Proposed Fixes" (Washington: 2006); Joseph Carroll, "Hispanics Views on Immigration Unchanged from Last Year," Gallup News Service, June 28, 2007.

10. Alan Greenblatt, "Immigration Debate: Can Politicians Find a Way to Curb Illegal Immigration?" *CQ Researcher,* February 1, 2008, pp. 97–120.

11. Ibid.

four

The Decline of the White Working Class and the Rise of a Mass Upper-Middle Class

ALAN ABRAMOWITZ AND RUY TEIXEIRA

Dramatic shifts have taken place in the American class structure since the World War II era. Consider education levels. Incredible as it may seem today, in 1940, 75 percent of adults twenty-five-years old and over were high school dropouts (or never made it as far as high school), and just 5 percent had a four-year college degree or higher. But educational credentials exploded in the postwar period. By 1960 the proportion of adults lacking a high school diploma was down to 59 percent; by 1980 it was less than a third; and by 2007 it was only 14 percent. Concomitantly, the proportion with a bachelor's degree or higher rose steadily, reaching 29 percent in 2007. Moreover, those with some college (but not a four-year degree) constituted another 25 percent of the population, making a total of 54 percent who had at least some college education.[1] Quite a change, moving from a country in which the typical adult was a high school dropout (more accurately, never even reached high school) to a country in which the typical adult not only has a high school diploma but some college as well.

Or consider the occupational structure. In 1940 only about 32 percent of employed U.S. workers held white-collar jobs (professional, managerial, and clerical-sales). By 2006 that proportion had almost doubled to 60 percent, including rises from 8 percent to 20 percent among professionals and from 17 percent to 26 percent among clerical-sales. On the other end of the occupational distribution, manual workers (production workers, operatives, crafts people, and laborers) declined from 36 percent to 23 percent.[2] So the country has moved from an occupational structure in which there were more manual than white-collar workers to one in which there are nearly three times as many white-collar as manual workers.

Finally, consider income levels. In 1947 the median family income (in 2005 dollars) was around $22,000. By 2005 median family income was around $56,000, two and a half times as high as in 1947. Looked at another way, in 1947, 60 percent of families made under $26,000. But in 2005 only 20 percent made less than that figure and 40 percent made over $68,000, a figure that was exceeded by less than 5 percent of families in 1947.[3] In this chapter we discuss these shifts in the class structure and analyze their political implications, primarily by focusing on the decline of the white working class. We also take a look at another aspect of the shifting class structure, the rise of a mass upper-middle class. We then assess whether and to what extent the trends reshaping our class structure are likely to continue in the future. We conclude with a discussion of how these changes are likely to shift the political terrain facing the parties and present new challenges for policymakers.

Defining the White Working Class

Before we can discuss the decline of the white working class, it is necessary to define it. Perhaps the first thing to observe is that there is no "correct" way to do this. Reasonable cases can be made for defining the white working class by any of these three criteria: education, occupation, and income. Below we note the advantages and disadvantages of each.

There are several arguments for using education to define the working class. First, educational level is a proxy for skill level, or human capital, which in turn is a central determinant of not only the job a worker holds today but also the kind of job that worker can expect to hold in the future. Thus educational level tends to shape a worker's economic and life trajectory in profound ways. Moreover, this relationship has strengthened in the years since 1979. In particular, the economic fates of those with a four-year college degree and those without have diverged sharply. Between 1979 and 2005 the average real hourly wage for those with a college degree went up 22 percent and for those with advanced degrees, 28 percent. In contrast, average wages for those with only some college went up a mere 3 percent; for those with a high school diploma wages actually fell 2 percent; and for high school dropouts wages declined a stunning 18 percent.[4]

A final reason to use education to define the working class is practical. Educational data are almost always collected in political surveys, and the categories used are usually commensurate across surveys. Moreover, such data are typically collected for all survey respondents, not just those who currently hold a job, so it is possible to categorize all individuals in the survey. That said, education by definition does not capture the actual job a given individual holds and, therefore, departs from the traditional definition of class, which is rooted in a worker's role in the economy. This can create anomalies: some individuals with low levels of education may have powerful or highly skilled jobs, while some with high levels of education may have very menial jobs.

Using occupation data to define the working class has the advantage of tapping directly into this traditional definition. A manual worker clearly belongs in the working class; a professional or businessman does not; and so on. But occupation data typically are not collected on political surveys. And when they are, the categories used vary widely and typically leave out those not in the labor force or even all those not holding a full-time job.

The third way to define the working class is to use income data. This method connects to the popular conception that one's class is determined by the amount of money one makes. By that measure, the working class is simply those who do not have much money. One problem this approach creates is whether to use income relationally or absolutely. Are people working class because they do not have much money relative to others or because they do not have much money period? By the latter criterion, the size of the working class—the bottom 20 (or 40 or 60) percent of the income distribution—could not change over time no matter how affluent a society becomes. By the former criterion, the size of the working class can change as society itself changes, which seems preferable. There are also technical problems with using income data. Although they are more commonly collected on political surveys than occupation, these data are usually categorical, and the categories vary substantially across surveys. And then there is the problem of inflation, which makes comparison of categorical income data from different time periods problematic.

It seems clear there is no perfect way to measure class; each way has its virtues and drawbacks. In this chapter we therefore use all three indicators in our analysis, sometimes singly, sometimes combined into a summary measure. In addition, in analyzing survey data we make use of another measure, subjective class identification, which is related to all three of our more objective measures of class status.

How then should we define the white working class using these indicators? In each case, there is a both a broad and a narrow definition that can be used. For education, a broad definition of the white working class would include all whites with less than a four-year college degree—the dividing line between high and medium to low skill levels and, as we saw above, between positive and flat to negative economic trajectories since 1979. A narrower definition would assign only whites with a high school degree or less to the white working class.

For occupation, a broad definition of the white working class would include all whites without a professional or managerial job—that is, all whites with manual, service, or low-level white-collar occupations. A narrower definition would include only those whites with manual or service jobs.

Income is trickier, since the potential cutoff points are less obvious and harder to assign. A broad definition of the white working class might include whites with household incomes below $60,000. A narrower definition might include only those whites with incomes below $30,000. Whether one uses a broad or narrow definition is, to some extent, a matter of taste. In popular terms, if one believes only the poor really belong in the working class, then a narrow definition is appropriate. But if one believes that the working class can and should overlap with the middle class—that a decent standard of living does not disqualify those of modest skill from membership in the working class—then a broader definition is appropriate. But as we shall see, whether a broad or narrow definition is used, the story of the white working class since the World War II era is one of profound change and substantial decline. That story is sketched below.

Change and Decline in the White Working Class

Let us start with the basic numbers on the size of the white working class in the World War II era and the size of the white working class today. Using the broad education-based definition, America in 1940 was an overwhelmingly white working-class country. In that year 86 percent of adults twenty-five-years old and over were whites without a four-year college degree. By 2007, with the dramatic rise in educational attainment and the decline in the white population, that percentage was down to 48 percent. A similar trend can be seen using the narrow education-based definition. In 1940, 82 percent of adults ages twenty-five and over were whites with a high school diploma or less. By 2007 that figure was down to 29 percent.[5]

Turning to a broad occupation-based definition, in 1940, 74 percent of employed workers were whites without professional or managerial jobs. By 2006 the steady climb in professional and managerial jobs, combined with the decline in the white population, had brought that percentage down to 43 percent. A narrow occupation-based definition yields a decline of similar magnitude. In 1940, 58 percent of workers were whites without professional, managerial, or clerical-sales jobs (or looked at another way, whites who held manual, service, or farm jobs). By 2006 that figure had fallen to 25 percent.[6]

The final class indicator to look at is income. Using a broad, income-based definition of the white working class, 86 percent of American families in 1947 were white families with less than $60,000 in income (2005 dollars). With rising affluence—especially rapid in the period from 1947 to 1973—and the decline in the white population, that percentage had declined to 33 percent by 2005. Using a narrow income-based definition, 60 percent of families in 1947 were white families with less than $30,000 in income. That figure had dropped to 14 percent by 2005.[7]

So each indicator that can be used to define the white working class, whether applied broadly or narrowly, shows huge declines from the World War II era to today—declines roughly in the 30–50 percentage point range. Income-based definitions show the sharpest declines and occupation-based definitions the least, with education-based definitions somewhere in between. And in each case, these shifts have moved the white working class from being the solid and sometimes overwhelming majority of U.S. adults (or workers or families) to being a minority.

But the story of the white working class in the post–World War II era is not just one of sharp decline but also one of profound transformation. This is true no matter what indicator one uses to define the white working class. That is, whether one looks at white families with less than $60,000 income, at whites who do not hold professional-managerial jobs, or at whites without a four-year college degree, there have been dramatic shifts in the character and composition of the white working class.

Consider the following shifts among whites without a four-year college degree. In 1940, 86 percent of these working-class whites had never graduated from high school (or even reached high school). But today just 14 percent of the white working class are high school dropouts. About 40 percent have some education beyond high school, with 13 percent having achieved an associate degree.[8] (Note, however, that the economic situation of those with an associate degree is very similar to those with some college but no degree: the median household income of whites with an associate degree is only a few thousand dollars more than those with some college only.)[9]

While data unavailability precludes a precise estimate, the economic situation of the white working class has altered dramatically. A reasonable guess is that the median family income of the white working class rose from around $20,000 to $50,000 between 1947 and 2005, a 150 percent increase.

And the jobs the white working class holds have also changed. Today most white working-class jobs are not manual or blue-collar but are rather in low-level white-collar (technical and clerical-sales) and service occupations. And the blue-collar jobs that remain are increasingly likely to be skilled positions: only about a sixth of the white working class holds unskilled blue-collar jobs (even among white working-class men, the figure is less than one-quarter). Today only about a sixth of the white working class holds manufacturing jobs (even among men, the proportion is still less than one-quarter). In fact, the entire goods-producing sector, which includes construction, mining, and agriculture as well as manufacturing, provides less than three in ten white working-class jobs. This leaves the overwhelming majority—over seven in ten—in the service sector, including government. There are about as many members of the white working class working in trade alone (especially retail) as there are in all goods-producing jobs.[10]

The White Working Class Abandons the Democratic Party

Accompanying the decline and transformation of the white working class was a very significant shift in its political orientation, from pro-Democratic in most respects to pro-Republican, especially on the presidential level. The story of this shift away from the Democratic Party starts with the New Deal Democrats and their close relationship with the white working class.

The New Deal Democratic worldview was based on a combination of the Democrats' historic populist commitment to the average working American and their experience in battling the Great Depression (and building their political coalition) through increased government spending and regulation and the promotion of labor unions. It was really a rather simple philosophy, even if the application of it was complex. Government should help the average person through vigorous government spending. Capitalism needs regulation to work properly. Labor unions are good. Putting money in the average person's pocket is more important than rarified worries about the quality of life. Traditional morality is to be respected, not challenged. Racism and the like are bad, but not so bad that the party should depart from its main mission of material uplift for the average American.

That worldview had deep roots in an economy dominated by mass production industries and was politically based among the workers, overwhelmingly white, in those industries. And it helped make the Democrats the undisputed party of the white working class. Their dominance among these voters was, in turn, the key to their political success. To be sure, there were important divisions among these voters—by country of origin (German, Scandinavian, Eastern European, English, Irish, Italian, and so on), by religion (Protestants, Catholics), and by region (South, non-South)—that greatly complicated the politics of this group, but New Deal Democrats mastered these complications and maintained a deep base among these voters.

The prototypical member of the New Deal coalition was an ethnic white worker in a unionized factory; the coalition also included, though, nonunion workers, most blacks, and such groups as Jews and southerners. It was these voters who provided the numbers for four FDR election victories and Harry Truman's narrow victory in 1948 and who provided political support for the emerging U.S. welfare state, with its implicit social contract and greatly expanded role for government.

Even in the 1950s, with Republican Dwight Eisenhower as president, the white working class continued to put Democrats in Congress and to support the expansion of the welfare state, as a roaring U.S. economy delivered the goods and government poured money into roads, science, schools, and whatever else seemed necessary to build up the country. This era, stretching back into the late 1940s and forward to the mid-1960s, was the era that created the first mass middle class in the world—a middle class that even factory workers could enter, since they could earn relatively comfortable livings even without high levels of education or professional skills. A middle class, in other words, that members of the white working class could reasonably aspire to and frequently attain.

So New Deal Democrats depended on the white working class for political support and the white working class depended on New Deal Democrats to run the government and the economy in a way that kept that upward escalator to the middle class moving. Social and cultural issues were not particularly important to this mutually beneficial relationship; indeed, they had only a peripheral role in the uncomplicated progressivism that animated the Democratic Party of the 1930s, 1940s, and 1950s. But that arrangement and that uncomplicated progressivism could not and did not survive the decline of mass production industries and the rise of postindustrial capitalism.

First, there was the transformation of the white working class itself, discussed in detail above. The white working class became richer, more educated, more white-collar and less unionized (to get a sense of how important the latter factor was, consider the fact that in the late 1940s unions claimed around 60 percent or more of the northern blue-collar workforce).[11]

Second, as this great transformation was changing the character of the white working class, reducing the size and influence of the Democrats' traditional blue-collar constituencies, the evolution of postindustrial capitalism was creating new constituencies and movements with new demands. These new constituencies and movements wanted more out of the welfare state than steady economic growth, copious infrastructure spending, and the opportunity to raise a family in the traditional manner.

During the 1960s these new demands on the welfare state came to a head. Americans' concern about their quality of life overflowed from the two-car garage to clean air and water and safe automobiles; from higher wages to government-guaranteed health care in old age; and from access to jobs to equal opportunities for men and women and blacks and whites. Out of these concerns came the environmental, consumer, civil rights, and feminist movements of the 1960s. As Americans abandoned the older ideal of self-denial and the taboos that accompanied it, they embraced a libertarian ethic of personal life. Women asserted their sexual independence through the use of birth control pills and through exercising the right to have an abortion. Adolescents experimented with sex and courtship. Homosexuals "came out" and openly congregated in bars and neighborhoods.

Of these changes, the one with most far-reaching political effects was the civil rights movement and its demands for equality and economic progress for black America. Democrats, both because of their traditional, if usually downplayed, antiracist ideology and their political relationship to the black community, had no choice but to respond to those demands. The result was a great victory for social justice but one that created huge political difficulties for the Democrats among their white working-class supporters. Kevin Phillips captures these developments in his 1969 book, *The Emerging Republican Majority:*

> The principal force which broke up the Democratic (New Deal) coalition is the Negro socioeconomic revolution and liberal Democratic ideological inability to cope with it. Democratic "Great Society" programs aligned that party with many Negro demands, but the party was unable to defuse the racial tension sundering the nation. The South, the West, and the Catholic sidewalks of New York were the focus points of conservative opposition to the welfare liberalism of the federal government; however, the general opposition . . . came in large part from prospering Democrats who objected to Washington dissipating their tax dollars on programs which did them no good. The Democratic

party fell victim to the ideological impetus of a liberalism which had carried it beyond programs taxing the few for the benefit of the many . . . to programs taxing the many on behalf of the few.[12]

But if race was the chief vehicle by which the New Deal coalition was torn apart, it was by no means the only one. White working-class voters also reacted poorly to the extremes with which the rest of the new social movements became identified. Feminism became identified with bra burners, lesbians, and hostility to the nuclear family; the antiwar movement with appeasement of third world radicals and the Soviet Union; the environmental movement with a Luddite opposition to economic growth; and the move toward more personal freedom with a complete abdication of personal responsibility. Thus the New Deal Democrat mainstream that dominated the party was confronted with a challenge. The uncomplicated commitments to government spending, economic regulation, and labor unions that had defined the Democrats' progressivism for over thirty years suddenly provided little guidance for dealing with an explosion of potential new constituencies for the party. Their demands for equality and for a better—as opposed to merely a richer—life were starting to redefine what progressivism meant, and the Democrats had to struggle to catch up.

Initially, Democratic politicians responded to these changes in the fashion of politicians since time immemorial: they sought to co-opt these new movements by absorbing many of their demands while holding onto the party's basic ideology and style of governing. Thus Democratic politicians did not change their fundamental commitment to the New Deal welfare state but grafted onto it support for all the various new constituencies and their key demands. After Lyndon Johnson signed the Civil Rights Act in 1964, the party moved over the next eight years to give the women's, the antiwar, the consumer's, and the environmental movements prominent places within the party. This reflected both the politician's standard interest in capturing the votes of new constituencies and the ongoing expansion in the definition of what it meant to be a Democrat, particularly a progressive one.

But there was no guarantee, of course, that gains among these new constituencies would not be more than counterbalanced by losses among their old constituency—the white working class—who had precious little interest in this expansion of what it meant to be a progressive and a Democrat. And indeed that turned out to be the case in 1972, with the nomination and disastrous defeat of George McGovern, who enthusiastically embraced the new direction taken by the party. McGovern's commitment to the traditional

Democratic welfare state was unmistakable. But so was his commitment to all the various social movements and constituencies that were reshaping the party, whose demands were enshrined in McGovern's campaign platform. That made it easy for the Nixon campaign to typecast McGovern as the candidate of "acid, amnesty, and abortion." The white working class reacted accordingly and gave Nixon overwhelming support at the polls, casting 70 percent of their votes for the Republican candidate.[13]

Indeed, just how far the Democratic Party fell in the estimation of the white working class over this time period can be seen by comparing the average white working-class (whites without a four-year college degree) vote for the Democrats in 1960–64 (55 percent) to the average vote for the Democrats in 1968–72 (35 percent).[14] The Democrats were the party of the white working class no longer.

With the sharp economic recession and Nixon scandals of 1973–74, the Democrats were able to develop enough political momentum to retake the White House in 1976, with Jimmy Carter's narrow defeat of Gerald Ford. But their political revival did not last long. Not only did the Carter administration fail to do much to defuse white working-class hostility to the new social movements, especially the black liberation movement, but economic events—resulting in the stagflation of the late 1970s—conspired to make that hostility even sharper. Though stagflation (a combination of inflation and unemployment, along with slow economic growth with its slow wage and income growth) first appeared during the 1973–75 recession, it persisted during the Carter administration and was peaking on the eve of the 1980 election. As the economy slid once more into recession, the inflation rate in that year was 12.5 percent. Combined with an unemployment rate of 7.1 percent, it produced a "misery index" of nearly 20 percent.

By that time, white working-class voters had entered an economic world radically different from the one enjoyed by the preceding generation. Slow growth, declining wages, stagnating living standards, high and variable inflation, and high home mortgage interest rates were really battering them economically. The great postwar escalator to the middle class had drastically slowed down and, for some, even stopped.

These economic developments fed resentments about race: about high taxes for welfare (which were assumed to go primarily to minorities) and about affirmative action. But they also sowed doubts about Democrats' ability to manage the economy and made Republican and business explanations of stagflation (blaming it on government regulation, high taxes, and spending) more plausible. In 1978 the white backlash and doubts about Democratic economic policies had helped to fuel a nationwide tax revolt. In 1980 these factors reproduced the massive exodus of white working-class voters from the Democratic tickets first seen in 1968 and 1972. In the 1980 and 1984 elections Reagan averaged 61 percent support among the white working class, compared to an average of 35 percent support for his Democratic opponents, Jimmy Carter and Walter Mondale.[15]

Such a thrashing, coming not that long after the debacle of the McGovern campaign, led many Democrats, spearheaded by a new organization, the Democratic Leadership Council (DLC), to propose a reconfiguration of the Democratic approach. These "New Democrats" (as they called themselves) argued that in the late 1960s the liberalism of the New Deal had degenerated into a "liberal fundamentalism," which

> the public had come to associate with tax and spending policies that contradict the interests of average families; with welfare policies that foster dependence rather than self-reliance; with softness toward the perpetrators of crime and indifference toward its victims; with ambivalence toward the assertion of American values and interests abroad; and with an adversarial stance toward mainstream moral and cultural values.[16]

The DLC advocated fiscal conservatism, welfare reform, increased spending on crime through the development of a police corps, tougher mandatory sentences, support for capital punishment, and policies that encouraged traditional families. This new approach did not really take off until it was embraced by Democratic presidential candidate Bill Clinton in 1992, who synthesized these views with a moderate version of New Deal–style economic populism. It proved to be an electorally successful approach in 1992 and, riding some good economic times, in 1996 as well. But despite Clinton's electoral success, it was not the case that he received a great deal of white working-class support. He averaged only 41 percent across his two election victories. But he did, at least, prevent these voters from siding with his Republican opponents in large numbers, eking out 1-point pluralities among the white working class in both elections (the rest went to Ross Perot).[17]

His designated successor, Al Gore, was not so successful. He lost white working-class voters in the 2000 election by 17 points. And the next Democratic presidential candidate, John Kerry, did even worse, losing these voters by a whopping 23 points in 2004.[18] One could reasonably ascribe the worsening deficit for Democrats in 2004 to the role of national security and terrorism after 9/11, but the very sizable 2000 deficit cannot be explained on that basis.

Apparently, the successes of the Clinton years, which included a strong economy that delivered solid real wage growth for the first time since 1973, did not succeed in restoring the historic bond between the white working class and the Democrats.

It is worth asking what Democratic performance in 2004 looked like when one adds income to education for a more fine-grained consideration of white working-class voting, as exit poll data do permit (occupation cannot be looked at with exit poll data). Here is what we find: those voters who seem to correspond most closely to one's intuitive sense of the heart of the white working class—that is, white voters who have a moderate income and are non-college-educated—are precisely the voters among whom Democrats did most poorly. For example, among non-college-educated whites with $30,000–$50,000 in household income, Bush beat Kerry by 24 points (62 to 38); among college-educated whites at the same income level, Kerry actually managed a 49 to 49 tie. And among non-college-educated whites with $50,000–$75,000 in household income, Bush beat Kerry by a shocking 41 points (70 to 29), while leading by only 5 points (52 to 47) among college-educated whites at the same income level. Thus the more voters looked like hardcore members of the white working class, the less likely they were to vote for Kerry in the 2004 election.[19]

How Can I Miss You If You Won't Go Away?; or, Did the White Working Class Really Abandon the Democratic Party?

As noted above, white working-class support for the Democratic Party from the New Deal to the Great Society was based primarily on economic self-interest: Democrats stood for economic policies such as full employment and social programs such as Social Security and Medicare that benefited the white (and nonwhite) working class. Starting from the idea that voting for the Democrats would still be in these voters' economic self-interest, some analysts like Thomas Frank argue that Republicans' inroads among white working-class voters in recent decades are entirely attributable to the GOP's emphasis on cultural issues like abortion and gay marriage.[20] This led to a decline in class-based voting. Frank further argues that this decline has occurred not because white working-class voters have become more conservative on cultural issues but because they have been persuaded by Republican propaganda to weigh these issues more heavily than economic self-interest.

In contrast to Frank, Larry Bartels argues that the white working class never abandoned the Democratic Party in the first place.[21] In fact, according to Bartels, data from the American National Election Studies (ANES) show that "white voters in the bottom third of the income distribution have actually become more reliably Democratic in presidential elections over the past half-century, while middle- and upper-income white voters have trended Republican."[22] This is a counterintuitive and interesting finding, but there are a number of problems with it, having to do with Bartels's definition of the white working class and with the indicators of Democratic orientation he chose to look at.

Start with his definition of the white working class. As noted above, family income is only one indicator of an individual's position in the class structure, and it is not necessarily the most valid one. Compared with characteristics such as educational attainment and occupational status, income is more likely to fluctuate over the course of an individual's life. This may explain why, according to ANES data, subjective class identification is more strongly related to both occupational status and education than to family income. For all years between 1952 and 2004 the average correlation between class identification and family income was .28, while the average correlation between class identification and occupational status was .34, and the average correlation between class identification and educational attainment was .37.

Another problem with equating low income with membership in the working class is that, as David Gopoian and Ralph Whitehead point out, the large majority of low-income white voters are not currently working.[23] According to data from the 2004 ANES only 39 percent of white voters in the low-income group were currently employed, compared with 73 percent of white voters in the middle-income group and 78 percent of white voters in the upper-income group. The majority of low-income white voters in 2004 were retired, disabled, homemakers, or students. Similarly, data from the 2004 national exit poll show that low-income white voters were disproportionately young or elderly—44 percent were either under twenty-five years of age or over sixty-four years of age, compared with 19 percent of all other white voters. Only 15 percent of white voters in their prime earning years (twenty-five to sixty-four) reported family incomes of less than $30,000, compared with 38 percent of those under twenty-five years of age and 37 percent of those over sixty-four years of age.

In addition, it should be stressed that Bartels's definition of the white working class as those whites who fall in the bottom third of the income distribution is based on overall income distribution, not income distribution among whites. Thus among whites we are talking about a substantially smaller group than one-third. According to Bartels's own data, over the 1984–2004 time period, whites in the lower third of the income distribution amounted to only about 23 percent of white voters (and about 17 percent of all voters).

Finally, defining the white working class as, in essence, the white poor throws out of the white working class, the very kind of workers who traditionally are most associated with that group. Using Bartels's definition, for example—while one must make inferences from inadequate historical data—it appears highly unlikely that the typical autoworker, steelworker, construction worker, mechanic, and so on back in the late 1940s and 1950s could have qualified for Bartels's white working class. They just were not poor enough. And today? Not too different. Consider these data from the Economic Policy Institute: the average unionized blue-collar job in the United States in 2003 paid $22.74 an hour (presumably the average wage of whites in these jobs was somewhat higher). That is way too high to qualify for Bartels's white working class—and that is leaving out any possible income from a spouse.

These results suggest that an analysis of the relationship between social class and partisanship should include other indicators of class in addition to family income. The ANES include four variables that measure different aspects of social class: family income, education, occupational status, and subjective class identification. These variables were moderately correlated with each other in every decade, indicating that they were all measuring some aspect of an individual's status in society. The average correlation (Pearson's r) among these four variables was .34 for 1952–60, .32 for 1962–70, .32 for 1972–80, .31 for 1982–90, and .31 for 1992 to 2004. All of the individual coefficients were statistically significant. As a result, rather than relying on any one of these variables to measure social class, we created an index that combines all four.

All of the components of our socioeconomic status (SES) index except family income show a marked upward shift over time among white voters, and the only reason that the income variable did not show such a shift was that the ANES recoded the original income categories into lower, middle, and upper terciles for each year in order to facilitate over-time comparisons (table 4-1). As a result, even though the real median family income of white voters increased substantially between the 1950s and the beginning of the twenty-first century, the proportion of white voters in each of the ANES income groups was fairly stable. However, the proportion of white voters with no college education fell from 78 percent to 35 percent between 1952–60 and 1992–2004, the proportion with blue-collar occupations fell from 47 percent to 28 percent, and the proportion identifying with the working class fell from 56 percent to 38 percent.

Despite the fact that the income component of the ANES index was artificially constrained, the overall index shows a marked shift over time: the pro-

Table 4-1. Distribution of White Voters on SES Index, by Decade, 1952–2004

Percent except where indicated

SES index	1952–60	1962–70	1972–80	1982–90	1992–2004
Lower	52	47	43	35	33
Middle	30	32	33	34	32
Upper	18	21	24	31	35
N	1,708	1,737	3,655	3,306	2,833

Source: ICPSR, American National Election Studies (Institute for Social Research, University of Michigan, cumulative file).

portion of white voters in the lower SES group fell from 52 percent to 33 percent, while the proportion in the upper group rose from 18 percent to 35 percent. Thus the ANES data, like the census data examined earlier, indicate that since the end of World War II the white working class has been slowly but steadily shrinking as a proportion of the overall white electorate due to rising levels of education and changes in the American occupational structure.

Despite the trends evident in the data, lower SES individuals still make up a large share of the white electorate in the first decade of the twenty-first century. We would therefore like to know whether the political loyalties of this group have shifted over time. Have white working class voters remained solidly in the Democratic camp, as Bartels argues, or have they been moving toward the GOP, as Frank claims and as other data adduced earlier suggest? Rather than relying on presidential voting to measure partisan loyalties, however, we use party identification. We believe that party identification provides a broader and more accurate measure of the partisan orientations of voters than the presidential vote.[24] The presidential vote can fluctuate dramatically from election to election in response to short-term forces such as the state of the economy, the popularity of the incumbent president, and the relative appeal of the presidential candidates.

This is particularly important when looking at the white working class and when starting in 1952 and 1956, as Bartels does. In these two elections, where Eisenhower, the Republican candidate, prevailed, Democrats drew unusually low presidential support, including among white working-class voters, however defined, and especially outside the South. To underscore the anomalous nature of the Eisenhower elections in the New Deal era, consider the fact that Democrats averaged 55 percent support in the five New Deal elections from 1932 to 1948 and then an identical 55 percent in the 1960–64 elections, which closed the era. That compares with an average of only 43 percent in the 1952–56 elections. Thus starting with the Eisenhower elections sets up one's analysis (if the focus is the presidential vote) to see relatively little decline in Democratic support among working-class whites.

In contrast, shifts in party identification tend to be gradual and reflect long-term changes in the images and ideological positions of the parties. Using party identification avoids the problems that can be created by the vagaries of the presidential vote, as with the Eisenhower elections. Moreover, party identification strongly influences voting for many offices, from the presidency down to the state and local level. The trend in party identification among lower, middle, and upper SES white voters between the 1960s and the first decade of the twenty-first century shows that, over this time period, there has been a dramatic decline in support for the Democratic Party among both lower and middle SES white voters, while party loyalties of upper SES white voters have changed very little (figure 4-1). Using the terminology introduced earlier, lower SES white voters correspond roughly to a narrow definition of the white working class and match up best with the definition used by Bartels. Lower and middle SES white voters together correspond roughly to a broad definition of the white working class.

Figure 4-1. Democratic Identification, Lower, Middle, and Upper SES White Voters, by Decade, 1962–2004[a]

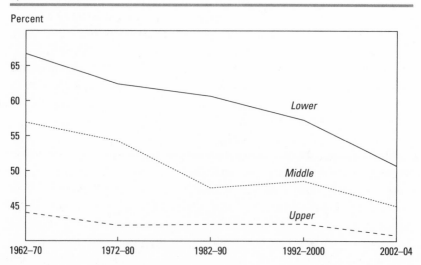

Percent

Source: American National Election Studies cumulative file.
a. Percentage of Democratic identifiers based on Democratic identifiers and leaners divided by all party identifiers and leaners.

Between 1962–70 and 2002–04 Democratic identification fell from 67 percent to 51 percent among lower SES white voters and from 57 percent to 45 percent among middle SES white voters. Thus whether a narrow or broad definition of the white working class is used, there has been a substantial decline in Democratic identification over the past several decades. In contrast, Democratic identification fell only from 44 percent to 41 percent among upper SES white voters over the same time period. This means that the difference in Democratic identification between the lower and upper SES groups declined from 23 percentage points in the 1960s to just 10 percentage points in the first decade of the twenty-first century, while the difference between the middle and upper SES groups declined from 13 percentage points to a mere 4 percentage points. As a result, lower and middle SES white voters have come more and more to resemble upper SES white voters in their party loyalties. Class differences in party identification have not disappeared but are considerably smaller than they were thirty or forty years ago.

A related question is whether the decline in Democratic identification among white working-class voters has been a national phenomenon or a regional phenomenon. In a recent article using education rather than family income to measure social class, Bartels argues that this decline was confined entirely to the South.[25] Outside of the South white working-class voters have remained loyal to the Democrats. However, our data do not support this claim (figure 4-2).[26] We compare the trend in Democratic identification in the South with the trend in the rest of the country among lower SES white voters (the closest analogue in our scheme to Bartels's definition of the white working class). These data show that while the decline in Democratic identification was much steeper in the South than in the rest of the country, there was a substantial drop in support for the Democratic Party among lower SES white voters in the North. Between 1962–70 and 2002–04 Democratic identification among lower SES white voters fell from 76 percent to 42 percent in the South and from 64 percent to 53 percent outside of the South.

These findings raise the question of why support for the Democratic Party has declined dramatically among lower SES white voters since the 1960s while remaining fairly stable among upper SES white voters. They also raise the question of why this decline has been much greater in the South than in the rest of the country. It is not surprising to find that forty years ago Democratic identification was much higher among lower SES white voters in the South than in the rest of the country. This presumably reflected the traditional loyalty of southern white voters to the Democratic Party—a loyalty that traced its origins back to the Civil War and Reconstruction. However, it is not clear

Figure 4-2. Democratic Identification, Lower SES White Voters, by Decade and Region[a]

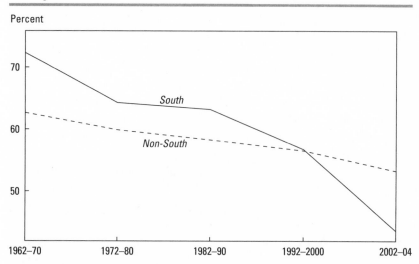

Source: American National Election Studies cumulative file.
a. Percentage of Democratic identifiers based on Democratic identifiers and leaners divided by all party identifiers and leaners.

why, by the first decade of the twenty-first century, Democratic identification among lower SES white voters in the South had fallen well below the level found in the rest of the country.

One explanation for the changes in party identification over the past several decades, including the dramatic decline in Democratic identification among white southerners, is that they reflect an ideological realignment within the American electorate. According to this theory, the increasing clarity of ideological differences between Democratic and Republican elected officials and candidates has made it much easier for voters to choose sides based on their own ideological predispositions. As a result there is now a much closer correspondence between ideology and party identification and a much greater degree of ideological polarization within the electorate.[27]

Ideological realignment theory provides a potential explanation for why the decline in Democratic identification among lower SES white voters has been much greater than the decline among upper SES white voters. It is possible that this realignment took place earlier among better educated and more affluent whites than among less educated and affluent whites. Conservative upper SES whites may have largely shifted their loyalties to the Republican Party by the 1970s or 1980s, while conservative lower SES whites may not have fully shifted to the Republicans until the 1990s or the first decade of the twenty-first century.

Changes in party identification since the 1970s among lower and upper SES white voters—depending on their ideological identification—are shown in figure 4-3.[28] The trends evident in this figure are consistent with our expectations. Among both lower and upper SES whites, Democratic identification declined among self-identified conservatives but remained stable or increased among self-identified moderates and liberals. However, the patterns of change among lower and upper SES voters were quite different. Upper SES whites were already largely divided along ideological lines during the 1970s: 70 percent of moderate-to-liberal voters identified with the Democratic Party, compared with less than 20 percent of conservatives. Over the next thirty years, the gap in party identification between these two ideological groups increased modestly. In contrast, lower SES whites were not as clearly divided along ideological lines during the 1970s: over 70 percent of moderate-to-liberal voters identified with the Democratic Party, but so did almost half of conservative voters.

Over the next three decades, however, the gap between these two ideological groups increased dramatically, as conservative voters shifted decisively into the Republican camp while moderate-to-liberal voters moved even further toward the Democrats. By the first decade of the twenty-first century, ideological realignment was largely complete among lower as well as upper SES whites. In both groups almost 80 percent of moderate-to-liberal voters identified with the Democratic Party, while close to 90 percent of conservative voters identified with the Republican Party.

One question raised by these findings is whether the ideological realignment of lower SES white voters has been driven primarily by cultural issues, as Frank argues. To test this hypothesis, we used data from the 2004 ANES to examine the relationship between the attitudes of lower, middle, and upper SES white voters on abortion—the most divisive cultural issue of the past quarter century—and their party identification. Respondents were classified as pro-life if they indicated that abortion should never be allowed or allowed only under exceptional circumstances such as rape, incest, or danger to the life of the mother. They were classified as pro-choice if they indicated that abortion should always be a woman's choice or should be allowed under a variety of circumstances beyond rape, incest, or danger to the mother's life. The results are displayed in table 4-2.

Figure 4-3. Democratic Identification by Ideology, Lower and Upper SES White Voters, by Decade

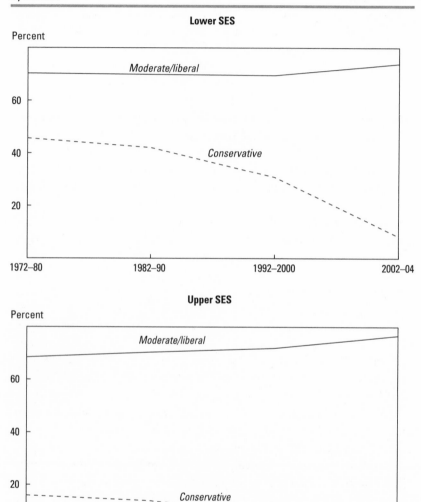

Source: American National Election Studies cumulative file.

Table 4-2. Abortion Position, Democratic White Voters, by SES Index, 2004[a]

Percent, except where indicated

SES index	Pro-life	Pro-choice	Kendall's *tau-b*	Significance
Lower	43	57	.14	.05
Middle	33	55	.22	.01
Upper	8	60	.50	.001

Source: American National Election Studies cumulative file.
a. Democratic identifiers and leaners, divided by all party identifiers and leaners.

The results, displayed in the table, do not support Frank's hypothesis that Republicans have relied primarily on cultural issues such as abortion to lure working-class white voters away from the Democratic Party. Lower SES white voters were somewhat more conservative on abortion than upper SES white voters: 45 percent of them chose the two pro-life options in the survey, compared with 35 percent of upper SES white voters. However, the relationship between abortion attitudes and party identification was actually much stronger among upper SES whites than among lower SES whites. On the pro-choice side, similar proportions of lower and upper SES whites identified with the Democratic Party—57 percent versus 60 percent. On the pro-life side, however, only 57 percent of pro-life lower SES whites identified with the Republican Party, compared with 92 percent of upper SES whites. Based on these results, it appears that Republicans have been much more successful in attracting support from culturally conservative upper SES whites than from culturally conservative lower SES whites. It does not appear that cultural issues like abortion have played a major—and certainly not *the* major—role in the decline of Democratic identification among lower SES white voters. The story of declining white working-class support for Democrats is, as we outlined earlier, far more complex than that.

The Geography of the White Working Class

White working-class dominance, as we have seen, has eroded. The minority population has burgeoned, and the upgrading of education, occupation, and income has also cut into the white working class's population share. But these changes have not been uniformly distributed across the United States. Thus we need to understand not only how today's white working-class lives differently from its predecessors but also how it lives in different places. This is particularly important for assessing the political impact of the white working class.

Start with distribution by state. Using a broad definition of the working class (non-college-educated), white working-class voters range from lows of 3 percent in Washington and 15 percent in Hawaii to highs of 70 percent in Iowa and Wyoming and 72 percent in West Virginia. Of course, given that these voters are roughly half of voters nationally, they tend to be a significant percentage of the electorate everywhere, but there is substantial variation between those extremes. The lowest percentages tend to be in states with high Hispanic populations (New Mexico, 34 percent white working class, California, 36 percent), states with high black populations (Maryland, 37 percent, Georgia, 42 percent, Mississippi, 45 percent, Louisiana, 45 percent), states with substantial segments of both (Texas, 37 percent), and states with unusually large college-educated populations (Colorado, 45 percent, Virginia, 45 percent). The highest percentages of white working class voters are in states in which the minority population is small to minimal, typically rural, with small college-educated populations (West Virginia, 72 percent, Wyoming and Iowa, both 70 percent, South Dakota and Maine, both 69 percent; North Dakota and Idaho, 67 percent; and Montana and Kentucky, both 66 percent).[29]

Significantly, with the exceptions of New Mexico and Florida (48 percent working class), the twelve most contested states in the last couple of presidential elections all have levels of white working-class voters well above the national average. These are the five states carried by Democrats by an average of less than 5 points in the two elections (Michigan, 59 percent, Minnesota, 58 percent, Oregon, 64 percent, Pennsylvania, 56 percent, and Wisconsin, 64 percent), two of the three states that changed hands across elections (Iowa, 70 percent and New Hampshire, 60 percent) and three of the four states the GOP carried by an average of less than 5 points in the two elections (Missouri, 58 percent; Nevada, 56 percent; Ohio, 60 percent).[30]

Of course, the white working class is not equally distributed *within* states either. Over time, the white working class has tended to migrate out of cities as minorities have moved in and, as a result, is now seriously underrepresented in urban areas (comprising less than a third of voters). The white working class has also tended to migrate out of America's rapidly dwindling rural areas but is still, at 68 percent of rural voters, overrepresented in these areas due to lack of minority in-migration to change the mix. It is the suburbs that have been the recipient of white working-class migration from both cities and rural areas, and here the white working class now represents about half of voters.[31] Since the suburbs are clearly the battleground of U.S. politics today, this is not an insignificant fact.

White working-class voters on average favor the GOP, as we have discussed at length. But the extent to which they do varies considerably by area of the country and type of community. Our previous analysis suggests that these differences in white working-class support for the Democratic Party reflect differences in the ideological orientations of white working-class voters in different regions of the country. The South, the most conservative region of the country, is the Democrats' worst region, where they lost white working-class voters by 44 points (72 to 28) in 2004. Outside the South they did better, losing by a comparatively small 15-point margin overall. Their best region is the Northeast, the most liberal region of the country, where they lost these voters by 9 points, followed by the Midwest, where they lost by 11 points, and the West, where they trailed by 26 points.[32]

Nationally, Democrats tend to fare best among white working-class voters in either large cities (over 500,000), where they ran a 13-point deficit in 2004, or the suburbs, where they had an 18-point deficit. They run worst in rural areas, where they lost two to one among the white working class (66 to 33) in 2004. In the Northeast and Midwest they ran closer than nationally among the suburban white working class (trailing by 12 points) and ran particularly well in small cities and towns in the East and Midwest, where they generally broke even among these voters.

Looking at the most competitive states mentioned above, in the five states that have been carried by Democrats by an average of less than 5 points in the last two elections (Michigan, Minnesota, Oregon, Pennsylvania, and Wisconsin), the Democrats ran fairly close among white working-class voters in 2004, losing by an average of 8 points. This is considerably better than the national average. And in the four states that the GOP carried by an average of less than 5 points in the two elections (Florida, Missouri, Nevada, and Ohio), the Democrats averaged a 13-point deficit. The relative closeness of the white working-class vote in these states is clearly part of what puts them in play (and the differences between them in degree of closeness help explain why one group has leaned blue and the other red in the last two elections).

Finally, it is worth noting the difference between these groups of states and another group of states that are viewed as potentially being in play, albeit more distantly. These are the five states—Arizona, Arkansas, Colorado, Tennessee, and West Virginia—that the GOP won by an average of less than 10 points (but more than 5) in the last two elections. In these states the Democrats lost the white working-class vote in 2004 by an average of 25 points.[33] There are other factors, of course, that put some of these states in play, but the size of the Democratic deficit among these states' relatively conservative white working-class voters is clearly a significant obstacle in the way of shifting them out of the GOP column.

The White Working Class and the 2008 Election

During the 2008 Democratic primary season, Hillary Clinton generally ran far ahead of Barack Obama among white working-class voters. But due to the structure of the Democratic primary electorate, with its heavy minority and college-educated representation, this did not translate into electoral dominance, and she ultimately failed to secure the nomination.

The story will be different in the November general election, however. Here the voting proclivities of the white working class will make a huge difference and could well determine who the next president will be. At the most general level, Bush carried white working-class voters by 23 points in 2004. A replication of this performance by the GOP candidate in 2008 would make it quite unlikely that the Democrat could prevail. Indeed, given the structure of the rest of the electorate, the Democrats have to get that deficit down to around 10–12 points to achieve a solid popular vote victory. How feasible is this?

The results of the 2006 congressional election indicate that this is possible. In that election the Democrats dramatically improved their performance among white working-class voters, running only a 10-point deficit, down from a 20-point deficit in 2004 congressional voting. Moreover, the Democrats reduced their deficit from 32 to 21 points among non-college-educated whites with $50,000 to $75,000 in household income and completely eliminated their deficit among non-college-educated whites with $30,000 to $50,000 in household income, going from 22 points down in 2004 to dead even.[34]

Looked at in terms of states—and of course the presidential election is fought out on a state-by-state basis (though popular vote results typically track electoral vote results and in fact are amplified by them)—the challenge for the Democrats will be to hold the line at roughly 8 points on average of the white working-class vote in the highly competitive states they won in 2000 and 2004 (Michigan, Minnesota, Oregon, Pennsylvania, and Wisconsin). To carry the four highly competitive states they lost in 2000 and 2004 (Florida, Missouri, Nevada, and Ohio), they will have to cut their average 13-point deficit at least in half.

The issue environment that favored the Democrats in 2006 and led to significant pickups (Senate, governor, state legislature, and House) in almost all of these states—especially Ohio, where white working-class voters backed both the Democrats' senatorial and gubernatorial candidates—remains in place for 2008. Negative views of the economy and the Iraq War, anxiety about health care, and disapproval of President Bush continue to run high among white working-class voters, making it quite plausible that the Democrats could replicate their 2006 margin among these voters. That would all but guarantee a bad outcome for the GOP in 2008.

Moreover, the pattern of election results in 2006 and 2007 suggests that appeals to cultural conservatism and generic toughness on national security, divorced from concrete problems like Iraq, are of diminishing effectiveness in steering white working-class voters away from the Democrats. If so, this could make the GOP's task in 2008 even harder.

The Future of the White Working Class

The decline of the white working class is likely to continue, since current trends are likely to persist. First, there is the continuing decline in the white population. By the presidential election of 2020, Census Bureau projections indicate that non-Hispanic whites will be down to around 61 percent of the population. By 2050 that share will have dropped to almost exactly half.

Education upgrading is also likely to continue, though it may slow down. A Census Bureau paper predicts a 4–7-point increase in high school completion rate, a 7–12-point increase in college attendance (some college or higher) rate, and a 4–5-point increase in four-year-college completion rate by 2028.[35]

Occupational upgrading will continue, though here too the rate at which it will increase may slow. Bureau of Labor Statistics occupational projections to 2016 indicate that while professional (and service) jobs will grow at the fastest rate among major occupational groups, professional occupations will increase their share of jobs by only about a percentage point, a slowdown from the rate of share increase in the 1950–2000 period (changes in occupation coding make the comparison inexact). In addition, managerial occupations will grow at the second fastest rate (though their share will remain flat).

Income upgrading should also continue, though the rate is very difficult to assess. Recall that median family income increased about 150 percent from 1947 to 2005. But most of that increase was in the twenty-six-year period between 1947 and 1973, when family income more than doubled, with an annual growth rate of 2.8 percent. In the thirty-two years between 1973 and 2005, income went up only 23 percent, an annual growth rate of 0.6 percent.[36] So how much income goes up in the future will depend very much on whether income growth follows the pre- or post-1973 pattern or something in between.

Since we do not know the answer to this question and recent history is inconclusive—there was a period of rapid growth in median family income from 1995 to 2000 (up 11 percent), followed by negative growth from 2000 to 2005 (down 2 percent)—one approach is to use the growth rate over the entire 1947–2005 period (1.6 percent), which in effect averages the growth rates in the "good" (1947–73) and "bad" (1973–2005) periods. Applying this rate to median family income produces an estimate of $83,000 for the year 2030 (2005 dollars). Moreover, if one applies this rate to the 40th percentile of the family income distribution, the 40th percentile would move up to around $67,000 by 2030, meaning that roughly 65 percent of families in that year would have more than $60,000 in income. In 2005 the corresponding figure was about 47 percent.

The downward trajectory of the white working class therefore seems assured, even if its rate of decline is uncertain. As with the trend data between World War II and the contemporary era (reviewed at the beginning of this chapter), the future rate of decline is likely to be fastest under an income-based definition, slowest under an occupation-based definition, and intermediate under an education-based definition. More precise statements about the projected population share of the white working class are difficult, but some educated guesses can be made.

Looking first at the broad education-based definition (whites without a four-year college degree), the rate of decline of the white working class since the World War II era has been 0.57 percentage points a year. Adjusting this rate downward a bit to allow for the expected slowdown in educational upgrading and projecting it forward to the presidential election of 2020 yields an estimate of 41 percent of adults in the white working class and perhaps a percentage point more of voters. Under the occupation-based definition (whites without a professional or managerial job), the rate of decline since the World War II era has been 0.47 percentage points a year. Adjusting the rate downward to allow for the projected slowdown in occupational upgrading and projecting forward to 2020 yields an estimate of 37 percent of workers in the white working class. Finally, under the income-based definition (white families with incomes under $60,000), the rate of decline since 1947 has been 0.91 percentage points a year. Keeping the rate the same and projecting forward to 2020 yields an estimate of 20 percent of families qualifying as white working class.[37]

These estimates suggest that the white working class, particularly under the broad education- and occupation-based definitions, will remain a substantial force in American society and politics even as it continues to decline.

Indeed, the 2020 estimates above may, if anything, be underestimating white working-class density in that year, since the rates of decline used here seem more likely to be too high than too low (observed rates of decline in this decade appear to be a bit lower than the historic rates of decline used as a base for these projections). Looking forward, then, what challenges will this still-substantial group of voters present to the political parties?

For the Democrats, the electoral challenge will be to keep their deficit among white working-class (non-college-educated) voters as close to single digits as possible. Allowing the GOP to run up supermajorities among these voters will remain a recipe for electoral defeat for many election cycles to come. This suggests that Democrats need a way of connecting with the white working class, a way that has mostly been lacking for forty years.

Certainly, Democrats' current emphasis on issues like health care and other aspects of economic security could be part of reestablishing that connection. There is no doubt that white working-class voters are profoundly troubled by the insecurities of the new economic world they find themselves in and wish to see some serious reforms. And they are especially worried that the pressures of globalization could make their situations even more tenuous. But simply calling for programs that would enhance economic security, leavened with a hefty dose of economic populist rhetoric, may not be enough. Indeed, the whole populist approach, where the privileged are portrayed as stacking the deck against the economic security of ordinary hard-working people, has some serious problems.

Perhaps the most serious is that it fails to take into account the extent to which many in the working class aspire to be among the more privileged—and to believe that they will be, eventually. In a March 2005 *New York Times* survey, for example, 84 percent of Americans described themselves as middle class or poorer, but 45 percent of them believed it was very or somewhat likely that they would become wealthy in the future. These findings are consistent with polls over many decades that show Americans to be great believers in class mobility (despite the reality that such mobility is probably no higher in the United States than in the supposedly class-bound nations of Western Europe).

In aspiring to rise higher on the economic ladder, Americans, including white working-class Americans, generally adopt a bifurcated view of their economic situation, which is not clearly reflected by populist rhetoric. On the one hand they tend to believe that things have changed for the worse: that the economy is doing poorly, that the security that families once enjoyed is disappearing, and that leaders just do not get it. On the other hand this very same white working class believes that they are holding up their end of the economic bargain, that they are working hard and doing right by their families, that their story is one of optimism and hope, not pessimism and despair. Even today, with most white working-class voters embracing a negative economic story overall, many still believe that a positive economic story applies to their own lives. Although populism appeals to one side of these voters' outlook—their pessimism—it frequently falls short in appealing to the other side—their optimism. These are voters who, after all, are more and more likely to have at least some college education and, over time, have become decidedly more affluent than the New Deal working class for whom Democratic economic appeals were crafted. The white working class today is an *aspirational* class, not a downtrodden one.

This suggests that Democrats may have to go a step farther to reach white working-class voters and connect economic security to economic opportunity. When Democrats talk about social insurance and economic security, they tend to focus on how programs like Social Security and Medicare help prevent financial disaster. But there is another, more positive way to talk about insurance: as a way for families to get ahead. Just as businesses and entrepreneurs are encouraged by basic protections against financial risk to invest in economic growth, so adequate security encourages families to invest in their own future, which many now find quite difficult. It is not easy to invest in the future, after all, when a sudden drop in income or rise in expenses could completely blow away the family budget. That sense of insecurity will make a person less likely to invest in specialized training, cultivate new career paths, and readily change jobs, the very things that are likely to allow that person to get ahead.

Democrats could therefore connect more positively to the white working class by speaking convincingly about the need to provide economic security to expand opportunity. Efforts to increase health coverage and contain health care costs (including the cost of prescription drugs), to improve the quality and availability of child care, to defend and extend guaranteed retirement benefits (including Social Security), to provide middle-class families with strong incentives to save and build wealth, and to make college and specialized training available to all are the subjects of countless and competing policy prescriptions. But it is critical that these policies be put in the context of helping Americans get ahead. These are measures that could allow the typical white working-class family to raise its head from the day-to-day struggle in an insecure world and concentrate on its most heartfelt wish: to achieve the American Dream.

And there is no doubt that the white working class still believes it is feasible to attain this goal. In a March 2006 Greenberg Quinlan Rosner/Economic Resliency Group (GQR/ERG) poll, 69 percent of white working-class respondents said they had already attained the American Dream or would attain it in their lifetimes.[38] An interesting perspective on this optimism is provided by looking at a question in the poll on whether increasing uncertainty or achieving the American Dream characterizes the economy today and comparing respondents' answers to their views on whether they themselves would achieve the American Dream. Here are the choices posed by the uncertainty question:

—Most people today face increasing uncertainty about employment, with stagnant incomes, paying more for health care, taxes, and retirement, while those at the top have booming incomes and lower taxes.

—Our economy faces ups and downs, but most people can expect to better themselves, see rising incomes, find good jobs and provide economic security for their families. The American Dream is very much alive.

By almost two to one (63 to 32 percent), white working-class respondents selected the first statement about increasing uncertainty as coming closer to their views. But of that group an amazing 60 percent nevertheless thought that they themselves would achieve the "dream."

The GOP, for its part, has been more successful in connecting to white working-class aspirations than to its very real economic difficulties. There has been a tendency to deny these difficulties on the one hand and on the other to insist that the magic of the market, spurred on by tax cuts, will solve whatever minor difficulties there might be. This reflexively antigovernment approach may have reached its limits, as a restless white working class finds more and more to like in the Democrats' economic approach.

To continue this approach going forward could create severe electoral problems for the Republicans. Currently, they are dependent on a supermajority of the white working class to cobble together a majority coalition. And the portion of the supermajority that the GOP needs will only increase in the future as the white working class continues to shrink. Moreover, as it shrinks, it is likely to become more socially liberal, as younger cohorts of the white working class replace older ones. This makes a reliance on social issues as a counterweight to economic ones, already a faltering strategy, seem very suspect over the long run and suggests that the GOP in the future will have to engage the Democrats directly on economic issues and programs if they wish to retain high levels of support among the white working class. Moreover, that engagement will have to go beyond support for tax cuts and a generic insistence that government programs do not really work. The white working class moving forward is asking, as they asked of the Democrats in the 1970s and 1980s, What have you done for us lately? The GOP needs an answer.

There are voices in the GOP that recognize this challenge and are trying to address it. A book by conservative writers Ross Douthat and Reihan Salam, *Grand New Party: How Republicans Can Win the Working Class and Save the American Dream,* directly acknowledges the need to retain supermajorities of the white working-class vote and argues that the current Republican anti-government, tax-cutting philosophy is inadequate for doing so.[39] They propose a new approach based on a series of substantial government programs that directly address health care and other aspects of economic insecurity but do so in a way that reflects conservative principles—market friendly, reliant on individual initiative, and family oriented. It remains to be seen whether the GOP can and will embrace such an approach, but it seems a promising one, given the demographic dilemma the party faces.

The Rise of a Mass Upper-Middle Class

This chapter focuses on the decline of the white working class—past, present and future. It is worth taking a few moments to consider other changes in the class structure that have accompanied this decline. Most of these changes have been covered in passing in our discussion: increasing affluence, the rise of the college educated, the growth of the professional-managerial class (especially professionals), and so on.

We focus here on one particular aspect of these changes: the rise of a mass upper-middle class. That is, it is not only true that more and more Americans over time have attained what might be called a middle-class standard of living, it is also true that more and more Americans have reached a level of affluence we might call upper-middle class. This term serves to differentiate them from the truly rich on the one hand and the ordinary middle class on the other.

Consider the following. In 1947 the 80th percentile of family income was less than $37,000 and the 95th percentile was around $60,000 (2005 dollars). At most a few percent could have had family incomes above $100,000. By 2005 the 80th percentile was around $103,000 and the 95th percentile was about $185,000.[40] If we use $100,000 income as a dividing line for the upper-middle class, we have gone from a situation in which the upper-middle class was a tiny fraction of families to one in which it qualifies as a mass grouping (even subtracting out a few percent for the truly rich).

On the face of it, this might seem a straightforward benefit for the GOP, since more affluent voters tend to lean Republican. But there are some complications. As this group has gotten larger it has become a mix of affluent, liberal-leaning professionals, on the one hand, and managers, small business owners, and midlevel white-collar workers on the other, and who are much more conservative. Indeed, one of the big stories of American politics in the last several decades is the diverging paths of professionals, who have shifted from the Republicans to the Democrats, and managers, who have remained Republican in their loyalties.

The 2004 and 2006 elections, in which voters with over $100,000 in income have been, respectively, 18 percent and 23 percent of voters, revealed a split in political behavior among the mass upper-middle class that reflects this difference between managers and professionals. In the 2004 election, upper-middle-class voters with a four-year college degree only (likely to be a managerial credential) favored Bush over Kerry by 60 to 39 percent. But upper-middle-class voters with postgraduate study (likely to be a professional credential) favored Bush by only 51 to 48 percent. Similarly, in 2006 college-degree-only, upper-middle-class voters favored Republicans for Congress by 56 to 42 percent, while postgraduate-study, upper-middle-class voters favored Democrats by 50 to 48 percent. Between them, those with a four-year college degree only and those with postgraduate study make up the great majority of upper-middle-class voters and are roughly equal in size to that group, so this split is of potentially great significance, as this group continues to increase its share of the American electorate.[41]

Just how much that share is likely to increase can be estimated by the same procedure used earlier. Assuming a 1.6 percent annual increase in family income at the 60th percentile, by the year 2030 the 60th percentile will actually be slightly over $100,000. That would put roughly 40 percent of families in the upper-middle class. Even by the year 2020 that rate of increase would be enough to put roughly one-third of families in the upper-middle class.[42]

So the influence of the upper-middle class on our politics will only grow larger as time goes on. Much will depend on how the political inclinations of the professional and managerial components of this group sort themselves out. The professional component could be especially significant, since Bureau of Labor Statistics projections suggest that this is the strongest growth group within the professional-managerial class. At any rate, the comparatively liberal leanings of upper-middle-class professionals should blunt the conservative politics that one might expect from this group sheerly on the basis of income.

This suggests, once again, that the GOP may have to back off a hard right stand on social issues if it hopes to build a strong base among the emerging upper-middle class. Such a stance runs the risk of alienating the sizable professional contingent. In addition, professionals' views on economic issues tend to be more moderate than those of managers—less emphasis on tax cuts and more emphasis on government programs that serve the public good (albeit in a fiscally responsible manner). The same Reaganite program found wanting by Douthat and Salam for the white working class is likely also a poor fit for affluent professionals.

For the Democrats' part, traditional economic populism, which has serious problems as a program for the white working class, is even more poorly suited for affluent professionals. Such a stance could work at cross-purposes to Democrats' liberal stand on social issues, which is generally attractive to this group. This suggests that, as with the white working class, an economic approach that melds security and opportunity—a sort of aspirational populism—is a better bet for expanding their base in the upper-middle class.

Whether either party will effectively respond to the long-term challenges posed by the decline of the white working class and the rise of the upper-middle class remains to be seen. All that one can say with certainty is that these challenges will sorely test both parties' political strategies. In the end, the party that is most adaptable and sees the future most clearly is likely to emerge victorious.

Notes

1. Data in this paragraph are based on authors' analysis of the 1940–2000 census and the 2007 Current Population Survey Annual Social and Economic Supplement, education.

2. Data in this paragraph are based on authors' analysis of the 1940 census and the 2006 American Community Survey, occupation. Occupational categories used by the government have shifted between 1940 and 2007, but at this very broad level of occupational aggregation the effects on trend should be small.

3. Data in this paragraph are based on authors' analysis of the 1947 and the 2005 Current Population Survey Annual Social and Economic Supplement, income.

4. Lawrence Mishel, Jared Bernstein, and Sylvia Allegretto, *The State of Working America, 2006/2007* (Cornell University Press, 2007).

5. Data in this paragraph are based on authors' analysis of the 1940 census and the 2007 Current Population Survey Annual Social and Economic Supplement, education.

6. Data in this paragraph are based on authors' analysis of the 1940 census and the 2006 American Community Survey, occupation.

7. Data in this paragraph are based on authors' analysis of the 1947 census and the 2005 Current Population Survey Annual Social and Economic Supplement, income.

8. Authors' analysis of the 1940 census and the 2007 Current Population Survey Annual Social and Economic Supplement, education.

9. Ruy Teixeira and Joel Rogers, *America's Forgotten Majority: Why the White Working Class Still Matters* (New York: Basic Books, 2000).

10. Data in this paragraph are conservative extrapolations from ibid., pp. 16–17.

11. John B. Judis and Ruy Teixeira, *The Emerging Democratic Majority* (New York: Scribner, 2002).

12. Kevin Phillips, *The Emerging Republican Majority* (New York: Arlington House, 1969), p. 37

13. Judis and Teixeira, *The Emerging Democratic Majority*, p. 63.

14. Teixeira and Rogers, *America's Forgotten Majority*.

15. Judis and Teixeira, *The Emerging Democratic Majority*; Teixeira and Rogers, *America's Forgotten Majority*.

16. William Galston and Elaine Kamarck, *The Politics of Evasion* (Washington: Progressive Policy Institute, 1989).

17. Data in this paragraph are based on authors' analysis of the 1992 and 1996 Voter News Service (VNS) national exit polls.

18. Data in this paragraph are based on authors' analysis of the 2000 VNS and the 2004 National Election Pool (NEP) exit polls.

19. Data in this paragraph are based on authors' analysis of the 2004 NEP exit polls.

20. Thomas Frank, *What's the Matter with Kansas? How Conservatives Won the Heart of America* (New York: Metropolitan Books, 2004).

21. Larry M. Bartels, "What's the Matter with What's the Matter with Kansas?" paper prepared for the annual meeting of the American Political Science Association, Washington, 2005.

22. Ibid., abstract.

23. David Gopoian and Ralph Whitehead Jr., "Will the Real White Working Class Please Stand Up?" (www.emergingdemocraticmajorityweblog.com/donkeyrising/archives/001317.php).

24. The congressional vote can also serve much the same function as an indicator of partisan loyalties. Our analysis of the congressional vote shows a very similar pattern to the one reported here for party identification. To simplify the exposition, we omit congressional vote results and present only party identification results.

25. Larry M. Bartels, "What's the Matter with What's the Matter with Kansas?" *Quarterly Journal of Political Science* 1 (2006): 201–26.

26. There are some other problems with this version of Bartels's analysis, including his use of the presidential vote, which replicates the Eisenhower elections problem in his earlier analysis. In addition, his use of the two-party instead of the popular vote tends to overstate the strength of the Democratic vote in the elections of 1968, 1992, and 1996. The fact that large numbers of white working-class voters supported George

Wallace in the former election and Ross Perot in the latter two elections, leading to quite low Democratic popular votes in these elections, is surely some kind of indicator of diminishing white working-class support for Democrats. But the two-party vote in effect throws out this information.

27. See Alan I. Abramowitz, "Constraint, Ideology, and Polarization in the American Electorate: Evidence from the 2006 Cooperative Congressional Election Study," paper prepared for the annual meeting of the American Political Science Association, Chicago, 2007; Alan I. Abramowitz and Kyle L. Saunders, "Ideological Realignment in the U.S. Electorate," *Journal of Politics* 60 (1998): 634–52.

28. To simplify the presentation, we do not present the results for middle SES white voters, but the trends in this group fall between those in the lower and upper SES groups: the decline in Democratic identification among conservatives is larger than for upper SES whites but smaller than for lower SES whites.

29. Data in this and the following paragraph are based on authors' analysis of the 2004 Current Population Survey Voter Supplement. Figures are estimates for 2008 voters. These estimates use the 2004 figures as a base and then adjust them for trend— that is, the continuing decline of the white working class since 2004.

30. A similar pattern of results across states is obtained when one uses a broad occupation-based definition of the white working class, that is, white workers without a professional-managerial degree. The levels, however, are lower: as a rule of thumb subtract 8 percentage points from the state estimate for the percentage of non-college-educated white voters to get the state estimate for the percentage of whites without a professional-managerial job (among working voters, however—not among all voters).

31. Data in this paragraph are based on authors' analysis of the 2004 Current Population Survey Voter Supplement, adjusted for trend.

32. Data in this paragraph and subsequent three paragraphs are based on authors' analysis of 2004 NEP national exit poll and various 2004 NEP state exit polls.

33. This is true for states for which data are available. No data are available for Arkansas and Tennessee.

34. Data in this paragraph are based on authors' analysis of the 2006 NEP national exit poll.

35. Jennifer Cheeseman Day and Kurt J. Bauman, "Have We Reached the Top? Educational Attainment Projections of the US Population," Working Paper 43 (Washington: Census Bureau Population Division, 2000).

36. Data in this and the following paragraph are based on authors' analysis of the 1947–2005 Current Population Survey Annual Social and Economic Supplement, income.

37. Data in this paragraph are based on authors' analysis of the 1940–2000 census data and the 2007 Current Population Survey Annual Social and Economic Supplement, education; on authors' analysis of the 1940 census data and the 2006 American Community Survey, occupation; and on authors' analysis of the 1947–2005 Current Population Survey Annual Social and Economic Supplement, income.

38. Data in this paragraph are based on authors' analysis of the March 2006 GQR/ERG survey.

39. Ross Douthat and Reihan Salam, *Grand New Party: How Republicans Can Win the Working Class and Save the American Dream* (New York: Doubleday, 2008).

40. Data in this paragraph are based on authors' analysis of the 1947 and 2005 Current Population Survey Annual Social and Economic Supplement, income.

41. Data in this paragraph are based on authors' analysis of the 2004 and 2006 NEP exit polls.

42. Data in this paragraph are based on authors' analysis of the 2005 Current Population Survey Annual Social and Economic Supplement, income. Judging from current patterns, it looks as though the higher propensity of the upper-middle class to vote is roughly cancelled out by the fact that family income tends to be higher than household income, which in turn is closer to the income of the typical voter. So the family-share figure, assuming the projection is right, should closely approximate the share of voters corresponding to that income group—perhaps slightly overestimating it, but not by much.

Family, Religion, and Generational Change

five

Changes in Family Structure, Family Values, and Politics, 1972–2006

TOM W. SMITH

Over the last three decades the American family has been undergoing a profound and far-reaching transformation. Both family structure and family values have been changing and, as a result of these changes, the American family is a much-altered institution. As the core institution of society, the family affects all other aspects of society. This is especially true of politics. Political leanings are notably influenced by both family structure and family values. Moreover, the relationship is dynamic, with the connection between the family and politics changing over the last generation.

First, this chapter traces these developments and examines how household and family composition, family roles, and attitudes and beliefs about the family have changed. Second, it examines how family structure and family values relate to political leanings (presidential voting, party identification, and political ideology). Finally, it considers what the future prospects are for the political impact of family structure and values.[1]

Overall Trends

Affecting overall trends are both the structural changes in marriage, in child-bearing and child rearing, and in labor-force participation and the changes in attitudes and values.

Marriage

Although it is still a central institution in American society, marriage plays a less dominant role than it once did: the proportion of adults who have never been married rose from 15 percent in 1972 to 24 percent in 2006 (see appendix, table 5A-1). When the divorced, separated, and widowed are added in, 75 percent of adults were married in the early 1970s, but by the 2000s only 56 percent were.

The decline in marriage comes from four main sources. First, people are delaying marriage. Between 1960 and 2003 the median age at first marriage rose from 22.8 to 27.1 years for men and from 20.3 to 25.3 years for women. Second, divorces have increased. The divorce rate per 1,000 married women more than doubled between 1960 and 1980, from 9.2 divorces a year to 22.6 a year. This rise was at least in part caused by increases in female labor-force participation and decreases in fertility.[2] The divorce rate then slowly declined, to 17.7 in 2005. The drop in the divorce rate in the 1980s and 1990s was smaller than the large rise from the 1960s to the early 1980s, and as a result the divorce rate in the 2000s is still almost twice as high as it was in 1960. Even with the recent moderation in the divorce rate, the proportion of ever-married adults who have been divorced more than doubled between 1972 and 2006: 17 to 37 percent.[3]

Third, people are slower to remarry than previously. While most people divorced or widowed before the age of fifty remarry, the length of time between marriages has grown.[4] Fourth, the delays in both first marriage and remarriage are facilitated by an increase in cohabitation. Cohabitators represented only 1.1 percent of couples in 1960 but 9.0 percent in 2004 (table 5A-2). The cohabitation rate is still fairly low overall because most cohabitations are short term, typically leading to either a marriage or a breakup within a year.[5] But cohabitation has become the norm for both men and women both as their first form of union and after divorce. For women born in 1933–42 only 7 percent first lived with someone in cohabitation rather than marriage, but for women born in 1963–74, 64 percent started off cohabiting rather than marrying. The trend for men is similar. Among the currently divorced 16 percent are cohabiting, and of those who have remarried 50 percent report cohabiting with their new spouse before their remarriage.[6]

Children

Along with the decline of marriage has come a decline in childbearing and child rearing. The fertility rate peaked at 3.65 children per woman at the height of the baby boom in 1957 and then declined rapidly to a rate of 1.75 children in 1975. This is below the replacement level of about 2.11 children (needed for a population to hold its own through natural increase). The rate then slowly gained ground, to 2.0–2.1 children in the early 1990s, and has stayed around that level to the present (table 5A-3). In 1972 the average adult had 2.4 children; this number slipped to a low of 1.8 children in the mid-1990s and has remained around this level to the present. This decline has resulted mostly from the decline in people having 4 or more children (from 25 percent in 1972 to 13 percent in the 2000s), with only a small increase in the childless (from 24 percent in 1972 to 28 percent in the 2000s). Likewise, while only 45 percent of 1972 households had children under eighteen years of age living at home, these households climbed to 65–70 percent in the 2000s. Thus the typical American household currently has no minor children living in it.[7]

Accompanying this decline in childbearing and child rearing has been a drop in a preference for larger families. In 1972, 56 percent of adults thought that the ideal number of children was three or more. By 1996–98 only 39 percent thought so. By 2006 larger families had gained in popularity, with 47 percent favoring having three or more children. Despite the net decline in a preference for large families, there was little or no increase in a preference for small families. Over the last three decades, just 3–5 percent have favored families with no children or only one child.

Moreover, during the last generation, childbearing increasingly became disconnected from marriage. In 1960 a little more than 5 percent of births were to unmarried mothers; by 2005 over 36 percent of all births were outside of marriage.[8] Similarly, the birth rate for unmarried mothers is more than twice as high in the 2000s as it was in 1960.

The rise in divorce and the decline in fertility and marital births have had a major impact on the type of household in which children are raised. There has been a decline in the proportion of adults who are married and have children living at home (from 45 percent in 1972 to 23 percent in 2006) and a rise in the percentage of adults not married and with no children (from 16 percent in 1972 to 32 percent in 2006). By 1996 households with a married couple and children, the predominant living arrangement in the 1970s and earlier, had fallen to third place, behind households with 1) both no married couple and no children and 2) those with married couple and no children. This development has largely been traceable to two trends: a rise in empty nesters and a decline in parents of minors. Empty nesters (those with no children under eighteen years old in the household) rose from 27 percent in 1972 to 41–44 percent in the 2000s. Parents of minors dropped from 49 percent in 1972 to 28–31 percent in the 2000s.

Changes are even more striking from the perspective of who heads the households. In 1972 less than 5 percent of children under age eighteen were living in a household with only one adult present (table 5A-7). By 2002 this had increased to over 22 percent. Similarly, the portion of children in the care of two adults not currently married but previously married rose from less than 4 percent in 1972 to 8 percent in the 2000s. Also, the portion being raised by two parents with at least one having been divorced has tended upward, starting at 10 percent in 1972, reaching a high of 18 percent in 1990, and standing at 14–15 percent in 2004–06. Conversely, while in 1972, 73 percent of children were being reared by two parents in an uninterrupted marriage, this fell to 48 percent in 2002 and was at 50 percent in 2006. Thus the norm of the stable, two-parent family was close to becoming the exception for American children rather than the rule. Similarly, from 1980 to 2006 the portion of children being raised by two married parents (including stepfamilies) fell from 77 percent to 67 percent.

But within some of these major restructurings, some consistency does appear. While single-parent households rose appreciably, the gender of the custodial parent changed little. Across years about 90 percent of children in single-parent households were being raised by women, and about 85–90 percent of single parents were women.

Labor-Force Participation

Families involving an intact marriage have not avoided notable transformations. The biggest of these are the alterations in traditional gender roles in general and in the division of responsibility between husbands and wives in particular. Women have greatly increased their participation in the paid labor force outside of the home. In 1960, 42 percent of women in the prime working ages (twenty-five to sixty-four) were employed. This grew to 49 percent in 1970, nearly 60 percent in 1980, 69 percent in 1990, and 72 percent in 2005. Most of this growth was among mothers of children under the age of eighteen.[9] Among all married couples, the traditional home with an employed husband and a wife keeping house declined from 53 percent in 1972 to 21 percent in 1998–2002 (table 5A-10). Also gaining ground but still remaining relatively rare are married couples in which the wife works and the husband does not (rising from 3 percent in 1972 to nearly 8 percent in 2006). Conversely, the modern pattern of both spouses being employed grew from 32 percent to about 59 percent in 1996–2002. Showing little change are retired households, in which neither spouse works. This shift has been even slightly greater among married couples with children (table 5A-11). The traditional arrangement dropped from 60 percent in 1972 to 26 percent in 2004, while the modern arrangement doubled, from 33 percent to about 68 percent.

The data also seem to indicate a doubling, from 2 percent to 4 percent, in "Mr. Mom" arrangements. However, instances in which a husband kept house and the wife did not represented only 1 percent of married households in 2006 (table 5A-12). Similarly, even among married couples with children, in only 2 percent did the husband keep house with the wife otherwise engaged (table 5A-13). Thus some much-trumpeted shifts in family structure are still rare.[10]

In brief, America has shifted from a society in which households having a full-time homemaker were the norm to one in which the norm is households having no full-time homemaker but rather having both adults (and both parents, if there are children at home) work outside the home. Moreover, wives not only contribute to family income through their labor-force participation but also, among dual-earner couples, bring in an increasing share of the family's joint income. In 1970 wives and husbands in dual-earner couples contributed about equally to the household income 21 percent of the time; in only 4 percent of cases did the wife contribute more than 60 percent. By 2001 husbands and wives were about equal contributors for 35 percent of dual-earner couples, and wives were the predominant earner for 10 percent of them.[11]

Attitudes and Values

The American family has undergone fundamental changes over the last generation, and many of these changes have undermined the traditional family. Marriage has declined as the central institution under which households are organized and children are raised. People marry later and divorce and cohabitate more. In terms of childbearing, a growing portion of children are born outside of marriage. Even within marriage the changes have been profound, as women have entered the labor force and husbands' and wives' roles have become more homogeneous.

Partly in response to and partly as a cause of these structural changes, attitudes toward the family have also shifted.[12] Many important family values regarding marriage and divorce, childbearing and child rearing, and the duties and responsibilities of husbands and wives have changed. In addition, values closely related to the family have also been transformed. For example, views on and practices relating to sexual behavior are different from those of the previous generation.

Marriage, Divorce, and Cohabitation

Marriage is the core institution of the American family, but because of the structural changes described above it no longer occupies as prominent a role in people's lives. Moreover, its impact on the quality of people's lives is changing. On the one hand, married people are much happier with life as a whole than the unmarried are: 40 percent of the currently married rate their lives as very happy, while 23 percent of the widowed and the never married, 19 percent of the divorced, and 16 percent of the separated say the same. In addition, married people are happier in their marriages (62 percent very happy) than they are about life as a whole. On the other hand, there has been a small but real decline in how happy people are with their marriages, from about 68 percent very happy in the early 1970s to a low of 60 percent very happy in 1994 and 2002 (table 5A-14). Also, people are less likely to rate marriages in general as happy and are more likely to say there are few good marriages.[13]

The importance that people accord marriage is also shown by a reluctance to make divorce easier. Only 25–30 percent of people have favored liberalizing divorce laws over the last three decades, while on average 52 percent have advocated tougher laws, and 21 percent advocate keeping laws unchanged. This opposition to easier divorce probably contributed to a leveling off, and then a dip, in the divorce rate starting in the early 1980s, but such opposition has not led to a general tightening of divorce laws. In addition, favoring divorce as the "best solution" for couples with unresolved marital problems declined from 47 percent in 1994 to 41 percent in 2002. However, people also do not favor trapping couples in failed marriages. A plurality has consistently considered divorce to be the best solution for marriages that are not working. Additionally, in 1994, 82 percent agreed that married, childless couples who "don't get along" should divorce, and 67 percent thought that even when there were children, couples that do not get along should not stay together.

Not only has cohabitation become more common, but it has also become more acceptable.[14] From 1994 to 2002 the proportion of people favoring a couple living together before they married rose from a third to almost a half; and almost a half also thought cohabitation was all right even when a couple did not plan to eventually marry.

Children

While most people want to and eventually do have children, the desire for larger families has declined both in terms of the actual level of childbearing and in terms of preferences about family size.[15] The ambivalence toward children is also shown by a question in a 1993 survey on the things that people value and that are important to them: 24 percent said that having children was one of the most important things in life, 38 percent that it was very important, 19 percent somewhat important, 11 percent not too important, and 8 percent not at all important. While clearly most people saw having children as personally important, overall it was fourth on the list, behind having faith in God (46 percent), being self-sufficient and not having to depend on others (44 percent), and being financially secure (27 percent). Similarly, surveys in 1988, 1994, and 2002 generally show that people favored children but that some traditional attitudes toward children were declining (table 5A-16).

In terms of what children should be taught and how they should be raised, people have become less traditional over time, with a shift from emphasizing obedience and parent-centered families to valuing autonomy for children.[16] From 1986 to 2006 a majority (or near majority) of Americans selected thinking for oneself as the most important trait for a child to learn; the proportion mentioning obedience was less than half as popular and was declining further (from about 23 percent in 1986 to 17 percent in 2006; table 5A-17). Likewise, in line with the weakening of support for child obedience, approval for the corporal punishment of children declined during the last two decades, from 84 percent to 72 percent (table 5A-18).[17]

But another traditional value, hard work, gained ground, up from 11 percent in 1986 to 20–23 percent in 2002–06. This indicates that the switch from parental authority to juvenile autonomy describes only part of the evolving process. Some traditional values, like hard work, may be gaining ground while some, like obedience, are losing. Thus the shift from traditional to modern may not be as simple as depicted in previous research.

Gender Roles

Among the most fundamental changes affecting American society over the last generation has been the redefinition of the roles of men and women and husbands and wives.[18] A traditional perspective—in which women were occupied in the private sphere of life centered on running a home and raising a family, while men engaged in the public sphere of earning a living and participating in civic and political events—has been replaced by a modern perspective in which there is much less role specialization and women have increasingly been entering the labor force as well as other areas of public life.

First, the acceptance of women in politics has grown substantially over the last quarter of a century (table 5A-19). In 1972, 74 percent of people said they would be willing to vote for a woman for president; in 1998 that percentage was 94.[19] Similarly, disagreement with the statement that "most men are better suited emotionally for politics than are most women" climbed from about 50 percent in the early 1970s to 78 percent in the mid-1990s; and while in the early 1970s 64 percent opposed the idea that "women should take care of running their homes and leave running the country up to men," about 85 percent in 1998 disagreed with this sentiment. Of course, increased female representation in high elected office and Hillary Clinton's campaign for the presidency are concrete manifestations of this societal change.[20]

Second, people have reevaluated the participation of women in the labor force. In 1972, 67 percent approved of a wife working even if her husband could support her, and in the 1990s about 83 percent agreed (table 5A-20). Similarly, while 43 percent in 1977 disagreed that a wife should help her husband's career rather than have one of her own, 81 percent disagreed by 1998; and while only 34 percent in 1977 opposed the idea that "it is much better for everyone involved if the man is the achiever outside the home and the woman takes care of the home and family," more than 60 percent have disagreed since 1989. In fact, people increasingly think that both the husband and the wife should earn money (table 5A-21). In addition, work is increasingly seen as important to women. In 1988 only 39 percent disagreed with the idea that what women really want is a home and children, but by 2002, 52 percent rejected this idea. Likewise, agreement that a job is "the best way for a woman to be an independent person" climbed from 42 percent in 1988 to 53 percent in 2002.

Third, people have become more convinced that having a working mother does not negatively affect her children. In 1977, 49 percent felt that a working mother can have just as "warm and secure a relationship with her children" as a mother who does not work; and in 2006, 67 percent agreed (table 5A-20). Similarly, disagreement with the idea that children suffer when a mother works rose from 32 percent in 1977 to 59 percent in 2006. However, at the same time most people are not convinced that mothers of young children should have full-time jobs. In 2002, 81 percent felt that a wife should work before having children and 75 percent favored her being employed after her youngest child left home (table 5A-22). But only 41 percent endorsed a full-time job after the youngest had started school and just 14 percent were for such employment when there was a child under school age.

While the shift toward accepting nontraditional roles for women has grown notably over the last generation, over the last decade the increase has plateaued. Political, work-related, and child-related trends basically leveled off in the mid-1990s and have been stable since then.

Sexual Mores and Practices

America is commonly seen as having undergone a sexual revolution over the last generation, during which attitudes and behavior became more permissive. But, in fact, trends in sexual morality are more complex than that.[21]

First, there has been a notable growth in permissiveness toward premarital sex. The portion saying that sex between an unmarried man and woman is always wrong dropped from 36 percent in 1972 to 24 percent in 1996 (table 5A-23). (Most of the decline was in the 1970s, and the trend has not continued since the mid-1990s.) Reflecting the more permissive attitudes toward premarital sex, sexual activity among the young increased from the 1970s to the early 1990s, before leveling off and probably retreating slightly from its peak in the early 1990s.[22] More than 66 percent of people say that premarital sex between teenagers fourteen to sixteen years old is always wrong, and since 1986 there has been a slight increase in disapproval, to 71–73 percent in 2002–06. People prefer that teenagers postpone the initiation of sexual intercourse, but first and foremost they want the young to be well informed about sex in general and safe sex in particular. Support for sex education in the schools has been high throughout the last thirty years (table 5A-24). It grew from the 1970s to the early 1990s and has been at or near 90 percent approval since then. Birth control is also strongly supported. Since the mid-1980s a majority of people have consistently favored making contraception available to sexually active teens even without their parents' approval.

Second, over the time period attitudes toward homosexuality first became less tolerant and then became more accepting.[23] Approval of homosexual activity has never been high. In the mid-1970s, about 68 percent of people said that homosexuality was always wrong; this level moved upward to about 77 percent during the mid-1980s to early 1990s (table 5A-23). After 1991 disapproval began falling. By 2006 only 56 percent considered homosexuality always wrong. Likewise, objection to gay marriage fell from 73 percent in 1988 to 51 percent in 2006 (with 35 percent accepting it and 14 percent neither approving nor disapproving; table 5A-25). Also, discrimination against homosexuals has declined. In the 1970s, 53 percent opposed a homosexual person teaching at a college, but opposition fell to 20 percent in the 2000s. Likewise, opposition to a public library having a book favoring homosexuality decreased from 43 percent in the 1970s to 25 percent in the 2000s. But while opposition to homosexuality has appreciably decreased in recent decades, it is one of the issues on which Americans are sharply divided. Nearly unique among family values, views on homosexuality are highly polarized. In 2006, while 56 percent said it was "always wrong," another 32 percent said it was "not wrong at all," and only 12 percent were in the two middle categories ("almost always wrong" and "wrong only sometimes").

Third, disapproval of extramarital sex has always been high and has increased over the last generation. In the early 1970s about 70 percent thought infidelity was always wrong. This increased to about 80 percent from the late 1980s to the present.

While there has not been a sweeping sexual revolution like that depicted in the popular media, sexual attitudes and practices regarding premarital sex and cohabitation have become more permissive over the last three decades. Attitudes toward homosexual behavior also became more accepting (but only since the 1990s). Counter to these trends, extramarital relations are even more opposed today than in the 1970s.

Neighborhoods

Another hallmark of the traditional family is its rootedness in local communities and neighborhoods. This attachment has been weakening over the last three decades. Socializing with relatives and friends outside one's neighborhood has changed little, but social contacts with neighbors have plummeted from 30 percent reporting spending a social evening with neighbors at least several times a week in 1974 to only 20 percent doing so in 1998 (table 5A-26). This decline, however, has now leveled off. There was also some decline in socializing in a bar, from about 11 percent in the 1970s and early 1980s to 7 percent in 2006. It is likely, but there is no available evidence, that work-related contacts have grown over this period.

Summary

Over the last three decades modern values have gained ground over traditional values. But the changes have not been uniform across topics or decades. In one area, gender equality, the change has been both massive and comprehensive. The social role of men and women and husbands and wives has been redefined to accept women in the public spheres of employment and political life.

In other areas, the changes have been more limited, with a continuing balancing between old and new values. First, in terms of marriage and divorce, ending marriage has been accepted as preferable over enduring bad marriages, but people are reluctant to endorse quick-and-easy divorces, especially when children are involved. Second, regarding children, people favor small families. However, the change has only been from favoring three or more children to wanting only two children, with little change in those wanting fewer than two. Third, in child rearing there is a decreasing emphasis on obedience and corporal punishment, but hard work has gained ground as a top value for children. Fourth, people have become more sexually tolerant of premarital and homosexual sex but less approving of extramarital sex. The ambivalence shows clearly in terms of adolescent sexual activity: most people oppose teenage sex but want teenagers to be sexually educated and to have access to birth control even if their parents do not approve. Finally, families are not as grounded in their local neighborhoods. This is probably largely a function of the increased labor-force participation of women.

Family Structure and Family Values

Family values are in part shaped by the types of families that people live in. On marital status, the widowed uniformly hold the most traditional values regarding all family values (such as divorce, cohabitation, gender roles, sexual morality), followed closely by the currently married. The never married almost always hold the most modern viewpoints, with the separated and divorced always less traditional than the married but usually not as nontraditional as the never married (table 5A-27).

Traditional family values also increase with family size (table 5A-28). Those who have never had children are consistently the least traditional, while in almost every instance those with four or more children are the most traditional.

When marital status and the presence of children in the household are examined, one again sees the impact of family structure on family values (table 5A-29). On most items the married with no children present hold the most traditional values (due to many older, empty nesters in this category). The not married are the least traditional and the presence of children does not consistently affect traditionalism. For about half of the items the unmarried with children present are the least traditional and for the other half those without children are the least traditional. In most cases the differences are small between these two groups.

Family Structure and Politics

The connection between family structure and politics is more apparent now than in the past. For example, from 1968 to 2004 married people were more likely to vote in every presidential election than the divorced, the separated, and the never married (table 5A-30). Early in this period the married also outvoted the widowed, but since the 1992 election the widowed have voted at a higher level than the married.[24]

In each presidential election from 1968 to 2004 the married have been the most likely to vote Republican (table 5A-31). Up until the 2000 election those in first marriages voted Republican more than the remarried, but by a narrow margin the remarried were the most Republican in the 2000 and 2004 elections. Usually the separated voted the most Democratic, but occasionally the never married or the divorced voted more Democratic. The marriage gap has become quite large. For example, in the 2004 presidential vote Democrats lost by about 12 points among the married, while winning by about 25 points among the never married. In addition, the marriage gap is larger than the more frequently cited gender gap. Similarly, from the 1970s to the 2000s, the married have been the most likely to identify as Republican (table 5A-32). The separated have consistently had the highest Democratic identification. All marital groups became more Republican during that period, but even in the 1990s and 2000s only among the married did Republicans edge out Democrats.

In terms of political ideology, from the 1970s to the 2000s the married and the widowed have always tilted towards the right (table 5A-33). The widowed were the most conservative in the 1970s, but since then the married have been the most conservative. Except for the divorced in the 2000s, the other unmarried groups have been more liberal than conservative. Usually the never married have been the most liberal, followed by the separated, and then the divorced. Over time all groups except the widowed have become more conservative in their expressed political ideology. Political differences between the married and the not married are striking (table 5A-34). Among the married, Republican presidential voters, Republican Party identifiers, and conservatives predominate in the 2000s, while among the not married Democrats and liberals lead. For example, in the 2004 presidential election 40 percent of the married voted Democratic and 58 percent Republican, but among the unmarried 57 percent were Democratic voters and 41 percent were Republican.

Political leaning is also correlated with whether the family has children. In the 2000 and 2004 presidential elections those who never had children were most likely to vote Democratic, while those with two or more children in 2000 and three or more children in 2004 were most likely to vote Republican (table 5A-37). This pattern exists for political ideology as well: those with no children being the most liberal and those with three or more children the most conservative (table 5A-38).[25] But in terms of party identification the relationship is curvilinear, with those having had two children being the most Republican and those having no children or more than four children being the most Democratic (table 5A-39).

In terms of marital status and the presence of children, in the 2000 and 2004 elections those married with children were the most likely to vote Republican, followed by those married without children present. The unmarried with children were the top Democratic voters due in large part to single parents in this category. The same pattern prevails for party identification. On political ideology the married are much more conservative than the unmarried, and the presence of children makes little difference.

The connection between traditional family structures and values and political conservativism and Republicanism is not surprising given the natural association between traditionalism and conservativism and the references by Republicans and conservatives to so-called family values. But there is also a socioeconomic dimension. Married couples and those with low child dependency ratios have fewer problems, while the unmarried—and especially single parents and others with high child dependency ratios—have notably more problems.[26]

Socioeconomic Status

There is also a socioeconomic dimension to family structure. Married couples and those with low child dependency ratios have fewer financial problems, while the unmarried and especially single parents and others with high child dependency ratios have notably more.[27] This means that nontraditional families are in greater need of government assistance and more likely to lean to the left. Over the last generation socioeconomic status and family structure have become increasingly related. In the 1970s marital status varied little by class identification, but by the 2000s the middle class was more likely to be married than the working class, while the latter was more likely to be divorced, separated, or never married (table 5A-40). In terms of education, in the 1970s those with more than a high school education were the least likely to be married and the most likely to never have been married. But by the 2000s the college educated were the most likely to be married (59 percent of them, compared to only 46 percent of those without a high-school degree).

In terms of number of children ever had, there have been no appreciable class differences from the 1970s to the present decade (table 5A-41). Educational differences however have been large and consistent across time. The college educated have been the most likely to have no children and the least likely to have four or more children. However, the childless gap between the least and best educated has narrowed from 18 percentage points in the 1970s to 11 points in the 2000s.

On marital status and the presence of children, the middle class has increasingly predominated among the married with no children present (from about 3 points in the 1970s to about 9 points in the 2000s). Conversely, the working class has expanded its lead over the middle class among the unmarried with children (from 1 point in the 1970s to about 7 points in the 2000s; table 5A-41). In terms of education, the college educated have always been the least likely to be unmarried with children, but the difference grew from −3 points in the 1970s to −10 points in the 2000s. Moreover, the educational difference shifted from the college educated being less likely than those without a high school diploma to be married with children in the 1970s to being more likely than the least educated to be married with children in the 2000s (from −10 points to 4 points).

Finally, there is an association of family structure with family income. Among households with children, those with two married parents or step-parents are the least likely to be below the poverty line (9–10 percent; table 5A-42). At the other extreme are single, female-headed households, 37 percent of which live below the poverty level. In between are two-parent, cohabiting households, with 27–32 percent of them below the poverty line.

Overall, family life has become more socially differentiated and stratified over time. Socioeconomic status and family structure are more linked than previously; middle-class households are increasingly likely to be married households, while the unmarried in general and single parents in particular are prone to be working class or poor.

Future Trends

In general, both family structure and family values have been changing in nontraditional directions for a generation. The duration and size of these trends and their mutual reinforcement make it unlikely that they will reverse themselves. Moreover, the continued shift to nontraditional family values is also predicted by age-cohort differences: the youngest cohort holds the most nontraditional views and the oldest cohort the most traditional (table 5A-43). For example, while 20 percent of the pre-1930 birth cohort supports gay marriage, 49 percent of those born since 1980 do so. Likewise, 51 percent of the oldest cohort believes that children are not harmed if their mothers work, while 75 percent of the youngest cohort thinks no harm occurs. As older cohorts die out and are replaced by younger cohorts, these differences should continue to push most family values in the nontraditional direction for the foreseeable future.

However, while this nontraditional shift is widespread, it is not universal. There are two main exceptions: approval of extramarital sex has not increased over time, and younger cohorts are not more supportive of adultery than older generations; and while from the 1960s to the 1980s there was a trend toward support for abortion rights, and while younger cohorts were supportive of abortion rights in the 1970s and 1980s, this support peaked in the baby boom generation and fell appreciably among postboomers.[28] While the abortion rights pattern is clearly the exception rather than the rule, it does indicate that social trends and cohort differences can reverse themselves. Still, the main expectation is that traditional family values will in general continue to decline and that, as a result, the political appeal of such positions will also diminish.

This expectation is also suggested by cross-national comparisons. Other economically advanced nations in Europe, North America, and elsewhere generally hold less traditional family values than Americans do.[29] While convergence between the United States and other first-world societies is not necessarily to be expected, America and other advanced countries have shown similar trends on a range of family changes, such as cohabitation, extramarital births, and divorce. Thus forces of modernization may be at work cross-nationally, and the less traditional family values of other advanced countries do suggest that evolving American attitudes have not hit a ceiling.

Conclusion

Major changes in family structure and in values feed off each other. Structural changes lead to the reassessment of traditional values and to the growth of values more in tune with current conditions. Likewise, changes in values facilitate the development of new forms of social organization and the growth of those forms most consistent with the emerging values. Structural and value changes reinforce one another, so that social transformations are sped along and newer forms and viewpoints replace older ones. Several examples of this mutual process of societal change apply to the contemporary American family.

First, the decline in birth rate and family size parallels a decrease in ideal family size. Second, the rise in female labor-force participation follows along with increased acceptance of women being involved in the public sphere in general and, in particular, of combining employment with raising children. In turn, the growth in dual-earner families (and the decline in single-earner couples) was accompanied by first acceptance of and then even a preference for families with both parents employed. Third, the climb in divorce and the liberalization of divorce laws went along with public support for the idea that divorce was preferable to continuing failed marriages. Finally, greater tolerance of premarital sex coincided with gains in teenage sexual activity, cohabitation, and nonmarital birth. In brief, changes in family structure and values have gone hand in hand over the last generation to transform the American family in both forms and norms.

The way that attitudes differ by family type shows that society is moving away from the values favored by traditional families to those endorsed by modern families.[30] Attitudes held by single-earner families are losing ground, while the attitudes favored by single-parent and dual-earner families are growing in popularity. In some cases, both types of modern family—single-parent and dual-earner—differ from the traditional, single-earner family. For example, support for gender equality in general and the employment of women in particular is gaining ground—and both positions are more supported by single-parent and dual-earner families than by single-earner families. In other cases, only single-parent families differ from families of couples (both dual and single earners). For example, single-parent families are more accepting of nonmarital births and the idea that children interfere with parental freedom than couples of either ilk. However, in those frequent cases when dual- and single-earner families differ, trends are away from single earners' points of views and toward the position of the dual earners.

In addition, birth cohort affects family values: more recent cohorts are more modern on most family values than earlier generations are.[31] Moreover, the shift in family type is likely to create even more modern attitudes in future generations, since children raised by employed mothers are more supportive of gender equality and other modern viewpoints and since more and more children are being raised in such circumstances.[32]

Overall, the shift from traditional to modern family structures and values is likely to continue. The basic trends have shown little sign of subsiding, cohort turnover will continue to push things along, and cross-national differences indicate ample room for further movement. This is especially true of the shift to dual-earner couples and egalitarian gender roles. The impetus toward single-parent families is less certain. The divorce rate has stopped rising and has even come down, although it is still at a high level; nonmarital births have slowed their increase; and premarital sexual activity has apparently peaked and may be falling. These factors will tend to curb the continued growth of single-parent families, although they are not likely to lead to their decline.

As important as the changes in family structure and family values are on their own, they take on added significance because they are tied to political attitudes and behaviors. First, family structure is related to political participation. The married and the widowed, for example, are more likely to vote in presidential elections. Second, those living in traditional families and those holding traditional family values are more likely to vote for Republican presidential candidates and to identify as Republican and conservative rather than Democratic and liberal. In general, the currently married and parents lean to the right; most nonmarried groups (the never married, the separated, and the divorced), those never having had children, and single parents tilt to the left.

The political role of family structure has increased over time in part because class and family type have come into closer alignment. Traditional family structure has become more associated with the middle class, while nontraditionally organized families have become more closely tied to the working class and the poor.

The changes in family structure and values have been large and enduring. Moreover, it is likely that nontraditional families will continue to grow and that family values will further liberalize. The smaller segment of the population living in traditional family structures naturally means fewer voters from such families.[33] The family values of the twenty-first century are not our parents' family values. These changes may undermine static, political appeals to traditional family values, and the changing nature of the family will mean that appeals to family values will also have to evolve to remain effective.

One is tempted to think that the prevalence of divorce among three of the 2008 Republican presidential contenders might be both a symbol and harbinger of a diminished role of family values in 2008 and beyond, until one recalls that Reagan was both America's first divorced president and estranged from some of his children. Personal biography is thus not a good predictor of the political appeal of family values.

Of course, there are public policy implications of the family changes as well as the political repercussions. Nontraditional families have different needs than traditional families. Policies to assist them might accept the reality of the new family structure and promote such measures as quality affordable daycare; after-school programs for those who would otherwise be latchkey children; financial and other assistance for single parents; and workplace nondiscrimination on the basis of gender, marital/cohabitation status, and parental status. Or policies might try to slow or even reverse the changes by such steps as tax breaks for stay-at-home parents; promarriage incentives, especially for unmarried mothers; divorce-avoidance programs; and various faith-based initiatives.

Few areas of society have changed as much as the family has over the last generation. The basic structure of the family has been reshaped, and family values and related attitudes have also undergone paradigmatic shifts. Families are smaller and less stable, marriage is less central and cohabitation more common, the value of children and values for children have altered, and within marriages gender roles have become less traditional and more egalitarian in both word and practice. Collectively, these alterations mark the replacement of traditional family types and family values with the emerging, modern family types and a new set of family values.

The changes that the family has been experiencing have in turn transformed society. As Meng-tzu has noted "the root of the state is the family," and the transplanting that the family has been undergoing has uprooted society in general. Some changes have been good, others bad, and still others both good and bad. But given the breadth and depth of changes in family life, the changes both for the better and the worse have been disruptive. Society has had to readjust to continually evolving structures and related new attitudes. It is through this process of structural and value change and adaptation to these changes that the modern, twenty-first-century family is emerging.

Notes

1. Most of the data in this chapter come from the 1972–2006 General Social Surveys (GSS). The GSS are conducted by the National Opinion Research Center (NORC) at the University of Chicago. The surveys are full-probability, in-person samples of adults (eighteen years old and older) living in households in the United States. The annual response rates have ranged from 70 percent to 82 percent. From 1972 to 1993 each survey interviewed about 1,500 people. Since a change to a biennial design in 1994, nearly 3,000 people have been interviewed for each survey. For more details on sampling and survey design, see James A. Davis, Tom W. Smith, and Peter V. Marsden, *General Social Surveys: 1972–2006 Cumulative Codebook* (Chicago: NORC, 2007) (www.gss.norc.org). The surveys are directed by James A. Davis (NORC, University of Chicago), Tom W. Smith (NORC, University of Chicago), and Peter V. Marsden (Harvard University).

2. Robert T. Michael, "Why Did the U.S. Divorce Rate Double within the Decade?" *Research in Population Economics* 6 (1988): 367–99.

3. The 37 percent level is lower than the commonly cited figure of 50 percent ("half of all marriages end in divorce"). The latter is a projection of how many married people will eventually divorce. In effect, these projections indicate that of the about 63 percent of ever-married people who have not yet been divorced at least 20 percent will end their marriages with divorces.

4. Andrew J. Cherlin, *Public and Private Families* (New York: McGraw-Hill, 1996).

5. Frances K. Goldscheider and Linda J. Waite, *New Families, No Families? The Transformation of the American Home* (University of California Press, 1991); Linda Waite and Christine Bachrach, *The Ties that Bind: Perspectives on Marriage and Cohabitation* (Piscataway, N.J.: Aldine Transaction, 2000).

6. Tom W. Smith, "American Sexual Behavior: Trends, Socio-Demographic Differences, and Risk Behavior," GSS Topical Report 25 (Chicago: NORC, 2006).

7. The term *children* refers to those ever born; in the household, it refers to children under the age of eighteen.

8. Dramatic as this trend is, it is similar to that in other advanced industrial nations. Between 1960 and 1995 births to unmarried women in the United States rose from 5 to 32 percent, in Great Britain from 5 to 34 percent, in Canada from 4 to 26 percent, and in France from 6 to 37 percent. Smith, "American Sexual Behavior."

9. Goldscheider and Waite, *New Families, No Families?*

10. Lisa Takeuchi Cullen and Lev Grossman, "Fatherhood 2.0," *Time*, October 15, 2007, pp. 63–66.

11. Sara B. Raley, Marybeth J. Mattingly, and Suzanne M. Bianchi, "How Dual Are Dual-Income Couples? Documenting Change from 1970 to 2001," *Journal of Marriage and the Family* 68 (2006): 11–28; Thomas Exter, *The Official Guide of American Incomes*, 2d ed. (Ithaca, N.Y.: New Strategist, 1996); Anne E. Winkler, "Earnings of Husbands and Wives in Dual-Earner Families," *Monthly Labor Review* 121 (1998): 42–48.

12. Arland Thornton and Linda Young-DeMarco, "Four Decades of Trends in Attitudes toward Family Issues in the United States: The 1960s through the 1990s," *Journal of Marriage and the Family* 63 (2001): 1009–37.

13. Arland Thornton, "Changing Attitudes toward Family Issues in the United States," *Journal of Marriage and the Family* 51 (1989): 87–93. Some research indicates that decline in marital happiness and satisfaction may result from the increased labor-force participation of women and the difficulty families have adjusting to changes in gender roles and division of domestic work. Norval D. Glenn, "Quantitative Research on Marital Quality in the 1980s: A Critical Review," *Journal of Marriage and the Family* 52 (1990): 818–31; Norval D. Glenn, "The Recent Trend in Marital Success in the United States," *Journal of Marriage and the Family* 52 (1990): 261–70; Dolores A. Stegelin and Judith Frankel, "Families of Employed Mothers in the United States," in *Families of Employed Mothers: An International Perspective*, edited by Judith Frankel (New York: Garland, 1997); Jane Riblett Wilkie, Myra Marx Ferree, and Kathryn Strother Ratcliff, "Gender and Fairness: Marital Satisfaction in Two-Earner Couples," *Journal of Marriage and the Family* 60 (1998): 577–94.

14. Alan Booth and Ann C. Crouter, *Just Living Together: Implications of Cohabitation on Families* (Mahwah, N.J.: Lawrence Erlbaum, 2002); Laura Spencer Loomis and Nancy S. Landale, "Nonmarital Cohabitation and Childbearing among Black and White American Women," *Journal of Marriage and the Family* 56 (1994): 949–62; Thornton and Young-DeMarco, "Four Decades of Trends."

15. W. Keith Bryant and Cathleen D. Zick, "Are We Investing Less in the Next Generation? Historical Trends in Time Spent Caring for Child," *Journal of Family and Economic Issues* 17 (1996): 365–92; Child Trends, Facts at a Glance, June 2007 (www.childtrends.org).

16. Duane Alwin, "Historical Changes in Parental Orientations to Children," *Sociological Studies of Child Development* 3 (1990): 65–86; Christopher G. Ellison and Darren E. Sherkat, "Obedience and Autonomy: Religion and Parental Values Reconsidered," *Journal for the Scientific Study of Religion* 32 (1993): 313–29.

17. Christopher G. Ellison and Darren E. Sherkat, "Conservative Protestantism and Support for Corporal Punishment," *American Sociological Review* 58 (1993): 131–44.

18. Catherine I. Bolzendahl and Daniel J. Myers, "Feminist Attitudes and Support for Gender Equality: Opinion Change in Women and Men, 1974–1998," *Social Forces* 83 (2004): 759–90; Clem Brooks and Catherine Bolzendahl, "The Transformation of U.S. Gender Role Attitudes: Cohort Replacement, Social-Structural Change, and Ideological Learning," *Social Science Research* 33 (2004): 106–33; Glenn Firebaugh, "Social Change and Gender Role Ideology," paper prepared for the annual meeting of the American Sociological Association, Miami Beach, August 1993; Karen Oppenheim Mason and Yu-Hsia Lu, "Attitudes toward U.S. Women's Familial Roles, 1977–1985," *Gender and Society* 2 (1988): 39–57; Thornton, "Changing Attitudes."

19. The item was dropped from the surveys due to this skew but is included in the 2008 survey due to the Hillary Clinton candidacy.

20. Research at the time of Geraldine Ferraro's vice presidential nomination in 1984 indicates that the embodiment of the abstraction of women in politics by a particular candidate of one party can also lead to a reaction. Tom W. Smith, "Did Ferraro's Candidacy Reduce Public Support for Feminism?" GSS Social Change Report 22 (Chicago: NORC, 1985).

21. David J. Harding and Christopher Jencks, "Changing Attitudes toward Premarital Sex: Cohort, Period, and Aging Effects," *Public Opinion Quarterly* 67 (2003): 211–26; Edward O. Laumann and others, *The Social Organization of Sexuality: Sexual Practices in the United States* (University of Chicago Press, 1994); Smith, "American Sexual Behavior"; Tom W. Smith, "The Sexual Revolution?" *Public Opinion Quarterly* 54 (1990): 415–35; Tom W. Smith, "Attitudes toward Sexual Permissiveness: Trends, Correlates, and Behavioral Connections," in *Sexuality across the Lifecourse,* edited by Alice Rossi (University of Chicago Press, 1994); Thornton, "Changing Attitudes."

22. Smith, "American Sexual Behavior."

23. Jeni Loftus, "America's Liberalization in Attitudes toward Homosexuality, 1973–1998," *American Sociological Review* 66 (2001): 762–82.

24. Laura Stocker and M. Kent Jennings, "Life-Cycle Transitions and Political Participation: The Case of Marriage," *American Political Science Review* 89 (1995): 421–33; Paul W. Kingston and Steven E. Finkel, "Is There a Marriage Gap in Politics?" *Journal of Marriage and the Family* 49 (1987): 57–64; Krzysztof Kulakowski and Maria Nawojczyk, "The Galam Model of Minority Opinion Spreading and the Marriage Gap" (AGH University of Science and Technology, 2007); Eric Plutzer and Michael McBurnett, "Family Life and American Politics: The 'Marriage Gap' Reconsidered," *Public Opinion Quarterly* 55 (1991): 113–27; Herbert F. Weisberg, "The Demographics of the New Voting GAP: Marital Differences in American Voting," *Public Opinion Quarterly* 51 (1987): 335–43; Lena Edlund and Rohini Pande, "Why Have Women Become Left-Wing? The Political Gender Gap and the Decline of Marriage," *Quarterly Journal of Economics* 117 (2002): 917–61; Janet Box-Steffensmeier, Suzanna de Boef, and Tse-Min Lin, "The Dynamics of the Partisan Gender Gap," *American Political Science Review* 98 (2004): 515–28.

25. Ruy Teixeiria, "Trends among American Parents: The 1950s to 1996," in *Taking Parenting Public: The Case for A New Social Movement,* edited by Sylvia Ann Hewlett, Nancy Rankin, and Cornel West (Lanham, Md.: Rowman and Littlefield, 2002).

26. Tom W. Smith, "Troubles in America: A Study of Negative Life Events across Time and Subgroups" (Washington: Russell Sage Foundation, 2006).

27. Ibid.

28. Ted G. Jelen and Clyde Wilcox, "Causes and Consequences of Public Attitudes toward Abortion: A Review and Research Agenda," *Political Research Quarterly* 56 (2003): 489–500; Ted Mouw and Michael E. Sobel, "Culture Wars and Opinion Polarization: The Case of Abortion," *American Journal of Sociology* 106 (2001): 913–43.

29. Sara O'Sullivan, "Gender and Attitudes to Women's Employment, 1988–2002," in *Changing Ireland in International Comparison,* edited by Betty Hilliard and Maire Nic Ghiolla Phadraig (Dublin: Liffey Press, 2007); Tom W. Smith, "The Emerging 21st Century American Family," GSS Topical Report 42 (Chicago: NORC, 1999); Carrie Yodanis, "Divorce Culture and Marital Gender Equality: A Cross-National Study," *Gender and Society* 19 (2005): 644–59.

30. Smith, "The Emerging 21st-Century American Family."

31. Brooks and Bolzendahl, "The Transformation of U.S. Gender Role Attitudes"; Firebaugh, "Social Change and Gender Role Ideology"; Mason and Lu, "Attitudes toward U.S. Women's Familial Roles"; Thornton and Young-DeMarco, "Four Decades of Trends in Attitudes toward Family Issues."

32. Smith, "Did Ferraro's Candidacy Reduce Public Support for Feminism?"

33. Teixeira, "Trends among American Parents."

Appendix

Sources for data in the following tables include General Social Surveys, 1972–2006; Current Population Surveys, 1987–1997; Federal Interagency Forum on Child and Family Statistics, 2007; J. C. Abma and others, "Fertility, Family Planning, and Women's Health: New Data from the 1995 National Survey of Family Growth," *National Center for Health Statistics Vital Health Statistics* 23 (1997); Paul C. Glick and Graham B. Spanier, "Married and Unmarried Cohabitation in the United States," *Journal of Marriage and the Family* 42 (February 1980): 19–30; Edward O. Laumann and others, *The Social Organization of Sexuality: Sexual Practices in the United States* (Chicago: University of Chicago Press, 1994); Tom W. Smith, "American Sexual Behavior: Trends, Socio-Demographic Differences, and Risk Behavior," GSS Topical Report 25 (Chicago: NORC, 2006); Graham B. Spanier, "Married and Unmarried Cohabitation in the United States," *Journal of Marriage and the Family* 45 (May 1983): 277–88; and Arland Thornton, "Cohabitation and Marriage in the 1980s," *Demography* 25 (November 1988), 497–508.

Table 5A-1. Marital Status, Various Years, 1972–2006
Percent

Year	Never married	Not now married	Ever divorced (all)	Ever divorced (ever married)
1972	15.0	26.0	14.0	17.0
1973	15.0	26.0	13.0	15.0
1974	14.0	25.0	15.0	17.0
1975	16.0	28.0	15.0	19.0
1976	16.0	30.0	15.0	18.0
1977	16.5	31.0	16.0	19.0
1978	15.0	30.0	18.0	21.0
1980	17.0	33.0	18.0	21.0
1982	19.0	35.0	19.5	24.0
1983	17.0	33.0	19.0	23.0
1984	20.0	36.0	20.0	25.0
1985	18.0	35.0	20.0	25.0
1986	19.0	37.0	21.0	26.0
1987	20.0	39.0	21.0	26.0
1988	22.0	40.0	22.0	28.0
1989	21.0	38.0	21.0	26.0
1990	20.0	39.0	25.0	31.0
1991	21.0	39.0	22.5	29.0
1993	19.0	39.0	24.5	30.0
1994	20.0	40.0	26.0	32.0
1996	22.0	43.0	26.5	34.0
1998	23.0	44.0	26.0	33.0
2000	24.0	46.0	25.0	34.0
2002	24.0	46.0	27.0	35.0
2004	24.0	40.0	26.0	33.0
2006	24.0	44.0	28.0	37.0

Table 5A-2. Cohabitation, Various Years, 1960–2006

Percent

Year	All couples	All households	All adults
1960	1.1	0.8	n.a.
1970	1.1	0.8	n.a.
1975	1.8	1.2	n.a.
1977	2.0	1.3	n.a.
1978	2.3	1.5	n.a.
1980	3.1	2.0	n.a.
1981	3.5	2.2	n.a.
1982	3.6	2.2	n.a.
1983	3.6	2.3	n.a.
1984	3.8	2.3	n.a.
1985	3.7	2.3	n.a.
1986	4.1	2.5	3.5
1987	4.3	2.6	4.0
1988	4.7	2.8	n.a.
1989	5.0	3.0	n.a.
1990	5.1	3.1	n.a.
1991	5.4	3.2	n.a.
1992	5.8	3.5	n.a.
1993	6.1	3.6	4.2
1994	6.3	3.8	4.3
1995	6.3	3.7	n.a.
1996	6.8	4.0	6.0
1997	7.0	4.1	n.a.
1998	7.1	4.1	n.a.
1999	7.4	4.1	n.a.
2000	8.8	4.3	10.8
2001	n.a.	n.a.	n.a.
2002	n.a.	n.a.	n.a.
2003	8.7	5.0	n.a.
2004	9.0	5.2	8.7
2005	n.a.	n.a.	n.a.
2006	n.a.	n.a.	9.2

Addendum:

Cohabited with present spouse before marriage
1988: 23.4
1994: 28.0

Currently cohabiting
1988: 5.0
1995: 7.0

Ever cohabited
1988: 34.0
1995: 41.0

Cohabited before first marriage
1988: 25.0
1995: 24.0

First union was cohabitation, by birth cohort, men
1933–42: 16.4
1943–52: 30.3
1953–62: 53.1
1963–74: 65.7

First union was cohabitation, by birth cohort, women
1933–42: 6.9
1943–52: 21.8
1953–62: 42.4
1963–74: 64.0

Table 5A-3. Children and Households, Various Years, 1972–2006

Percent, unless otherwise noted

Year	No children under 18 in house	Mean number of children born	Ideal number of children for a family to have		
			0–1	2	3+
1972	45.0	2.4	3.0	41.0	56.0
1973	48.0	2.3	n.a.	n.a.	n.a.
1974	47.0	2.2	3.0	45.0	52.0
1975	49.0	2.1	3.0	49.0	48.0
1976	50.0	2.1	5.0	51.0	44.0
1977	52.0	2.1	3.0	49.0	48.0
1978	50.0	2.1	3.0	51.0	46.0
1980	54.5	2.1	n.a.	n.a.	n.a.
1982	58.0	2.0	3.0	55.0	42.0
1983	53.0	2.1	3.0	51.0	46.0
1984	57.5	2.0	n.a.	n.a.	n.a.
1985	58.0	2.1	4.0	55.5	40.5
1986	56.5	2.1	3.0	51.5	45.5
1987	58.5	2.0	n.a.	n.a.	n.a.
1988	59.0	2.0	3.0	51.0	46.0
1989	57.5	1.9	4.0	54.0	42.0
1990	63.0	1.9	3.0	55.0	42.0
1991	61.0	1.9	4.0	54.0	42.0
1993	60.0	1.8	4.0	58.0	38.0
1994	60.0	1.9	4.0	54.0	42.0
1996	61.0	1.8	4.0	57.0	39.0
1998	62.0	1.8	4.0	57.0	39.0
2000	59.0	1.8	5.0	52.0	43.0
2002	70.0	1.8	4.0	50.0	46.0
2004	68.0	1.8	3.0	50.0	47.0
2006	65.0	1.9	3.0	50.0	47.0

Questions asked:

How many children have you ever had? Please count all that were born alive at any time (including any you had from a previous marriage).

What do you think is the ideal number of children for a family to have?

Table 5A-4. Out-of-Marriage Births, Various Years, 1960–2005

Year	Percent of all births to unmarried mothers	Birth rates for unmarried mothers
1960[a]	5.3	21.6[b]
1965[a]	7.7	23.5
1970	10.7	26.5
1975	14.2	24.5
1980	18.4	29.4
1985	22.0	32.8
1986	23.4	34.3
1987	24.5	36.1
1988	25.7	38.6
1989	27.1	41.8
1990	28.0	43.8
1991	29.5	45.2
1992	30.1	45.2
1993	31.0	45.3
1994	32.6	46.9
1995	32.2	45.1
1996	32.4	44.6
1997	32.4	42.9
1998	32.8	43.3
1999	33.0	43.3
2000	33.2	44.1
2001	33.5	43.8
2002	34.0	43.7
2003	34.2	44.9
2004	35.8	47.1
2005	36.8	47.6

a. In 1960 and 1965 figures are for non-whites. This slightly underestimates the rate for blacks only.
b. Number to births to unmarried women per 1,000 unmarried women age 15–44.

Table 5A-5. Living Arrangements of Households, Various Years, 1972–2006
Percent

Year	Married, no children	Married, children	Not married, no children	Not married, children
1972	29.0	45.0	16.0	10.0
1973	32.0	42.0	16.0	10.0
1974	31.0	44.0	16.0	9.0
1975	31.0	41.0	18.0	11.0
1976	32.0	38.0	19.0	12.0
1977	33.0	37.0	19.5	11.0
1978	31.0	39.5	19.0	11.0
1980	32.0	35.0	22.0	10.5
1982	33.0	32.0	25.5	10.5
1983	31.0	35.5	22.0	11.5
1984	31.0	32.0	26.0	10.0
1985	33.0	32.0	25.0	10.0
1986	30.0	33.0	27.0	10.0
1987	30.0	31.0	28.0	10.5
1988	31.0	28.0	28.0	13.0
1989	30.5	31.0	27.0	11.0
1990	33.0	28.0	30.0	10.0
1991	31.0	30.0	29.0	10.0
1993	32.0	29.0	29.0	10.0
1994	31.0	29.0	29.0	11.0
1996	30.0	26.0	30.0	13.0
1998	30.0	26.0	32.0	12.0
2000	26.0	27.5	33.0	14.0
2002	35.0	19.0	35.0	11.0
2004	38.0	23.0	30.0	10.0
2006	33.0	23.0	32.0	12.0

Table 5A-6. Childbearing and Child Rearing, Various Years, 1972–2006

Percent

	Empty nest	Childless	Parent	Stepparent
1972	27.0	18.0	49.0	6.0
1973	28.0	20.0	46.0	6.0
1974	29.0	18.0	48.0	5.0
1975	29.0	20.0	45.0	6.0
1976	31.0	19.0	43.0	7.0
1977	32.0	20.0	42.0	6.0
1978	29.0	21.0	44.0	6.0
1980	33.0	22.0	41.0	5.0
1982	35.0	23.5	37.0	5.0
1983	32.5	21.0	41.0	6.0
1984	32.0	25.0	38.0	5.0
1985	36.0	22.0	36.0	5.0
1986	34.0	23.0	39.0	5.0
1987	34.0	24.0	38.0	4.0
1988	35.0	24.0	37.0	4.0
1989	35.0	23.0	37.0	6.0
1990	38.0	25.0	33.0	4.0
1991	36.0	25.0	36.0	3.0
1993	36.0	24.0	35.5	4.0
1994	36.0	24.0	36.0	4.0
1996	36.5	24.0	35.0	4.0
1998	38.0	24.0	35.0	3.0
2000	34.0	25.0	37.0	4.0
2002	44.0	26.0	27.5	3.0
2004	43.0	25.0	29.0	3.0
2006	41.0	24.0	31.0	4.0

Empty nest = Parent of 1 or more children; none under 18 in household.

Childless = No children ever; no one under 18 in household.

Parent = Parent of 1 or more children; 1 or more children under 18 in household.

Stepparent = No children ever; 1 or more children under 18 in household (many in this group are stepparents, but group also includes partners and other adults living in households with children under 18).

Table 5A-7. Children in Five Types of Family, Various Years, 1972–2006

Percent

Year	Single parent	Two parents continuing	Two parents remarried	Two adults ex-married	Two adults never married
1972	4.9	73.0	9.9	3.8	8.6
1973	6.4	71.8	9.2	6.4	6.2
1974	6.0	71.4	12.0	4.1	6.6
1975	8.3	65.1	14.8	4.8	7.0
1976	10.8	63.8	11.0	3.8	10.6
1977	12.5	63.4	13.1	3.2	7.9
1978	10.3	65.3	13.6	4.0	6.9
1980	13.2	61.7	12.7	5.8	6.8
1982	14.3	59.3	13.7	5.2	7.3
1983	13.6	61.8	12.2	4.6	7.8
1984	15.0	58.4	14.2	6.5	5.9
1985	14.1	61.4	12.2	4.6	7.7
1986	11.4	61.0	13.6	6.6	7.4
1987	10.3	60.4	14.9	8.3	6.1
1988	18.6	54.7	13.0	5.0	8.7
1989	15.9	56.5	12.2	7.3	8.1
1990	15.0	56.1	17.9	5.1	6.0
1991	18.7	53.6	15.5	5.2	7.0
1993	15.9	57.7	13.2	6.6	6.7
1994	18.5	52.8	14.7	7.1	7.0
1996	19.7	48.8	14.4	8.5	8.7
1998	18.2	51.7	12.3	8.6	9.2
2000	20.7	48.9	13.6	7.8	9.0
2002	22.5	48.1	11.2	8.5	9.8
2004	17.4	51.0	14.7	8.2	8.6
2006	16.2	50.0	14.4	7.5	12.0

Single parent = only one adult in household.

Two parents, continuing = married couple, never divorced.

Two parents, remarried = married couple, at least one remarried (unknown if remarriage came before or after children born).

Two adults, ex-married = two or more adults; previously, but not currently, married.

Two adults, never married = two or more adults; never married (this category also includes some complex family structures).

Table 5A-8. Children in Three Types of Family, Various Years, 1980–2006

Percent

Year	Two married parents	One parent	No parent
1980	77	20	4
1985	74	23	3
1990	73	25	3
1995	69	27	4
2000	69	26	4
2001	69	26	4
2002	69	28	4
2003	68	28	4
2004	68	28	4
2005	67	28	4
2006	67	28	5

Two parents = includes parents and stepparents.

One parent = includes married parents not living with spouse.

No parent = no parent in household with child.

Table 5A-9. Gender of Single Parents in Households with Children under 18 and One Adult, Various Years, 1972–2006

Percent

	Adults with female	Children with female
1972[a]	98.0	98.0
1973	86.0	91.0
1974	89.0	89.0
1975	90.0	92.0
1976	89.0	92.5
1977	82.0	89.0
1978	87.0	86.0
1980	89.0	93.5
1982	92.0	94.0
1983	93.0	93.0
1984	89.0	91.0
1985	82.0	86.0
1986	90.0	92.0
1987	88.0	89.0
1988	87.5	89.0
1989	89.0	91.0
1990	91.0	93.0
1991	89.0	92.0
1993	89.5	90.0
1994	89.0	90.5
1996	89.0	90.0
1998	85.0	87.0
2000	87.0	90.0
2002	88.0	87.5
2004	85.0	87.0
2006	84.5	86.5

a. This year appears to be an outlier.

Table 5A-10. Labor Force Participation of Married Couples, Various Years, 1972–2006
Percent

Year	Traditional: husband works, wife home	Modern: both work outside home	Nontraditional: wife works, husband home	Retired: neither works[a]
1972	53.0	32.0	3.0	11.5
1973	48.5	34.0	4.5	13.0
1974	47.0	35.0	3.0	14.0
1975	45.0	37.0	4.5	14.0
1976	46.0	35.0	3.0	16.0
1977	41.0	40.0	5.0	14.0
1978	45.0	40.0	3.5	12.0
1980	37.0	44.0	4.0	14.5
1982	35.0	45.0	5.0	15.5
1983	35.0	47.0	4.0	13.5
1984	34.0	48.0	4.0	14.0
1985	30.0	49.0	4.0	16.0
1986	29.0	49.0	4.0	18.0
1987	25.5	55.0	6.0	14.0
1988	25.0	52.0	4.0	18.5
1989	26.0	53.0	4.0	17.0
1990	25.0	55.0	4.0	15.0
1991	26.0	51.0	5.0	18.0
1993	22.5	56.0	5.0	16.0
1994	23.0	56.0	5.0	15.0
1996	24.0	59.0	5.0	12.0
1998	21.0	58.5	6.0	14.0
2000	23.0	58.0	6.0	14.0
2002	21.0	58.5	5.5	15.0
2004	23.0	57.0	7.0	13.0
2006	26.0	52.0	7.5	15.0

a. Households in which neither spouse is in the labor force. While retired couples are the largest group, this category includes any combination of persons retired or disabled, students, and those keeping house.

Table 5A-11. Labor Force Participation of Married Couples with Children under 18 in Household, Various Years, 1972–2006

Percent

Year	Traditional: husband works, wife home	Modern: both work outside home	Nontraditional: wife works, husband home	Retired: neither works[a]
1972	60.0	33.0	2.0	4.0
1973	58.0	34.5	2.0	5.0
1974	57.0	39.0	0.5	4.0
1975	54.0	40.0	2.0	3.5
1976	54.5	48.0	3.0	5.0
1977	52.0	41.5	2.0	4.0
1978	54.5	42.0	1.0	2.5
1980	46.0	49.0	2.5	2.0
1982	43.0	50.0	3.0	4.5
1983	45.0	52.0	1.0	2.0
1984	40.0	54.0	3.0	3.0
1985	37.0	58.0	4.0	1.5
1986	34.0	60.0	2.0	5.0
1987	31.0	63.0	2.5	4.0
1988	33.0	64.0	2.0	1.5
1989	32.0	63.0	3.0	2.0
1990	33.0	62.0	2.0	3.0
1991	33.0	61.0	2.0	4.0
1993	27.0	67.0	3.0	2.0
1994	28.0	66.0	4.0	2.0
1996	29.0	66.0	3.0	2.0
1998	27.0	67.0	4.0	2.0
2000	28.0	65.0	5.0	2.0
2002	29.0	66.0	3.0	2.0
2004	26.0	67.5	4.5	2.0
2006	32.0	62.0	4.0	2.0

a. Households in which neither spouse is in the labor force. While retired couples are the largest group, this category includes any combination of persons retired or disabled, students, and those keeping house.

Table 5A-12. Keeping House for Married Couples, by Gender, Various Years, 1972–2006[a]

Percent

Year	Wife keeps house, husband other	Neither keeps house	Husband keeps house, wife other	Both keep house
1972	61.0	38.0	n.a.	n.a.
1973	58.0	42.0	n.a.	n.a.
1974	58.0	41.5	n.a.	n.a.
1975	55.0	45.0	n.a.	n.a.
1976	58.0	42.0	n.a.	n.a.
1977	52.0	47.0	n.a.	n.a.
1978	51.0	48.0	n.a.	n.a.
1980	47.0	52.0	1.0	n.a.
1982	45.5	54.0	n.a.	n.a.
1983	42.5	57.0	1.0	n.a.
1984	42.0	57.0	2.0	n.a.
1985	39.0	61.0	0.5	n.a.
1986	39.0	60.0	1.0	n.a.
1987	33.0	66.0	0.5	n.a.
1988	33.0	66.0	1.0	0.5
1989	33.5	66.0	1.0	n.a.
1990	31.0	68.0	1.0	n.a.
1991	32.0	67.0	n.a.	0.5
1993	27.0	72.0	1.0	n.a.
1994	28.0	72.0	1.0	n.a.
1996	26.5	72.0	1.0	n.a.
1998	24.0	75.0	1.0	n.a.
2000	25.0	73.0	1.0	n.a.
2002	23.0	75.0	1.0	0.5
2004	22.0	77.0	1.0	0.4
2006	26.0	72.0	1.0	0.2

a. This typology focuses on whether a person is "keeping house" and not on other labor force statuses.

Table 5A-13. Keeping House for Married Couples, by Gender, Households with Children under 18, Various Years, 1972–2006[a]

Percent

Year	Wife keeps house, husband other	Neither keeps house	Husband keeps house, wife other	Both keep house
1972	63.0	37.0	n.a.	n.a.
1973	61.0	38.5	n.a.	n.a.
1974	59.0	41.0	n.a.	n.a.
1975	56.0	44.0	n.a.	n.a.
1976	58.0	42.0	n.a.	n.a.
1977	56.0	44.0	n.a.	n.a.
1978	55.0	45.0	n.a.	n.a.
1980	46.0	53.0	1.0	n.a.
1982	45.0	54.0	1.0	n.a.
1983	44.0	55.0	0.5	n.a.
1984	40.5	57.0	2.0	n.a.
1985	36.0	63.0	1.0	n.a.
1986	37.0	63.0	n.a.	n.a.
1987	33.0	66.0	1.0	n.a.
1988	32.0	67.0	1.0	n.a.
1989	32.0	67.0	1.0	n.a.
1990	34.0	65.0	1.0	n.a.
1991	34.0	65.0	0.5	0.5
1993	26.0	72.5	1.5	n.a.
1994	28.0	71.0	1.0	n.a.
1996	28.0	71.0	1.0	n.a.
1998	26.0	72.0	1.0	1.0
2000	26.0	71.0	2.0	1.0
2002	27.0	71.0	1.0	n.a.
2004	22.0	76.0	1.0	n.a.
2006	30.0	68.0	2.0	n.a.

a. This typology focuses on whether a person is "keeping house" and not on other labor force statuses.

Table 5A-14. Attitudes toward Marriage and Divorce, Various Years, 1973–2006

Percent

Year	Very happy with marriage	Divorces should be easier	Divorce best if can't work out problems
1973	67.0	n.a.	n.a.
1974	69.0	33.5	n.a.
1975	67.0	29.0	n.a.
1976	66.0	29.0	n.a.
1977	65.0	29.0	n.a.
1978	65.5	28.0	n.a.
1980	67.5	n.a.	n.a.
1982	66.0	23.5	n.a.
1983	62.5	25.0	n.a.
1984	66.0	n.a.	n.a.
1985	56.0	24.0	n.a.
1986	63.0	28.0	n.a.
1987	65.0	n.a.	n.a.
1988	62.0	25.0	n.a.
1989	60.0	27.0	n.a.
1990	65.0	25.0	n.a.
1991	64.0	29.5	n.a.
1993	61.0	27.0	n.a.
1994	60.0	27.0	47.0
1996	62.0	28.0	n.a.
1998	64.0	25.0	n.a.
2000	62.0	25.0	n.a.
2002	60.0	26.0	41.0
2004	62.0	26.0	n.a.
2006	61.0	25.0	n.a.

Questions asked:

Taking things all together, how would you describe your marriage? Would you say that your marriage is very happy, pretty happy, or not too happy?

Should divorce in this country be easier or more difficult to obtain than it is now?

Divorce is usually the best solution when a couple can't work out their marital problems, yes or no?

Table 5A-15. Attitudes towards Cohabitation, 1994, 1998, 2002

Percent

Year	Should live together before marriage	Living together is all right
1994	33	41
1998	40	44
2002	48	47

Questions asked:

Do you agree or disagree?

It's a good idea for a couple who intend to marry to live together first.

It is allright for a couple to live together without intending to get married.

Table 5A-16. Attitudes about Children, 1988, 1994, 2002

Percent

Year	Disagree that those wanting children should get married	Disagree that children are life's greatest joy	Agree that children interfere with parents' freedom	Disagree that people w/o children lead empty lives
1988	14.8	4.1	10.7	44.8
1994	17.2	4.1	8.9	52.9
2002	20.2	3.2	n.a.	59.0

Questions asked:
Do you agree or disagree?
People who want children ought to get married.
Watching children grow up is life's greatest joy.
Having children interferes too much with the freedom of the parents.
People who have never had children lead empty lives.

Table 5A-17. Importance of Traits in Children, Various Years, 1986–2006

Percent

Year	To think for oneself	To obey	To work hard	To help others	To be well liked and popular
1986	51.0	23.0	11.0	14.0	n.a.
1987	54.0	20.0	12.0	13.0	1.0
1988	50.0	23.0	14.5	12.0	1.0
1989	53.0	19.0	14.0	12.0	1.0
1990	51.0	18.0	16.0	14.0	1.0
1991	51.0	20.0	15.0	14.0	n.a.
1993	53.0	19.0	14.0	13.0	1.0
1994	53.0	18.0	16.0	13.0	n.a.
1996	51.0	18.5	18.0	13.0	1.0
1998	49.0	18.5	18.0	13.0	1.0
2000	47.0	21.0	18.0	13.5	1.0
2002	48.0	14.0	22.5	15.0	n.a.
2004	47.0	12.0	22.0	17.0	1.0
2006	46.5	17.0	20.0	16.0	1.0

Questions asked:
If you had to chose, which thing on this list would you pick as the most important for a child to learn to prepare him or her for life?
A. To obey
B. To be well-liked or popular
C. To think for himself or herself
D. To work hard
E. To help others when they need help

Table 5A-18. Approval of Spanking Children, Various Years, 1986–2006

Year	Percent
1986	83.5
1988	80.0
1989	77.0
1990	79.0
1991	75.0
1993	74.0
1994	74.0
1996	73.0
1998	75.0
2000	74.0
2002	74.0
2004	72.0
2006	72.0

Questions asked:

Do you strongly agree, agree, disagree, or strongly disagree that it is sometimes necessary to discipline a child with a good, hard spanking?

Table 5A-19. Attitudes toward Women and Politics, Various Years, 1972–2006

Percent

Year	Willing to vote for women for president	Women emotionally suited for politics	Women help run country as well as homes
1972	74.0	n.a.	n.a.
1974	80.0	53.0	64.5
1975	80.0	50.0	64.0
1977	80.0	50.0	62.0
1978	83.0	57.0	69.0
1982	86.5	62.0	74.5
1983	86.5	64.0	77.0
1985	83.0	61.0	74.0
1986	86.5	63.0	77.0
1988	88.0	68.0	79.0
1989	86.5	69.0	80.0
1990	91.0	74.0	82.0
1991	91.0	74.0	81.0
1993	90.0	78.0	85.0
1994	92.5	79.0	87.0
1996	93.0	79.0	84.0
1998	94.0	77.0	85.0
2000	n.a.	76.0	n.a.
2002	n.a.	77.0	n.a.
2004	n.a.	74.5	n.a.
2006	n.a.	76.0	n.a.

Questions asked:

If your party nominated a woman for President, would you vote for her if she were qualified for the job?

Tell me if you agree or disagree with this statement: Most men are better suited emotionally for politics than are most women.

Do you agree or disagree with this statement: Women should take care of running their homes and leave running the country up to men.

Table 5A-20. Attitudes toward Women, Work, and Family, Various Years, 1972–2006

Percent

Year	Agree wife can work if husband can support her	Agree mom who works can be as close to children	Disagree wife should help husband's career first	Disagree better if man works woman at home	Disagree children suffer if mom works
1972	67.0	n.a.	n.a.	n.a.	n.a.
1974	70.0	n.a.	n.a.	n.a.	n.a.
1975	75.0	n.a.	n.a.	n.a.	n.a.
1977	67.0	49.0	43.0	34.0	32.0
1978	74.0	n.a.	n.a.	n.a.	n.a.
1982	75.0	n.a.	n.a.	n.a.	n.a.
1983	77.5	n.a.	n.a.	n.a.	n.a.
1985	n.a.	61.0	63.0	52.0	46.0
1986	79.0	62.5	64.0	53.0	48.0
1988	81.0	62.5	69.0	59.0	52.0
1989	79.0	64.5	72.0	60.0	52.0
1990	83.0	63.5	71.5	61.0	51.0
1991	80.0	66.0	71.0	59.0	52.0
1993	81.0	68.0	77.0	65.0	57.0
1994	82.0	70.0	79.0	66.0	59.0
1996	83.5	66.0	80.0	62.0	53.0
1998	82.0	68.0	81.0	66.0	58.0
2000	n.a.	62.0	n.a.	60.0	53.0
2002	n.a.	63.0	n.a.	61.0	54.0
2004	n.a.	65.0	n.a.	63.0	57.0
2006	n.a.	67.0	n.a.	65.0	59.0

Questions asked:

Do you approve or disapprove of a married woman earning money in business or industry if she has a husband capable of supporting her?

Now I'm going to read several more statements. As I read each one, please tell me whether you strongly agree, agree, disagree, or strongly disagree with it. For example, here is the statement:

A working mother can establish just as warm and secure a relationship with her children as a mother who does not work.

It is more important for a wife to help her husband's career than to have one herself.

It is much better for everyone involved if the man is the achiever outside the home and the woman takes care of the home and family.

A preschool child is likely to suffer if his or her mother works.

Table 5A-21. Gender Roles, 1988, 1994, 1996, 2002

Percent

Year	Disagree women really want home and kids	Disagree housework as fulfilling as job	Agree job is best for woman to be independent	Agree both spouses should earn incomes
1988	38.9	23.0	42.5	49.3
1994	43.6	21.9	45.0	57.6
1996	n.a.	n.a.	n.a.	67.0
2002	52.0	16.1	53.0	68.2

Questions asked:

Do you agree or disagree?

A job is allright, but what most women really want is a home and children.

Being a housewife is just as fulfilling as working for pay.

Having a job is the best way for a woman to be an independent person.

Both the husband and the wife should contribute to the household income.

Table 5A-22. Attitudes on Mothers Working Full Time, 1988, 1994, 2002

Percent

Year	Before first child	When has preschooler	After youngest in school	After children leave home
1988	76.8	10.7	36.0	73.8
1994	84.5	11.6	38.0	80.2
2002	80.6	14.1	41.3	75.3

Question asked:

Do you think that women should work outside the home full-time, part-time, or not at all under these circumstances:

a. After marrying and before there are children

b. When there is a child under school age

c. After the youngest child starts school

d. After the children leave home

Table 5A-23. Belief that Sexual Permissiveness Is Always Wrong, Various Years, 1972–2006

Percent

Year	Extramarital sex	Homosexual sex	Premarital sex	Teenage premarital sex
1972	n.a.	n.a.	36.0	n.a.
1973	70.0	72.5	n.a.	n.a.
1974	73.0	69.0	33.0	n.a.
1975	n.a.	n.a.	31.0	n.a.
1976	69.0	70.0	n.a.	n.a.
1977	74.0	73.0	31.0	n.a.
1978	n.a.	n.a.	29.0	n.a.
1980	71.0	74.0	n.a.	n.a.
1982	74.0	74.0	28.0	n.a.
1983	n.a.	n.a.	28.0	n.a.
1984	71.5	75.0	n.a.	n.a.
1985	75.0	76.0	28.0	n.a.
1986	n.a.	n.a.	28.0	67.0
1987	74.0	77.5	n.a.	n.a.
1988	81.0	77.0	26.0	68.5
1989	78.5	74.0	28.0	70.0
1990	79.0	76.0	25.0	69.0
1991	77.0	77.0	28.0	68.0
1993	78.5	66.0	27.0	68.5
1994	80.0	68.0	26.0	70.0
1996	78.5	61.0	24.0	70.0
1998	81.0	58.5	27.0	72.0
2000	79.0	59.0	28.0	72.0
2002	81.0	56.0	28.0	73.0
2004	82.0	58.0	27.0	71.0
2006	82.0	56.0	26.0	73.0

Questions asked:

There's been a lot of discussion about the way morals and attitudes towards sex are changing in this country. If a man and woman have sex relations before marriage, do you think it is always wrong, almost always wrong, wrong only sometimes, or not wrong at all?

What if they are in their early teens, say 14 to 16 years old? In that case, do you think sex relations before marriage are always wrong, almost always wrong, wrong only sometimes, or not wrong at all?

What is your opinion about a married person having sexual relations with someone other than the marriage partner? Is it always wrong, almost always wrong, wrong only sometimes, or not wrong at all?

What about sexual relations between two adults of the same sex—do you think it is always wrong, almost always wrong, wrong only sometimes, or not wrong at all?

Table 5A-24. Sexual Attitudes, Various Years, 1974–2006

Percent

Year	For sex education in schools	For birth control for teenagers
1974	82.0	n.a.
1975	80.0	n.a.
1977	78.5	n.a.
1982	85.0	n.a.
1983	86.0	n.a.
1985	85.0	n.a.
1986	85.0	57.0
1988	88.0	59.0
1989	88.0	56.0
1990	90.0	61.0
1991	87.5	61.0
1993	86.0	58.0
1994	88.0	57.0
1996	87.0	60.0
1998	87.0	58.0
2000	87.0	59.0
2002	88.0	57.0
2004	89.5	53.0
2006	89.0	54.0

Questions asked:

Would you be for or against sex education in the public schools?

Do you strongly agree, agree, disagree, or strongly disagree that methods of birth control should be available to teenagers between the ages of 14 and 16 if their parents do not approve?

Table 5A-25. Disagree with Gay Marriage, 1988, 2004, 2006

Year	Percent
1988	73
2004	55
2006	51

Question asked:

Aree or disagree that homosexual couples should have the right to marry one another?

Table 5A-26. Socialize at Least Several Evenings a Week, Various Years, 1974–2006

Percent

Year	With relatives	With neighbor	With other friend	At bar
1974	38.0	30.0	22.0	11.0
1975	39.0	26.5	21.0	9.0
1977	37.5	27.0	22.0	11.0
1978	36.0	28.5	21.0	10.0
1982	37.0	24.0	22.0	12.5
1983	33.0	25.0	21.0	12.0
1985	36.0	23.0	21.0	9.0
1986	37.0	28.0	21.0	9.5
1988	37.0	25.0	20.0	10.0
1989	34.0	22.0	22.0	8.0
1990	35.0	22.0	20.0	8.0
1991	36.0	23.0	24.0	9.0
1993	33.0	21.0	24.0	8.0
1994	34.0	21.0	23.0	8.0
1996	36.0	20.0	24.0	8.5
1998	37.0	20.0	22.0	8.0
2000	37.5	22.0	23.0	9.0
2002	38.0	23.0	25.0	10.0
2004	40.5	21.0	21.0	8.0
2006	40.5	21.0	23.5	7.0

Question asked:

How often do you do the following things?

a. Spend a social evening with relatives

b. Spend a social evening with someone who lives in your neighborhood

c. Spend a social evening with friends who live outside the neighborhood

d. Go to a bar or tavern

Table 5A-27. Family Values, by Marital State

Percent

Value	Married	Widowed	Divorced	Separated	Never married
Easier divorce	22.1	20.2	35.0	53.2	36.9
Cohabitation acceptable	35.6	16.1	53.4	51.3	65.8
Cohabit first, agree	32.3	15.4	49.1	51.1	59.0
Children joy, disagree	12.0	10.3	17.2	6.0	22.7
No child empty, disagree	48.3	44.6	52.9	50.4	63.5
Disapprove of spanking	24.2	23.4	24.5	23.9	26.9
Obedience, not top value	81.0	70.5	82.9	79.5	86.9
Teen contraception, agree	52.8	44.6	65.5	67.1	69.6
Teen sex, not always wrong	24.1	15.0	33.9	33.0	46.5
Premarital sex, not wrong	68.3	53.1	81.6	80.1	84.0
Infidelity, not always wrong	20.3	15.6	29.6	33.4	32.2
Gay sex, not always wrong	27.3	17.5	38.5	39.1	45.8
For gay marriage	21.8	20.5	31.8	32.2	50.1
Women suitable politics	66.4	56.7	74.6	69.6	75.5
Vote woman president	85.5	72.9	90.1	89.3	91.4
Women run home, not nation	63.2	56.7	82.0	73.9	85.0
Housewife fulfilling, disagree	19.4	13.6	21.7	24.5	24.9
Women work, family ok	45.1	36.3	49.2	51.6	57.4
Wife not first help husband	68.2	46.1	79.5	74.2	82.5
Mom work, preschooler ok	49.4	42.0	58.6	57.2	60.8
Man work, woman home, dis.	56.2	33.5	63.1	61.8	73.8
Women work, children ok	61.4	53.5	69.0	68.1	72.4
Visit relative weekly	65.0	61.6	62.0	60.3	59.9
Visit bar, never	45.2	19.5	60.9	56.6	65.6
Visit neighbor weekly	81.8	71.1	75.5	72.6	62.6

Table 5A-28. Family Values, by Number of Children Born

Percent

Value	None	1	2	3	4+
Easier divorce	31.3	30.3	24.4	23.3	23.1
Cohabitation acceptable	61.0	44.1	40.2	31.6	28.7
Cohabit first, agree	52.5	46.7	35.5	29.0	26.2
Children joy, disagree	37.8	11.5	9.5	9.5	9.1
No child empty, disagree	67.6	48.3	47.4	46.6	40.0
Disapprove of spanking	26.4	26.4	25.5	23.0	20.0
Obedience, not top value	85.4	81.4	82.9	80.0	72.1
Teen contraception, agree	67.5	61.4	56.2	49.1	47.0
Teen sex, not always wrong	43.7	31.4	25.0	21.0	18.5
Premarital sex, not wrong	81.5	75.1	71.8	66.9	58.6
Infidelity, not al. wrong	29.4	25.1	21.2	20.4	17.2
Gay sex, not always wrong	44.0	37.9	30.0	25.7	18.0
For gay marriage	38.1	30.5	25.5	18.4	15.6
Women suitable politics	73.4	69.1	68.4	67.1	61.1
Vote woman president	89.6	86.8	86.8	86.0	80.3
Women run home, not nation	82.8	77.4	78.0	74.6	65.5
Housewife fulfilling, disagree	22.6	22.6	20.3	17.0	19.0
Women work, family ok	54.7	51.6	46.3	42.1	40.7
Wife not first help husband	79.2	73.6	72.3	66.2	56.5
Mom work, preschooler ok	56.4	59.3	53.3	47.0	42.9
Man work, woman home, disagree	70.8	63.6	58.2	53.1	42.4
Women work, children ok	69.0	67.7	64.4	59.9	55.6
Visit relative weekly	64.0	60.3	64.4	66.1	61.3
Visit bar, never	63.4	50.7	47.2	42.6	34.1
Visit neighbor weekly	68.6	76.9	80.6	80.5	79.4

Table 5A-29. Family Values, by Marital State and Children

Percent

Value	Married no children	Married children	Not married no children	Not married children
Easier divorce	20.1	24.0	31.4	42.6
Cohabitation acceptable	32.2	39.3	53.8	46.8
Cohabit first, agree	29.9	34.8	47.0	56.8
Children joy, disagree	15.3	8.1	22.0	10.8
No child empty, disagree	50.2	46.4	58.0	54.9
Disapprove of spanking	22.3	25.9	26.5	22.9
Obedience, not top value	78.1	84.2	82.1	80.6
Teen contraception, agree	61.2	54.6	63.9	66.2
Teen sex, not always wrong	22.7	25.5	38.1	35.7
Premarital sex, not wrong	65.4	71.0	76.5	81.1
Infidelity, not always wrong	18.6	22.0	29.0	28.3
Gay sex, not always wrong	25.8	28.7	39.8	35.4
For gay marriage	27.2	21.6	36.1	31.3
Women suitable politics	64.3	68.7	70.5	74.6
Vote woman president	83.5	87.3	86.4	90.4
Women run home, not nation	72.2	78.4	77.0	81.6
Housewife fulfilling, disagree	18.3	20.9	19.8	28.0
Women work, family ok	42.2	48.5	50.3	55.4
Wife not first help hus.	62.7	73.9	72.5	81.0
Mom work, preschooler ok	45.0	54.0	54.2	63.8
Man work, woman home, dis.	50.8	61.7	61.6	69.2
Women work, children ok	58.2	64.7	65.9	73.9
Visit relative weekly	65.0	65.0	63.5	54.2
Visit bar, never	38.8	51.6	55.7	56.2
Visit neighbor weekly	81.6	81.8	67.8	67.5

Table 5A-30. Presidential Voting, by Marital Status, 1968–2004 Elections

Percent

Election	Widowed	Divorced	Separated	Never married
1968	+1.6	+11.3	+11.9	+50.3
1972	+2.1	+8.9	+21.2	+28.0
1976	+2.4	+10.1	+14.3	+23.0
1980	−2.8	+5.4	+11.4	+21.0
1984	+1.8	+12.3	+14.4	+28.5
1988	+1.6	+12.6	+18.4	+24.1
1992	−1.5	+6.6	+14.7	+25.3
1996	−5.3	+6.8	+14.1	+30.0
2000	−6.9	+9.9	+19.8	+33.8
2004	−2.0	+4.5	+23.9	+21.6

Note: + indicates more liberals, − indicates more conservatives.

Table 5A-31. Democratic and Republican Presidential Voting, by Marital Status, 1968–2004 Elections

Percent

Election	Married	Widowed	Divorced	Separated	Never married	Remarried
1968	−6.4	+5.8	+17.4	+23.1	+2.3	+ 3.1
1972	−27.1	−22.1	−6.5	−16.0	−9.4	−18.9
1976	+9.1	+24.3	+16.6	+44.4	+13.7	+15.6
1980	−7.9	+22.2	+19.8	+45.2	+ 5.8	−4.0
1984	−31.1	−8.7	−9.7	+0.2	−20.7	−26.4
1988	−28.6	−16.2	−23.9	−13.7	−8.1	−24.3
1992	−0.7	+17.2	+20.9	+42.1	+28.2	+5.1
1996	+12.3	+34.1	+32.0	+56.5	+43.5	+14.5
2000	−21.0	+2.9	−1.5	+29.3	+22.2	−24.7
2004	−12.3	+0.9	+3.1	+35.4	+25.2	−15.0

Note: + indicates more liberals, − indicates more conservatives.

Table 5A-32. Democratic and Republican Identifiers, by Marital Status and Decade, 1970–2000

Percent

Decade	Married	Widowed	Divorced	Separated	Never married
1970s	+19.4	+24.3	+24.8	+40.4	+20.6
1980s	+9.1	+22.1	+20.6	+28.8	+8.5
1990s	−0.2	+17.9	+13.0	+26.5	+9.6
2000s	−3.7	+19.9	+11.9	+23.4	+15.5

Note: + indicates more liberals, − indicates more conservatives.

Table 5A-33. Liberal and Conservative Ideology, by Marital Status and Decade, 1970–2000

Percent

Decade	Married	Widowed	Divorced	Separated	Never married
1970s	−8.2	−13.4	+7.0	+11.3	+24.2
1980s	−15.6	−11.3	+3.7	+8.7	+6.4
1990s	−17.3	−15.5	+1.3	+5.5	+8.0
2000s	−18.4	−14.5	−3.1	+1.9	+9.3

Note: + indicates more liberals, − indicates more conservatives.

Table 5A-34. Presidential Voting, by Marital Status, 1968–2004 Elections

Year	Married Democrat	Married Republican	Not married Democrat	Not married Republican
1968	39.8	46.2	48.9	40.0
1972	34.5	61.6	47.5	49.0
1976	53.6	44.5	59.2	38.9
1980	42.8	50.1	54.0	37.0
1984	33.8	64.1	42.2	55.7
1988	35.0	63.6	42.0	56.3
1992	41.2	41.9	54.5	30.0
1996	49.6	36.8	62.3	23.5
2000	38.4	59.4	52.8	41.7
2004	40.4	57.7	56.5	41.4

Table 5A-35. Political Party Identification, by Marital Status and Decade, 1970–2000

Percent

Decade	Married Democrat	Married Republican	Not married Democrat	Not married Republican
1970s	42.6	23.2	42.6	18.9
1980s	37.5	28.4	29.6	24.4
1990s	32.4	32.6	36.8	24.0
2000s	29.2	32.9	35.8	20.1

Table 5A-36. Political Ideology, by Marital Status and Decade, 1970–2000

Percent

Decade	Married liberal	Married conservative	Not married liberal	Not married conservative
1970s	25.3	33.5	38.4	26.1
1980s	22.5	38.1	31.3	28.6
1990s	22.8	40.1	32.4	30.0
2000s	21.5	39.9	31.5	29.1

Table 5A-37. Presidential Vote, by Party, Number of Children, Marital Status, 2000 and 2004

Percent

Measure	2000	2004
Number of children born		
0	+5.5	+12.6
1	−8.5	−8.2
2	−16.1	−7.7
3	−17.3	−16.9
4+	−12.6	−12.1
Marriage/children		
Married, no children	−18.9	−13.1
Married, children	−24.4	−24.2
Not married, no children	+8.6	+13.5
Not married, children	+21.9	+21.3

Note: + indicates more liberals, − indicates more conservatives.

Table 5A-38. Liberal and Conservative Identifiers, by Number of Children and Marital Status, 2000–06

Percent

Number of children born	
0	+8.5
1	−13.4
2	−14.6
3	−18.8
4+	−19.4
Marriage/children	
Married, no children	−18.1
Married, children	−18.6
Not married, no children	+2.7
Not married, children	+1.2

Note: + indicates more liberals, − indicates more conservatives.

Table 5A-39. Party Identifiers, by Number of Children and Marital Status, 2000–06

Percent

Number of children born	
0	+9.4
1	+2.9
2	+0.9
3	+2.1
4+	+7.9
Marriage/children	
Married, no children	–2.5
Married, children	–5.6
Not married, no children	+14.7
Not married, children	+18.4

Note: + indicates more liberals, – indicates more conservatives.

Table 5A-40. Family Structure, by SES and Marital Status, by Decade, 1970–2000

Percent

Decade and SES	Married	Widowed	Divorced	Separated	Never married
1970s					
Working class	73.5	5.2	4.5	2.5	14.4
Middle class	72.4	6.7	3.5	1.5	15.9
1980s					
Working class	64.7	5.8	8.9	2.8	17.9
Middle class	64.3	7.9	6.3	1.8	19.7
1990s					
Working class	55.9	5.4	13.0	2.9	22.8
Middle class	63.1	7.8	8.2	1.7	19.2
2000s					
Working class	51.6	4.6	13.1	3.7	27.0
Middle class	62.1	5.5	7.0	1.0	21.7
1970s					
LT high school	72.2	10.9	3.8	3.7	9.3
High school	74.4	3.8	4.5	1.8	15.5
GT high school	69.2	3.5	3.9	1.4	22.0
1980s					
LT high school	59.5	14.7	7.3	3.9	14.5
High School	67.9	5.0	7.5	2.0	17.5
GT high school	62.9	3.4	8.1	2.1	23.6
1990s					
LT high school	53.1	14.2	10.9	3.1	18.7
High school	60.3	7.4	10.8	2.6	18.9
GT high school	60.0	4.1	10.7	2.0	23.2
2000s					
LT high school	45.7	11.6	10.5	5.4	26.8
High school	56.9	7.2	12.3	2.6	21.0
GT high school	58.9	3.4	11.6	2.2	23.9

Table 5A-41. Family Structure, by SES and Marriage and Children, by Decade, 1970–2000

Percent

Decade and SES	Married, no children	Married, children	Not married, no children	Not married, children
1970s				
Working class	30.0	43.5	16.1	10.5
Middle class	32.8	39.6	18.2	9.4
1980s				
Working class	28.6	36.1	24.0	11.3
Middle class	34.6	29.5	26.9	9.0
1990s				
Working class	27.1	28.7	30.0	14.2
Middle class	35.2	27.9	29.1	7.8
2000s				
Working class	28.2	23.2	33.9	14.6
Middle class	37.5	24.3	30.1	8.0
1970s				
LT high school	37.0	35.2	16.9	10.9
High school	27.4	46.9	13.9	11.7
GT high school	28.5	40.7	22.3	8.5
1980s				
LT high school	34.7	24.8	26.8	13.7
High school	32.2	35.8	20.6	11.5
GT high school	28.2	34.5	29.3	8.0
1990s				
LT high school	33.9	19.1	32.1	15.0
High school	32.3	27.9	27.0	12.8
GT high school	29.1	30.8	31.1	8.9
2000s				
LT high school	29.1	16.3	35.8	18.8
High school	34.5	22.3	30.5	12.7
GT high school	32.9	25.6	32.5	8.9

Table 5A-42. Poverty Level of Children, by Household Type, 2004

Percent

Measure	Two parents, married	Two parents, cohabiting	Two stepparents, married	Two stepparents, cohabiting	One parent, female	One parent, male
Below poverty line	10.0	32.0	9.0	27.0	37.0	16.0
100–199% of poverty	19.0	30.5	22.0	32.5	29.0	23.0
200+% of poverty	70.0	28.0	69.0	33.5	32.5	61.0
Income missing	0.5	9.0	n.a.	7.0	2.0	1.0

Table 5A-43. Cohort Differences on Family Values, 2000–06, by Birth Year

Value	Pre-1930	1930–1945	1946–1964	1965–1979	1980+
For gay marriage	20.3	21.8	30.5	38.9	48.8
Homosexual sex not always wrong	21.0	33.4	43.0	49.8	52.1
Against spanking	24.1	28.3	28.1	25.1	38.1
For teen birth control	39.4	44.8	54.4	64.0	68.5
For sex education	75.7	86.3	87.9	91.1	94.4
Teen sex not always wrong	14.2	20.7	24.4	34.1	41.6
Premarital sex not always wrong	54.2	65.0	74.5	73.9	81.7
Extramarital sex not always wrong	14.6	20.0	19.1	19.0	16.8
Women suited for politics	63.7	68.5	79.4	78.1	76.0
Family doesn't suffer if mother works	31.3	27.7	37.8	40.1	55.3
Preschoolers don't suffer if mother works	43.6	46.9	54.1	63.4	66.6
Mother working doesn't hurt children	50.5	56.5	64.8	67.2	74.5
Not better if man works woman at home	28.8	47.0	66.5	68.7	78.7
For easier divorces	13.5	17.5	24.3	30.1	32.4
Cohabitation ok	18.8	19.2	49.1	57.7	77.6
Legal abortion for any reason	33.9	35.3	43.9	39.6	32.6
Legal all reasons	24.4	27.7	34.6	29.9	22.5

six

Religion and American Politics
MORE SECULAR, MORE EVANGELICAL, OR BOTH?

JOHN C. GREEN AND E. J. DIONNE JR.

Is American politics becoming more secular or more religious? Even casual observation reveals evidence for both these tendencies.[1] On the one hand, nonreligious Americans have become more prominent in recent times and have strongly supported the Democratic Party. But on the other hand, many of the most religious Americans have also become more prominent, strongly backing the Republicans. The simultaneous appearance of these apparently opposite trends has caused considerable confusion about the role of religion in American politics. Where did this mix of secular and religious politics come from? Is it contributing to the polarization of national politics? What will happen in the future? And of most immediate interest, what impact might religion have on the 2008 presidential campaign?

This chapter seeks to address these questions. Using survey data from 2004, and also from 1984, 1964 and 1944, it documents changes in the variety and size of the major religious groups in the postwar period as well as shifts in their partisan preference in presidential elections. On the first count, we find a substantial increase in both the number of Americans who are unaffiliated with organized religion and the number who are actively engaged in white evangelical Protestant churches. And on the second count, these growing groups have shifted their partisan preferences toward the Democrats and Republicans, respectively. Taken together, these developments have contributed to the polarization of national politics. However, there has also been a pluralist trend of increased religious diversity, so that faith-based polarization has been less than comprehensive.

We conclude by speculating about the political impact of religion in the future. In the longer term, the present trends may continue, but there are other possibilities, including a shift in the political agenda away from cultural issues. Although this basic structure of faith-based politics is likely to persist in the 2008 presidential election, the present mix of secular and religious politics could benefit either party depending on the circumstances and conduct of the campaign.

How Religion Matters in Politics

Over the last sixty years there have been at least three trends in American religious demography with potentially important political consequences.[2] One might be labeled as a secular trend. Prime evidence for this trend is the increasing number of individuals who report no affiliation, declining membership of mainline Protestant churches, and decrease in the frequency of worship attendance since the 1960s. This evidence fits well with theories of modernization, which posit secularization as an inevitable consequence. The United States is certainly a modern society, and perhaps increasingly so, and the secular trend could produce a more secular politics.[3]

However, the simple association between modernization and secularization has been challenged by the persistence of traditional forms of religion around the world. In the American context, the growth of evangelical Protestantism is prime evidence of this phenomenon. In addition, the level of traditional religiosity, including frequent worship attendance, has remained largely unchanged in the last decade. For simplicity's sake, this tendency might be labeled an evangelical trend. It may well be that these patterns are a reaction to modernization (and secularization), but they may also reveal the adaptation of traditional religious groups to modern circumstances. In any event, the evangelical trend could make American politics more religious.[4]

A third trend in American religion deserves attention as well: increased ethnic and religious diversity. In keeping with American history, immigration has continued to bring new religious groups into the country. Most immigrants have been affiliated with the major Christian traditions but practice their own versions of these faiths. Other immigrants—Muslims, Buddhists, Hindus—belong to world religions that have been less common in the United States. These developments might be labeled as a pluralist trend, which could reinforce—or mitigate—secular or evangelical trends. In fact, secular and evangelical trends could be understood as parts of a broader pluralism in American society.[5]

Secular, evangelical, and pluralist trends are relevant to the variety and size of religious communities in the United States, which can serve as the raw material for faith-based politics. But how is religion politicized in the United States? Here it is useful to recognize two levels of politicization: micropoliticization (the way religion is connected to politics) and macropoliticization (the broader political context in which such connections are formed). Put another way, micropoliticization is how religious people react to the political agenda at a particular point in time, while macropoliticization is how the political agenda to which religious people react changes over time.

In terms of micropoliticization, religious affiliation is the most common way that religion is linked to politics in the mass public.[6] Religious communities develop distinctive political perspectives, based in part on their special religious beliefs but also on their members' ethnic, racial, and regional values as well as their material interests. At the individual level, religious affiliation fosters such political connections directly or indirectly, and such connections are often strongest among members most engaged in religious life. The unaffiliated represent a special case of this phenomenon: the absence of religious belonging removes one kind of communal connection but also allows other kinds of communities to develop.

One of the clearest measures of the political connections of religious affiliation is voting in presidential elections.[7] Some religious groups are aligned with one or the other of the major political parties, while other groups are divided between them. These differences regularly produce large affiliation gaps in the presidential vote. As a consequence, religious groups have been among the building blocks of major party voter coalitions throughout American history. Such coalitions have varied by region and have shifted over time, with the best known example occurring in the New Deal era: the Democrats were in part an alliance of Catholics, Jews, and black and white evangelical Protestant voters, while the Republicans were in part an alliance of various white mainline Protestant groups. Economic issues were central to these coalitions, although foreign policy and cultural issues mattered sometimes as well.

In recent times, a new kind of micropoliticization of religion has appeared in the United States, with religious beliefs and practices having an impact apart from religious affiliation.[8] The best known example is the worship attendance gap, sometimes dubbed the God gap, wherein there are sharp political differences within religious communities based on religious practices and beliefs. Put another way, active engagement with faith did not simply reinforce the dominant political perspective within religious communities but instead fostered different—and rival—political perspectives. Such differences may reflect disputes within religious communities over traditional and progressive values but also may reflect the effect of regular social contact among coreligionists and explicit efforts to politicize religion, such as mobilizing voters in elections. In this regard, the nonobservant and nonbelievers alike are characterized by a low level of religious behavior and belief, which may in turn be associated with a particular set of values as well as the absence of the social effects of religious engagement.

The much discussed culture wars of the last two decades are a good example of these patterns. Individuals with higher levels of worship attendance were more likely to vote Republican in presidential elections, while their less-observant coreligionists were more likely to vote Democratic. This attendance gap was the strongest among white evangelicals, mainline Protestants, and white Catholics but appeared to a lesser extent among all religious communities. The net result has been the development of complex party coalitions, with religious observance and affiliation helping to define the key elements in the coalitions. The Republicans added the most observant members of many religious traditions to their coalition, while the Democrats added support from the less observant and the nonobservant to their constituencies. These changes were largely associated with cultural issues, such as abortion and homosexuality, but sometimes with foreign policy and domestic issues as well.

The history of these affiliation and attendance gaps points to the macropoliticization of religion. At any one time, the national political agenda can have an impact on both the types and consequences of the micropoliticization of religion. For example, the greater focus on economic issues during the 1930s and 1940s may well have encouraged an affiliation gap in the presidential vote. Likewise, the greater focus on cultural issues in the 1980s and later 1990s appears to have encouraged an attendance gap in presidential ballots. Such variations in macropoliticization help account for the 1928 election, when the key issues were Prohibition and the debate over the first Catholic major party nominee, Democrat Al Smith. They also help to account for the 1992 election, characterized by the economic appeal of the winning candidate ("It's the economy stupid!") and the independent candidacy of Ross Perot.

An extensive literature documents these changes in political agenda over time, and these patterns are often used to define political eras.[9] Agenda changes are determined in large measure by events, such as economic conditions, foreign conflicts, and broader societal shifts—including trends in the variety and size of religious communities. However, presidential candidates and allied political activists, including those in religious communities, play a critical role in applying the agenda to building winning coalitions. Indeed, such calculations include both a sense of how the agenda might be used to mobilize individual citizens and a knowledge of the types of citizens available for mobilization.

In sum, religion matters in American politics in at least three ways: demographically (by the size and variety of religious communities that can be connected to politics), micropolitically (by the particular linkage of religion to politics), and macropolitically (by the relevance of religion to the issue agenda). The secular, evangelical, and pluralist trends are the raw material for faith-based politics; the affiliation and attendance gaps are particular types of micropolitics among faith communities; and the relative mix of economic, cultural, and foreign policy issues are the macropolitical foundation for faith-based politics.

Religion and the Presidential Vote in 2004

An investigation of these issues should begin with a look at the impact of religion on the 2004 presidential election. We start with the variety and size of religious groups, then turn to their partisan preferences at the polls, and finally put both features together to look at Democratic and Republican voter coalitions. This description relies on data from the 2004 National Election Pool.[10]

Variety and Size of Religious Groups in 2004

Table 6-1 reports the relative size of the religious groups most relevant to the secular, evangelical, and pluralist trends. The eleven categories are defined by religious affiliation and worship attendance (the "observant" report attending worship at least once a week and the "less observant" attend less often). With one exception, these groups are ordered by the strength of the Kerry vote, broken into Democratic and Republican groups, plus swing groups that were divided between the major party candidates (see tables 6-2 and 6-3 for more details on this order of religious groups). These figures reflect both the relative size of these religious groups in the adult population as well as their level of turnout in 2004. However, because the exit polls asked only a limited number of questions on religion, these categories are fairly crude, with many of the smaller religious groups combined into composite categories.[11]

Table 6-1. Variety and Size of Religious Groups in the Electorate, 2004

Percent

Religious group	Share of the electorate
Democratic groups	
Unaffiliated	12.3
Less-observant black Protestants	3.2
Observant black Protestants	4.4
Less-observant other faiths	9.2
Swing groups	
Observant other faiths	9.7
Less-observant white mainline Protestants	14.0
Less-observant white Catholics	11.5
Republican groups	
Observant white mainline Protestants	4.5
Observant white Catholics	9.3
Less-observant white evangelical Protestants	7.5
Observant white evangelical Protestants	14.3

Source: See note 10.

The one exception in the table order is the very first category: voters unaffiliated with organized religion (and also less observant).[12] This group is at the heart of the secular trend. It was the largest of the Democratic groups in 2004 and the third largest group overall, accounting for one-eighth of the total vote cast. The unaffiliated are substantially larger than other Democratic groups, such as less-observant and observant black Protestants as well as less-observant other faiths, a composite category of many smaller religious communities, including Latino Protestants and Catholics, Mormons, Jews, and Muslims.

The composite category of other faiths was created out of necessity, but these apparently disparate religious communities have more in common than one might expect. For one thing, they all lie outside of the historically white Christian traditions and most voted Democratic in 2004. In addition, many of these communities grew rapidly in recent decades, embodying the pluralist trend in American religion. Finally, this composite category is large enough to subdivide by religious observance, facilitating an investigation of secular and evangelical trends.

Religious categories among swing groups are fairly large: less-observant, white mainline Protestants is the second largest group over all, at about one-seventh of the electorate; and less-observant white Catholics are the fourth largest, at a little less than one-eighth of the total. These less-observant groups are associated with the secular trend in the form of less religious engagement. The unaffiliated and the less observant categories among the Democratic and swing groups summed to roughly one-half of the electorate in 2004.

According to these data, the single largest group in the electorate is observant white evangelical Protestants, with about one-seventh of all 2004 voters. This group is central to the evangelical trend and, if added to less-observant white evangelicals, comes to more than one-fifth of all voters in 2004. Observant white Catholics and observant mainline Protestants round out the Republican groups, while the composite category of observant other faiths completes the swing groups. These last three categories are associated with the evangelical trend in general terms because of the impact of religious observance. Evangelicals and other observant white Christians accounted for a little less than one-half of the 2004 electorate.

The Presidential Vote in 2004

Table 6-2 reports the details of how these religious groups voted for president in 2004 (as a percentage of the two-party vote), providing evidence of micro-politicization in the form of large affiliation and attendance gaps. The unaffiliated are solidly Democratic, providing John Kerry with nearly three-quarters of their votes. However, they are not the strongest Democratic religious constituency. That honor goes to less-observant black Protestants, followed closely by observant black Protestants. The composite category of less-observant other faiths comes in a bit behind the unaffiliated in this regard.[13]

Table 6-2. Religious Groups and the Presidential Vote, 2004
Percent

	Share of the two-party vote	
Religious group	Kerry	Bush
Democratic groups		
Unaffiliated	72.9	27.1
Less-observant black Protestants	91.5	8.5
Observant black Protestants	83.1	16.9
Less-observant other faiths	65.8	34.2
Swing groups		
Observant other faiths	48.1	51.9
Less-observant white mainline Protestants	47.5	52.5
Less-observant white Catholics	46.8	53.2
Republican groups		
Observant white mainline Protestants	42.7	57.3
Observant white Catholics	38.2	61.8
Less-observant white evangelical Protestants	28.3	71.7
Observant white evangelical Protestants	17.6	82.4
Total	48.5	51.5

Source: See note 10.

George W. Bush won slim majorities among all of the swing groups, including the composite category of observant other faiths, less-observant white mainline Protestants, and less-observant white Catholics. Bush had even more success among the counterparts of these last two categories: observant white mainline Protestants and observant white Catholics. The two strongest Bush constituencies were less-observant white evangelical Protestants and observant white evangelical Protestants.

Thus the unaffiliated bolstered the Democratic cause in 2004, revealing an impact of the secular trend, while observant white evangelicals backed the GOP, revealing the impact of the evangelical trend. Each trend was extended somewhat by the impact of religious observance: the less observant always voted more Democratic than their observant counterparts, who always voted more Republican. This pattern is evident even among the strongest Democratic and Republican groups. For instance, there is an 8.4 percentage point attendance gap in the Kerry vote between less-observant and observant black Protestants and a 10.7 percentage point attendance gap between less-observant and observant white evangelicals. These gaps are often smaller than many of the affiliation gaps, such as the difference between observant white evangelical Protestants and observant white mainline Protestants (25.1 percentage points). But note that the combination of affiliation and observance typically had a larger impact on the vote. For example, there was a 55.3 percentage point gap in the Kerry vote between the unaffiliated and observant white evangelical Protestants. These gaps are larger than the better known gender or generation gaps.[14]

Presidential Voter Coalitions in 2004

How important were these religious groups to the Kerry and Bush coalitions in 2004? Table 6-3 addresses this question by listing the proportion of each party's voter coalition made up of the eleven religious groups, combining the relative size of the groups (from table 6-1) with their presidential preferences (from table 6-2).

The unaffiliated were the single largest source of Kerry's ballots in 2004, at almost one-fifth of the total. If one were to combine the unaffiliated with the less-observant Catholics and the white mainline and evangelical Protestants, the total would account for nearly one-half of all the Kerry votes. And if less-observant black Protestants and the composite category of less-observant other faiths were added as well, the total would swell to two-thirds of the Democratic vote. The remaining one-third of the Kerry vote came from the various observant groups, especially observant other faiths and black Protestants.

Table 6-3. Religious Groups and Voter Coalitions, Presidential Vote, 2004
Percent

Religious group	Share of candidate's vote	
	Kerry	Bush
Democratic groups		
Unaffiliated	18.5	6.5
Less-observant black Protestants	6.0	0.5
Observant black Protestants	7.6	1.5
Less-observant other faiths	12.5	6.0
Swing groups		
Observant other faiths	9.6	9.8
Less-observant white mainline Protestants	13.8	14.3
Less-observant white Catholics	11.1	11.9
Republican groups		
Observant white mainline Protestants	4.0	5.0
Observant white Catholics	7.3	11.2
Less-observant white evangelical Protestants	4.4	10.4
Observant white evangelical Protestants	5.2	22.9

Source: See note 10.

The source of Bush's ballots is a sharp contrast: observant white evangelical Protestants are the single largest group, with more than one-fifth (roughly the same as the contribution of the unaffiliated to the Kerry vote). If less-observant white evangelicals are added, the total rises to one-third of the Bush vote. And if observant white Catholics, white mainline Protestants, other faiths, and black Protestants are also included, then the total grows to about three-fifths of the Republican presidential vote. The remaining two-fifths of Bush's ballots came from the various less-observant groups, especially white mainline Protestants and Catholics.

Differences by Region

The first column in table 6-4 looks at these patterns in yet another way: the net advantage the candidates had in each religious group, taken as a percentage of all the votes cast in the 2004 election. Here a positive figure means a net Kerry advantage and a negative figure a net advantage for Bush. From this perspective, Kerry's largest net advantage was among the unaffiliated. Bush's biggest advantage was with observant white evangelicals.

The rest of table 6-4 reports the distribution of the net 2004 vote by religious groups across the four major regions of the country.[15] These patterns provide a rough measure of how the votes of religious groups translated into electoral votes. Kerry enjoyed a net advantage among the unaffiliated in every

Table 6-4. Religious Groups and Net Party Advantage, by Geographic Region, 2004

Percent

Religious group	National	Northeast	West	Midwest	South
Democratic groups					
Unaffiliated	5.6	1.7	1.5	1.2	1.2
Less-observant black Protestants	2.6	0.6	0.2	0.4	1.4
Observant black Protestants	2.9	0.5	0.1	0.5	1.8
Less-observant other faiths	2.9	1.4	0.7	0.5	0.3
Swing groups					
Observant other faiths	−0.4	0.6	−0.6	0.1	−0.4
Less-observant white mainline Protestants	−0.7	0.2	0.4	0.1	−1.4
Less-observant white Catholics	−0.7	−0.3	0.3	−0.1	−0.6
Republican groups					
Observant white mainline Protestants	−0.7	0.2	0.0	−0.1	−0.8
Observant white Catholics	−2.2	−0.8	0.1	−0.5	−1.0
Less-observant white evangelical Protestants	−3.3	−0.1	−0.8	−0.8	−1.5
Observant white evangelical Protestants	−9.3	−0.9	−1.4	−2.3	−4.7
Total	. . .	3.2	0.4	−1.0	−5.7

Source: See note 10.

region, but it was largest in the Northeast and West, the blue regions, where he did best at the polls. A similar pattern obtained for the composite category of less-observant other faiths, and in these two regions Kerry also won two of the three swing groups and one of the Republican groups. Interestingly, Kerry received the largest advantage from black Protestants in the South, a region won by Bush.

In an analogous fashion, Bush had a net advantage among the two groups of evangelicals in all regions, but it was largest in the South, a red region, where he was the most successful at the ballot box. In the South, Bush was also well ahead among observant white mainline Protestants, observant white Catholics, and all the swing groups. But in the highly competitive Midwest his net advantage was reduced overall and extended only to less-observant white Catholics among the swing groups. Interestingly, Bush obtained the largest net advantage among the Catholic groups in the Northeast, where Kerry won all the states.

These regional patterns reflect in part the geographic distribution of the religious groups. For example, the West contains the most unaffiliated voters, the Midwest and Northeast the most Catholics, and the South the largest number of evangelicals and black Protestants. Thus the political import of the religious groups varies enormously. In addition, the particular politics of each region—and each state—can affect the impact of faith-based politics. Table 6-5 illustrates this point with exit poll data from four states (Pennsyl-

Table 6-5. Religion and the Kerry Vote, Four States, 2004
Percent

	Pennsylvania		California		Iowa		Georgia	
Religious group	Voters	Kerry	Voters	Kerry	Voters	Kerry	Voters	Kerry
Unaffiliated	7.3	70.4	14.7	66.6	8.2	73.1	5.2	63.4
Black Protestants	8.1	80.5	4.5	76.4	1.0	86.4	14.5	86.0
Less observant	59.5	56.6	67.3	57.6	55.5	55.5	49.0	47.7
White Catholics	30.8	47.9	14.3	53.5	21.2	52.5	8.0	20.0
White evangelical Protestants	9.2	37.0	14.6	12.9	26.1	31.1	33.6	15.3

Source: See note 10.

vania, California, Iowa, and Georgia), one from each of the major regions. Because exit polls did not ask the same religion questions in every state, the table pieces together five common measures across the states using various surveys: unaffiliated, black Protestants, white Catholics, white evangelicals, and less-observant voters. For each state, the table reports the percentage of the religious group in the 2004 electorate and the percentage that voted for Kerry.

The first thing to note about table 6-5 is the variation in the size of the religious groups by state. The unaffiliated were the largest in California and the smallest in Georgia. And although Kerry won the unaffiliated vote everywhere, he did worst in the least competitive states—California and Georgia. In contrast, Kerry's support matched the national figures in highly competitive Iowa and approached that figure in competitive Pennsylvania. There was a similar variation in the size of black Protestants, ranging from a high in Georgia to a low in Iowa. Kerry did very well among this core Democratic constituency in Georgia and with the tiny black electorate in Iowa, but less well in California and Pennsylvania.

White Catholics and evangelicals also showed considerable state-by-state variation. Catholics were most numerous in Pennsylvania, where Kerry did most poorly among them, but he won majorities among the smaller Catholic electorates in California and Iowa—and lost the small group of Georgian Catholics by a large margin. As one might expect, Kerry also lost big with the large evangelical vote in Georgia and with the smaller evangelical vote in California. However, Kerry got one-third or more of the evangelical vote in Iowa and Pennsylvania. Some cross-state variation also occurred among the less-observant voters. Their numbers varied across states, from a high in California to a low in Georgia. Here Kerry did best in the states that he won and less well in the states that he lost. However, the differences for the worship attendance gap were relatively small.

These state-by-state patterns underscore the contingent nature of the political impact of religion. The special circumstances of the individual states are important, including the variety and size of religious groups and the levels of micro- and macropoliticization. If there is this much variation in the political impact of religious groups in the highly polarized and hard-fought 2004 election, it is likely that there would be more variation in other electoral circumstances and over time.

Religion and the Presidential Vote in the Postwar Period

Where did the 2004 patterns come from?[16] To answer this question, we turn to an investigation of secular, evangelical, and pluralist trends that use the results of four surveys conducted at twenty-year intervals (1944, 1964, 1984, and 2004). Despite the limitations of these data, they are a good deal more precise than the exit poll data that produced such powerful results in 2004. As before, we first review changes in the variety and size of the religious groups, look at changes in their presidential preferences at the ballot box, and then bring these patterns together to describe the major party voter coalitions.

These four surveys cover a variety of political contexts and different kinds of macropoliticization. The 1944 survey was taken right before the end of World War II, thus providing a data point at the very beginning of the postwar period. These four presidential elections varied considerably. Both 1944 and 2004 were relatively close, but 1964 and 1984 were landslides; the Democrats won the first two of these contests and the Republicans the last two. The political agenda was dominated by economic concerns in 1944 and to a somewhat lesser extent in 1964. By 1984, cultural issues had increased in prominence, a pattern that extended to 2004.

Variety and Size of Religious Groups, 1944–2004

Table 6-6 lists the religious categories used in the previous tables in a slightly different order. The first column of the table reports the percentage-point change in the size of each religious group in the postwar period. For ease of presentation, the results for 2004 are listed first, followed by 1984, 1964 and 1944—in essence, a look back over the previous sixty years. Each of these columns reports the relative size of the religious groups as a percentage of the adult population.

Table 6-6. Variety and Size of Religious Groups, Twenty-Year Intervals, 1944–2004

Percent

Religious group	Change	2004	1984	1964	1944
Unaffiliated	9.8	14.4	8.9	6.4	4.6
Less-observant other faiths	3.3	9.4	7.8	3.8	6.1
Observant other faiths	8.1	9.7	5.4	2.9	1.6
Less-observant black Protestants	−0.7	4.0	3.8	5.6	4.7
Observant black Protestants	2.2	5.7	5.1	5.4	3.5
Less-observant white Catholics	1.5	8.0	10.2	4.9	6.5
Observant white Catholics	−3.3	7.7	9.9	15.5	11.0
Less-observant white mainline Protestants	−19.9	11.4	17.1	18.2	31.3
Observant white mainline Protestants	−6.6	6.5	9.8	15.6	13.1
Less-observant white evangelical Protestants	−2.1	9.3	11.1	10.7	11.4
Observant white evangelical Protestants	8.0	14.1	11.0	10.9	6.1
Percent observant (weekly worship attendance)	0.9	43.3	41.1	50.6	42.4

Source: See note 16.

Overall, table 6-6 shows substantial change in the variety and size of these religious communities in the United States. The unaffiliated voters show the largest percentage increase over the postwar period, and the rate of increase was steady over the time period. The composite category of observant other faiths increased enormously, strong evidence of the pluralist trend. The third largest increase was for observant white evangelical Protestants, whose increase was also steady. By 2004 the unaffiliated and observant white evangelicals made up about the same proportion of the adult population.

Thus the religious groups at the center of the secular and evangelical trends expanded in relative terms in the postwar period. The patterns for other religious groups were more complex. For example, changes among the less observant varied considerably. Percentages of less-observant black Protestants and white evangelicals declined modestly over the sixty-year period, while the composite category of less-observant other faiths grew slightly. By far the biggest change was the decline of less-observant white mainline Protestants. This change is part of the much commented upon decline in mainline Protestantism in the postwar period.[17]

Disparate patterns also occurred among observant groups. Observant black Protestants grew modestly, while observant white Catholics and observant white mainline Protestants experienced declines.

The uneven change between the less observant and the observant groups reflects the overall pattern for religious observance in the postwar period. Note that there is very little change in the percentage of the adult population that reported attending worship once a week or more. The sharp increase in observance between 1944 and 1964 had dissipated by 1984. Between 1984 and 2004 the level of reported observance was essentially stable.[18] Overall, these patterns complicate the secular and evangelical trends, which became clearer after 1964.

What caused these changes in the relative size of religious groups between 1944 and 2004? Although a full assessment is beyond the scope of this essay, several factors are clearly important. One is differential birth rates. Some of the groups that declined, including white mainline Protestants and white Catholics, had fewer children during this sixty-year period, while some of the groups that grew had more children, such as observant white evangelicals and black Protestants. Immigration was also a factor, especially for many of the religious communities in the composite category of other faiths. A complex of modernizing factors, such as higher levels of education and geographic mobility, may have had an impact as well, especially for the growth of the unaffiliated. Finally, some religious communities, such as white evangelical Protestants, may have adapted more effectively to new social circumstances, while others, such as white mainline Protestants, may not have done so. Such adaptations may have helped evangelicals to retain their children in the faith and also to attract adherents from other faiths.[19]

Presidential Vote in the Postwar Period

Table 6-7 reports the percentage point change in the two-party presidential vote of religious groups in the postwar period, also looking back from 2004 to 1944. In the postwar period the unaffiliated voted more Democratic, a shift in partisan preferences that occurred at the same time that the unaffiliated were growing as a percentage of the adult population. However, this shift in partisanship was uneven, with the Democrats doing best among the unaffiliated in the 1964 landslide and the Republicans nearly breaking even in the 1984 landslide. During the same period, observant evangelicals moved sharply in a Republican direction, at the same time that they were increasing in relative size (although here the change was fairly even). In 2004 the unaffiliated were less strongly Democratic than the observant white evangelicals were Republican. It is worth noting these patterns of micropoliticization are fairly constant and occurred across periods of change in macropoliticization.

Table 6-7. Religious Groups and the Presidential Vote, Twenty-Year Intervals, 1944–2004

Percent

Religious group	Change[a]	2004		1984		1964		1944	
		Dem.	Rep.	Dem.	Rep.	Dem.	Rep.	Dem.	Rep.
Unaffiliated	+12.9	71.9	28.1	53.3	46.7	76.7	23.3	59.0	41.0
Less-observant other faiths	−16.5	65.9	34.1	68.5	31.5	94.4	5.6	75.0	25.0
Observant other faiths	−21.3	43.0	57.0	53.6	46.4	71.8	28.2	64.3	35.7
Less-observant black Protestants	+11.3	86.3	13.7	92.6	7.4	97.1	2.9	75.0	25.0
Observant black Protestants	+21.4	81.0	19.0	90.2	9.8	100.0	0.0	59.6	40.4
Less-observant white Catholics	−4.7	58.2	41.8	40.5	59.5	83.6	16.4	62.9	37.1
Observant white Catholics	−31.4	37.3	62.7	46.5	53.5	82.5	17.5	68.7	31.3
Less-observant white mainline Protestants	+7.8	49.5	50.5	28.8	71.2	58.7	41.3	41.7	58.3
Observant white mainline Protestants	+7.6	44.4	55.6	26.2	73.8	55.5	44.5	36.8	63.2
Less-observant white evangelical Protestants	−12.5	43.2	56.8	38.0	62.0	51.7	48.3	55.7	44.3
Observant white evangelical Protestants	−34.1	17.0	83.0	20.3	79.7	41.4	58.6	51.1	48.9
Total	−3.3	48.9	51.1	41.5	58.5	68.5	31.5	52.2	47.8

Source: See note 16.

a. Positive number means a Democratic gain and a Republican loss, while a negative number means a Democratic loss and a Republican gain.

Here, too, the religious groups that are central to the secular and evangelical trends display substantial and opposite shifts in partisan preferences at the polls. However, the patterns are once again less clear for the less-observant groups. Democrats gained among less-observant black Protestants over 1944 but in 2004 show a decline from the high points of 1984 and 1964. Note that these gains are about half the size of the increase among observant black Protestants. Democrats also improved among less-observant white mainline Protestants during the period, when this religious group experienced a sharp decline in size. Here the pattern is also uneven, with the 2004 figures representing a major gain over 1984. (The party made very similar gains among observant white mainline Protestants as well.) By contrast, Democrats also lost ground among the composite category of less-observant other faiths, less-observant white Catholics, and less-observant white evangelicals. The high-water mark for Democrats among less-observant other faiths and less-observant white Catholics was 1964, whereas the low point for less-observant white Catholics and less-observant white evangelicals was 1984. In fact, for less-observant white Catholics and white evangelicals the 2004 Democratic vote represents a recovery over 1984. These shifts may well reflect changes in macropoliticization.

Patterns are somewhat clearer among the observant groups. Republicans gained nearly as much among observant white Catholics as among observant white evangelicals. They also made gains among the composite category of observant other faiths. In all three cases, the trend is steady across the four elections. However, the GOP lost ground among observant white mainline Protestants, despite winning a majority of this group in 2004—a pattern very similar among less-observant white mainliners. Here the trend is quite unstable, fluctuating by year and shifting Democratic after 1984. As noted above, Republican ballots increased among less-observant white evangelicals and Catholics over the period and among black Protestants after 1984.

The patterns across the four presidential elections suggest that many factors were likely at work in these shifts: differences in the quality of the candidates and campaigns as well as macropolitical changes in the issue agenda, especially cultural issues.

Voter Coalitions in the Postwar Period

What was the combined impact of the change in religious demography and partisan preferences of the religious groups on voter coalitions? Table 6-8 reports the change in the proportion of the Democratic and Republican presidential ballots from these groups, also looking back from 2004 to 1944.

Table 6-8. Religious Groups and Presidential Vote Coalitions, 1944–2004

Percent

Religious group	Dem. change	Rep. change	2004 Dem.	2004 Rep.	1984 Dem.	1984 Rep.	1964 Dem.	1964 Rep.	1944 Dem.	1944 Rep.
Unaffiliated	13.7	3.4	18.2	6.8	9.8	6.1	7.7	5.1	4.5	3.4
Less-observant other faiths	0.9	1.7	10.6	5.2	10.2	3.3	5.7	0.7	9.7	3.5
Observant other faiths	6.2	9.0	8.0	10.1	6.1	3.8	3.1	2.7	1.7	1.3
Less-observant black Protestants	1.4	–0.7	5.5	0.8	5.1	0.3	7.3	0.5	4.1	1.5
Observant black Protestants	5.0	–0.4	8.0	1.8	9.4	0.7	8.1	0.0	3.0	2.2
Less-observant white Catholics	1.6	1.5	9.7	6.7	10.0	10.4	6.0	2.4	8.1	5.2
Observant white Catholics	–7.1	4.7	7.5	12.0	15.2	12.3	20.7	9.7	14.6	7.3
Less-observant white mainline Protestants	–12.6	–26.2	12.8	12.5	11.7	20.5	15.0	23.0	25.4	38.7
Observant white mainline Protestants	–3.5	–11.4	7.3	8.8	8.8	17.6	13.6	23.7	10.8	20.2
Less-observant white evangelical Protestants	–4.8	–1.4	6.7	8.5	7.8	9.0	6.9	14.0	11.5	9.9
Observant white evangelical Protestants	–0.9	20.0	5.7	26.8	5.7	16.0	5.9	18.2	6.6	6.8

Source: See note 16.

The unaffiliated increased their share of the Democratic voter coalition in the postwar period, mostly because of the increase in the size of this group. Fewer of their gains came from a Democratic shift at the ballot box (a point illustrated by a parallel Republican gain over the period). Observant white evangelicals became even more important to the Republican voter coalition, a change that was fairly steady. Both increased size of the group and a Republican shift at the ballot box contributed to this change (a point illustrated by the very modest loss the Democrats sustained over the period with this group).

Thus the secular and evangelical trends altered the shape of the major party coalitions in the postwar period. At the same time, the less-observant groups became relatively more important to the Democratic voter coalition, including the composite category of less-observant other faiths, black Protestants, and white Catholics. These gains were also fairly steady, reflecting for the most part changes in the relative size of these groups. Indeed, the Democrats also made gains among observant black Protestants and observant other faiths for this same reason. But Democrats lost ground among observant white Catholics because of a combination of the declining size of the group and shifting party preference.

Meanwhile less-observant white mainline Protestants became substantially less important to the Democratic presidential coalition. This shift occurred in the face of a pro-Democratic shift at the polls and was caused mostly by the sharp decline in the size of this group. A smaller decline occurred among less-observant white evangelicals, and here the change was due to both changes in relative size of the group and voting behavior.

The observant groups show a similar mixed pattern with regard to the Republican voter coalition. The GOP received relative gains from the composite category of observant other faiths and observant white Catholics. The former reflected both change in size and presidential vote, the latter largely represented a change in voting preferences. (The party also made some modest gains among the less-observant counterparts of these groups.) However, the Republican coalition lost ground among observant mainline Protestants and suffered an even sharper decline among less-observant mainliners. Here the major factor is also the declining size of mainline Protestantism. Finally, GOP candidates lost some ground among black Protestants largely because of shifts in partisan preference.

For the most part, it appears that changes in the size of religious groups had a larger impact on the parties' voter coalitions than shifts at the ballot box. This pattern is particularly true for the decline of white mainline Protestants and the growth of the composite category of other faiths. But for the unaffiliated and observant white evangelical Protestants increases in size were reinforced by large shifts at the ballot box. Changes in macropoliticization may have influenced these partisan shifts.

Differences by Region in the Postwar Period

Table 6-9 reports the changes shown in table 6-8 in a slightly different way, showing the net change in partisan advantage as a percentage of the total vote cast. In this table, a positive figure means a net Democratic advantage and a negative figure a net Republican advantage over time. By this measure, Democrats enjoyed the biggest net gains among the unaffiliated, and Republicans experienced the largest net gains among observant white evangelicals.

The net Democratic advantage among the unaffiliated grew in all the regions except the South; it is the largest in the West. The net Republican advantage grew for observant white evangelicals in all regions, but especially in the South and the Midwest. Republicans experienced a similar net gain for observant white Catholics in all regions, and especially in the Northeast and Midwest. All the other religious groups show a mixed pattern across the regions. For example, Democrats benefited from a gain in net advantage among white mainline Protestants in the Northeast and Midwest, while the

Table 6-9. Religious Groups and Change in Net Party Advantage, by Geographic Region, Twenty-Year Intervals between 1944 and 2004[a]
Percent

Religious group	National	Northeast	West	Midwest	South
Unaffiliated	+4.7	+1.6	+2.5	+0.9	−0.3
Less-observant black Protestants	+1.3	−0.2	+0.1	+0.3	+1.1
Observant black Protestants	+3.8	+0.5	+0.8	+0.4	+2.1
Less-observant other faiths	−1.3	−1.8	+0.4	−0.4	+0.5
Observant other faiths	−1.9	+0.0	−1.8	+0.0	−0.1
Less-observant white Catholics	−1.0	+0.6	−0.6	−0.3	−0.7
Observant white Catholics	−7.2	−3.1	−0.4	−2.9	−0.8
Less-observant white mainline Protestants	+4.1	+3.1	−0.3	+2.0	−0.7
Observant white mainline Protestants	+2.5	+0.9	−0.1	+3.0	−1.3
Less-observant white evangelical Protestants	−2.5	+0.8	−0.3	+0.1	−3.1
Observant white evangelical Protestants	−10.9	−1.1	−1.5	−3.3	−5.0
Total	−8.4	+1.3	−1.2	−0.2	−8.3

Source: See note 16.
a. Positive number means a Democratic gain and a Republican loss, while a negative number means a Democratic loss and a Republican gain.

GOP made such gains in the South. Thus the regional patterns observed in 2004 were in part the result of long-term changes in the size and partisanship of the religious groups. It is likely that these shifts reflect regional and state differences in micropoliticization and also shifts in macropoliticization.

Toward the Future

The results of these investigations can be summarized succinctly. In the postwar period, there is strong evidence for both secular and evangelical trends: the unaffiliated and the observant white evangelical Protestants became more numerous and shifted their partisan preferences in, respectively, Democratic and Republican directions. By 2004 each had become the single largest source of votes for their parties' presidential nominees, providing their parties with special regional strengths in the Electoral College. These trends contributed to the polarization of national politics. The effects of religious observance are not as clear-cut, producing a more complex set of religious coalitions, a pattern reinforced by the pluralist trend. Thus faith-based polarization has not been comprehensive.

What about the future? As we have seen, religion and faith-based politics can change substantially over a span of decades, so there is no reason to suppose that their relationship will remain static in the next several decades. Three possibilities suggest themselves. The easiest to imagine is a continuation of the present trend. An alternative is a reversal of that trend. Yet another possibility is a new trend. Each of these possibilities is worth considering briefly.[20]

A continuation of the present trend would mean the continued expansion of the unaffiliated and of the observant white evangelical population and the continued development of the attendance gap. Table 6-10 illustrates this possibility by reporting a straight-line projection of the 1984–2004 change for religious groups (see table 6-6) forward twenty years to 2024. If this pattern holds, the unaffiliated would account for almost one-fifth of the adult population, slightly more than observant white evangelicals. White mainline Protestants and white Catholics would continue to decline in relative size, while the other faiths would continue to grow.

If taken to its logical conclusion, the country would be further polarized between secular and traditionally religious politics. The attendance gap would widen in other religious communities to the point that religious affiliation would largely cease to matter politically. And eventually even the pluralist trend would be drawn into these divisions, with the less-observant

Table 6-10. Projected Size of Religious Groups in 2024

Percent

Religious group	2004	Projected to 2024
Unaffiliated	14.4	19.8
Less-observant other faiths	9.4	11.0
Observant other faiths	9.7	13.9
Less-observant black Protestants	4.0	4.2
Observant black Protestants	5.7	6.3
Less-observant white Catholics	8.0	5.7
Observant white Catholics	7.7	5.5
Less-observant white mainline Protestants	11.4	5.7
Observant white mainline Protestants	6.5	3.2
Less-observant white evangelical Protestants	9.3	7.5
Observant white evangelical Protestants	14.1	17.2

Source: Estimate by the authors in the second column; the first column is described in note 16.

members of ethnic faiths and new religious communities joining the unaffiliated and the observant joining the evangelicals. This future is envisioned by the sociologist James Davison Hunter in his book *Culture Wars.*[21] Such a future would likely require that cultural issues stay high on the political agenda—thus no significant change in the macropoliticization of religion. The continuing confrontation between secularists and white Christian conservatives over such matters as the legalization of same-sex marriage by the California supreme court point to this scenario.

A reversal of the present situation is another possibility. In effect, this would mean an abatement of the secular and evangelical trends and the redevelopment of a distinctive political perspective within religious affiliations. One possibility is the adaptation of religious denominations to contemporary society so that their membership becomes stable. This pattern might be achieved by the full incorporation of new ethnic minorities into established denominations, such as the full integration of Hispanics into the Roman Catholic Church, and by sorting of people with traditional and progressive values into particular denominations. Another feature might be a decline in the unaffiliated population, including its recruitment into religious communities. Under such a scenario, the attendance gap would fade and the affiliation gap would become stronger, so that the situation would resemble that of the 1940s and 1960s. This change might well require a change in the macropoliticization of religion, with the national agenda turning from cultural issues to economic concerns.

There are, in fact, new religious voices calling for such a change in priorities. The best known are among evangelicals, including Jim Wallis of the Sojourners community, the megachurch pastors Rick Warren and Joel Hunter, and Richard Cizik of the National Association of Evangelicals. Of course, such developments would require similar voices among the unaffiliated population and, indeed, among other religious groups. Other efforts aimed at finding common ground within and across denominations may fit this bill, including efforts aimed at mobilizing religious people around concepts of the common good.[22]

The final possibility is for another aspect of religion to become important politically, supplementing religious affiliation in much the way that religious behavior and beliefs did over the last several decades. Of course, it is difficult to imagine something that has not happened and might not occur. But for purposes of illustration one might imagine spirituality becoming politicized around an issue like protecting the environment. There is evidence of such changes in American religion in recent times, documented by the sociologist Robert Wuthnow, who writes about a reordering of Americans' understanding of the sacred.[23] And there is a growing awareness and concern over the environment among religious people, most recently among white evangelical Protestants.

Under such a scenario, a new spirituality gap would appear to compete with the attendance gap and eventually supersede it. Just as the attendance gap made mainline white Protestants and white Catholics less distinctive politically, so would the spirituality gap make the unaffiliated and the observant white evangelicals less politically distinctive. In all likelihood, such a change would require a fairly dramatic shift in macropoliticization, with the environment becoming a preeminent issue on the national agenda, replacing economic and cultural issues. A series of environmental catastrophes of the sort predicted by some environmentalists could achieve such a change.

2008 and Beyond

The basic political patterns found in 2004 are not likely to disappear abruptly. After all, these trends developed over a sixty-year period and will not be overturned in just four years. So the alignments in 2008 and beyond are likely to be a variation on those of 2004.

Still, a shift in the political agenda could alter the macropoliticization of religious voters. Here an important development is the declining prominence of cultural issues and the increased concern with economic and foreign policy problems.[24] This shift reflects in part a widespread exhaustion with cultural conflict, but also new challenges facing the country, from higher gasoline prices to the mortgage crisis to the ongoing conflicts in Iraq and Afghanistan. These changes do not mean that cultural issues will vanish from national politics, as the California Supreme Court's 2008 decision legalizing same-sex marriage reveals. But such controversies will be less of a preoccupation for most voters.

The 2008 campaign provided strong evidence that the country was focusing on a new mix of priorities. All of the major presidential candidates embraced "faith and values," but their focus was decidedly on economic and foreign policy questions. This pattern was clearest on the Democratic side, where Barack Obama and Hillary Clinton both linked religion to domestic economic issues such as job creation, health care, and education. On the Republican side, Mike Huckabee had some success with including social welfare issues in his appeal to evangelical voters, and John McCain won the nomination in the face of opposition from many leaders of the "religious right" with an emphasis on foreign policy and national security. Once the presidential nominations were secured, the Obama campaign expanded its efforts to reach religious voters, while the McCain campaign pursued a more circumspect approach designed to avoid an overidentification with religious conservatives.

The renewed importance of economic and foreign policy issues could well decrease the polarization around religious practice so visible in the 2004 election, and such a result might point to the development of the second scenario for the future outlined above, with a decline in the attendance gap and a revival of the affiliation gap.[25] Of course, these developments will also depend on the successful micropolitization of religious voters by the presidential campaigns. Some clues about the impact of religion in the future can be found in the results of the 2006 congressional campaigns. Thus it is instructive to review two accounts of the role of religion in that election.[26]

Writing in the November 26, 2006, *Philadelphia Inquirer,* the reporter Thomas Fitzgerald begins a front-page analysis of the role of religion in the midterm election with these arresting words: "A minor miracle occurred this month: The 'God Gap' in American politics narrowed." But ten days earlier, the Pew Research Center issued a postelection report by the analyst Scott Keeter that was just as positive in declaring "The 'God Gap' Widens."

Who is right? Both accounts are based on fact, not speculation. "While the most religious voters in recent years have tended to favor Republicans, a slice of them voted Democratic in the Nov. 7 midterm congressional elections,"

Fitzgerald writes. "The shift has raised eyebrows among pollsters and strategists." He reports that "Democrats took back the Catholic vote they lost in 2004" and "trimmed the GOP advantage among weekly churchgoers, and even gained ground with the most loyal segment of the Republican base: white evangelicals."

"In this year's campaign, same-sex marriage and abortion were less dominant issues than they were two years ago," he continues. "Post-election analyses also suggest that many religious voters were concerned most about the war in Iraq and corruption in Washington." He naturally focuses on the U.S. Senate contest in Pennsylvania, where Democrat Bob Casey, an economic progressive and an opponent of abortion, defeated Republican incumbent Rick Santorum, an across-the-board conservative. Fitzgerald notes that Casey "got 59 percent of the Catholic vote against fellow Catholic Santorum, and the Democrat also won a narrow majority of all those who said they attend religious services weekly. Casey won 29 percent of self-described evangelicals." He adds that while Bush "carried the Harrisburg television market, which encompasses much of the state's conservative middle, by 34 percentage points over Democratic Sen. John Kerry in 2004," in 2006, "Santorum won that essential Republican turf by just 10 percentage points over Casey, a 24-point shift."

By contrast, Pew's Keeter finds that the Democratic Party's gains in the election are "concentrated among non-Christians and secular voters, suggesting that there was a larger political divide between Christians and the rest of American society." Keeter offers ample support for this view: the GOP held on to voters who attend religious services at least once a week (55 percent voted Republican versus 58 percent in 2004). But less frequent churchgoers were much more supportive of Democrats than they were four years ago. Among occasional churchgoers, 59 percent voted Democratic. In 2002 just 51 percent did so. And among those who never go to church, 67 percent voted Democratic—four years ago, only 55 percent did so. Thus the gap in Democratic support between the most and least religious has grown from 16 percentage points in 2002 to 24 points today.

Republicans, Keeter says, "did very well among white evangelicals: 72 percent voted Republican in races for the U.S. House nationwide, and they gave strong support—about two-thirds or more—to Republican Senate candidates in several key states, including Tennessee, Pennsylvania, Ohio, Missouri, and Virginia." These levels of support, he notes, are comparable to those registered by evangelicals in 2004 and in 2002 (about 75 percent for Republican candidates).

As for Bush, his approval rating among evangelicals on Election Day 2006 "was 70 percent, far higher than in the general electorate." That was down 10 points from its level two years earlier, Keeter notes, "but the decline was no greater among evangelicals than among the rest of the electorate." Evangelicals were clearly more inclined to vote on the old moral issues than other voters. While 59 percent of these voters said that "values issues such as gay marriage and abortion" were "extremely important" to their vote, just 29 percent of other voters said this. Lest there be any doubt about who drove the Democratic victory, Keeter adds this: "In fact, the Democratic Party's gains came largely among non-Christians. Democratic House candidates gained 25 points among Jews and 7 points among those of other non-Christian faiths, compared with 2002. They also picked up 10 points among secular voters."

That two analysts could reach such starkly different conclusions reveals the complexity of faith-based politics. But reconciling the two views is not that difficult. Remember, the *Inquirer*'s Fitzgerald claims only that "a slice" of the religious vote had gone Democratic. Democrats did, in fact, post gains among religious voters in 2006, including white evangelicals. But as Keeter suggests, Democrats gained even more from less religiously inclined voters.

A fair way to summarize the results is that Keeter is quite right in asserting that the attendance gap between the more and less religious voters actually widened between 2004 and 2006; but the affiliation gap turned from being a disadvantage to the Democrats into an advantage. They modestly cut their losses among observant voters (all that new organizing among voters of faith paid off at least to some degree) while at the same time vastly expanding their advantages in the rest of the electorate. Put another way, Republicans did so badly among less observant and unaffiliated voters in 2006 that their continuing, if slightly diminished, advantage among white evangelicals and the observant voters was not enough to save them.

Part of the clue to what happened is the distinction between the affiliation gap and the attendance gap in the vote, which represent different kinds of micropoliticization of religion. In the 2006 election both gaps were in play. As Keeter suggests, the attendance gap expanded and did so in the Democrats' favor. And as Fitzgerald notes, the affiliation gap also expanded to the benefit of the Democrats, as they gained a majority of white Catholics while expanding their already large majorities among Jews and Latinos.

Students of religion and politics made much of the 2006 Democratic victories in Ohio, Virginia, and Pennsylvania. The first two states supported Bush over Kerry in 2004, and Pennsylvania saw the nomination of a Catholic Democrat opposed to legal abortion. So it is worth examining how much (and also how little) the religious gap changed from the first election to the second in these states.

Ohio, the state on which Bush's 2004 Electoral College victory hung, saw a massive swing toward the Democrats, fueled by local Republican corruption, the sharp decline in manufacturing jobs, and the same discontent over Iraq and the Bush administration that affected much of the rest of the nation. Ohio had significant races for both governor and the U.S. Senate, and both jobs shifted from the Republicans to the Democrats. The Democratic nominee for governor, Representative Ted Strickland, was a moderate liberal and also a Methodist minister who spoke often of his faith. He opposed Secretary of State Ken Blackwell, closely and proudly aligned with the religious conservative movement. In the Senate race, an outspoken liberal and tough critic of free trade, Representative Sherrod Brown, opposed Mike DeWine, the moderately conservative incumbent.

Both Democrats swept the state, Strickland with 60 percent of the vote, Brown with 56 percent. Strickland won 38 percent of Ohio's observant voters, a 7-point gain over Kerry's showing. He won 55 percent of those who attend religious services weekly, a 19-point gain over Kerry. But he did best of all among voters who say they never attend religious services, winning 81 percent of their ballots, an 18-point gain over Kerry. Strickland also did well among occasional worship attenders, winning 68 percent in this group, an 11-point gain over Kerry.

In other words, even though Strickland gained substantial ground over Kerry among the observant voters, the attendance gap was actually higher in 2006 because of profound Republican weakness among the less observant and nonreligious voters. The patterns were similar in Brown's victory, although the gains were generally smaller. Brown did gain as much ground as Strickland did among those who attended religious services more than once a week, somewhat less in the other groups. Interestingly, Brown, the more liberal candidate, ran 7 percentage points behind Strickland among voters who never attended religious services—partly, perhaps, because nonreligious voters were more inclined to cast ballots against the conservative and openly devout Blackwell than against the more moderate DeWine.

In Pennsylvania, as Fitzgerald's account suggests, Democrats were very pleased with the staunchly Catholic Casey's success over the equally staunchly Catholic (and much more conservative) Santorum. But the evidence suggests that Casey's strong showing was built by moderately religious voters or voters who are not religious at all. Casey actually won marginally fewer voters who attend religious services more than once a week (down 3 points from Kerry—though this is within the margin of error). He gained 7 points over Kerry among weekly worship attenders, 12 points among occasional attenders, and 10 points among those who never attend religious services. Casey, like Strickland and Santorum, did best among the nonobservant, securing 78 percent of their ballots. As we have seen, Casey did improve the Democrats' share of the Catholic vote by 8 points, to 59 percent. But he also gained 6 points among Protestants and a remarkable 14 points among the roughly one-tenth of voters who have no religion. A strongly anti-Republican secular vote played an important role in the Pennsylvania result, as it did in Ohio.

The key Virginia contest between incumbent Republican Senator George Allen and Democrat Jim Webb underscores how political change in 2006 cannot be ascribed simply to religious shifts. Webb won a 50 to 49 percent victory, defeating Allen by just over 7,000 votes out of more than 2.3 million cast. What is striking about the Virginia race is how minor the religious shifts were between 2004 and 2006. Allen's support among white evangelical Protestants in the home state of Pat Robertson and Jerry Falwell was as solid as George W. Bush's had been two years earlier. White evangelicals voted 80–20 for Allen, and his performance was a statistically insignificant single point better that Bush's two years earlier. Allen ran slightly better than Bush among those who attend religious services more than once a week, slightly worse among weekly attenders. Webb, like Democrats in the other states, gained the most ground on Kerry among the least observant voters—those who attend religious services a few times a year, or never.

A key feature in all these pivotal contests was a change in the political agenda. Complaints about corruption, the Iraq War, and the economy sharply eroded the weak Republican support on the secular side of the affiliation and attendance gaps. This new agenda also hurt the GOP with the religiously observant, but here the party's strength was sufficient to keep losses to a minimum. Given the economic problems, the Democrats may have an opportunity to make further gains among observant voters. Barack Obama clearly took these shifting priorities into account in developing his campaign strategy, which included overt appeals to observant voters, especially white evangelicals and Catholics.

If it is foolish to ignore history, it is equally foolish to assume that history always repeats itself. A particular mix of secular and religious politics has become important in recent years. But these patterns are not immutable.

American religion and American politics are both dynamic, and this dynamism suggests that a new pattern may be on the horizon.

Appendix: The U.S. Religious Landscape Survey

The 2007 U.S. Religious Landscape Survey (RLS) by the Pew Forum on Religion and Public Life (http://religions.pewforum.org/) provides a more precise estimate of the size of religious groups than other survey results presented in this chapter. Using the RLS, table 6A-1 lists an expanded set of religious categories. Unless otherwise noted, the categories in table 6A-1 match those in table 6-6; the notes in table 6A-1 report how smaller religious groups not listed in table 6-6 fit into the composite "Other faiths," "Black Protestant," and "Unaffiliated" categories. (The figures in table 6A-1 may not total to 100 percent due to rounding of small categories.)

Table 6A-1. Religious Affiliation and Worship Attendance, 2007

Percent

Religious group	All	Less observant	Observant
Unaffiliated	16.1	15.3[a]	0.8[b]
No response	0.8	0.6[a]	0.1[b]
Other faiths			
Jews[b]	1.7	1.4	0.3
Buddhists[b]	0.8	0.6	0.1
Muslims[b]	0.6	0.3	0.3
Hindus[b]	0.4	0.3	0.1
Other religions[b]	1.4	1.2	0.2
Mormons[b]	1.7	0.4	1.3
Orthodox Christians[b]	0.6	0.4	0.2
Other Christians[b]	1.0	0.4	0.7
Historic black Protestants[c]	6.3	2.6	3.7
Historic black Protestants, other races[b]	0.6	0.2	0.4
White Catholics	15.3	8.9	6.4
Hispanic Catholics[b]	6.8	4.0	2.8
Other nonwhite Catholics[b]	1.7	1.0	0.6
White mainline Protestants	16.1	10.6	5.5
Black mainline Protestants[c]	0.4	0.2	0.2
Hispanic mainline Protestants[b]	0.6	0.3	0.3
Other nonwhite mainline Protestants[b]	1.0	0.6	0.4
White evangelical Protestants	21.0	9.0	12.0
Black evangelical Protestants[c]	1.6	0.5	1.1
Hispanic evangelical Protestants[b]	1.9	0.6	1.3
Other nonwhite evangelical Protestants[b]	1.8	0.7	1.1
Total	100.0	60.3	39.7

a. "Unaffiliated" category in tables 6-1 through 6-9.
b. "Other faiths" category in tables 6-1 through 6-9.
c. "Black Protestants" category in tables 6-1 through 6-9.
Note: Categories shown in bold are those used in other tables in this chapter.

Notes

1. For good overviews of this evidence, see Andrew Kohut and others, *The Diminishing Divide: Religion's Changing Role in American Politics* (Brookings, 2000); E. J. Dionne, "Polarized by God? American Politics and the Religious Divide," in *Red and Blue Nation?* vol. 1, edited by David W. Brady and Pietro S. Nivola (Brookings, 2008).

2. For a fuller discussion, see John C. Green, *The Faith Factor* (Westport, Conn.: Praeger, 2007).

3. A good overview of these issues can be found in Pippa Norris and Ronald Inglehart, *Sacred and Secular: Religion and Politics Worldwide* (Cambridge University Press, 2004).

4. See Peter Berger, "Religion in a Globalizing World," Pew Forum on Religion and Public Life (http://pewforum.org/events/?EventID=136). On the special politics of evangelical Protestants in the United States, see John C. Green, "Seeking a Place: Evangelical Protestants and Public Engagement in the 20th Century," in *Toward an Evangelical Public Policy,* edited by Ronald Sider and Diane Knipper (Grand Rapids, Mich: Baker, 2005).

5. Robert Wuthnow, *America and the Challenges of Religious Diversity* (Princeton University Press, 2005).

6. Green, *The Faith Factor,* chap. 2.

7. Lyman A. Kellstedt and others, "Faith Transformed: Religion and American Politics from FDR to George W. Bush," in *Religion and American Politics: From the Colonial Period to the Present,* 2d ed., edited by Mark A. Noll and Luke E. Harlow (Oxford University Press, 2007).

8. See Green, *The Faith Factor,* chap. 3.

9. For a good overview of this literature, see James A. Stimson, *Public Opinion in America: Moods, Cycles, and Swings* (Boulder, Colo.: Westview, 1999).

10. The National Election Pool is the 2004 "exit poll" conducted by Edison/ Mitovsky. These data and more information can be obtained at www.ropercenter. uconn.edu. The NEP has fairly crude religion measures; they were used to construct the eleven categories: unaffiliated (no religious affiliation, less than weekly worship attendance); black Protestants (African American Protestants, divided into weekly and less-than-weekly worship attenders); white Catholics (divided into weekly and less-than-weekly worship attenders); white mainline Protestants (white non-born-again Protestants, divided into weekly and less-than-weekly worship attenders); white evangelical Protestants (white born-again Protestants, divided into weekly and less-than-weekly attenders); other faiths (composite category containing all other religious groups and divided into weekly and less-than-weekly attenders). Weekly attenders are labeled *observant* and less-than-weekly attenders *less observant.*

11. A fuller estimate of these religious categories is found in the appendix, table 6A-1.

12. To be consistent, the handful of unaffiliated respondents who report weekly worship attendance are in the other faiths category.

13. On the voting behavior of the religious communities in this composite category, see John C. Green and others, "The American Religious Landscape and the 2004 Presidential Vote: Increased Polarization," Pew Forum on Religion and Public Life (http://pewforum.org/docs/indes.php?docid=64).

14. On the size of the various gaps, see Laura R. Olson and John C. Green, "Symposium: Voting Gaps in the 2004 Presidential Election," *PS* 39 (2006): 443–72.

15. For a more detailed look at religion by region, see Green, *The Faith Factor*, chap. 6.

16. The 1944 data come from a Gallup Poll (AIPO335) conducted November 1944 (N = 2,529); the 1964 data come from the survey Anti-Semitism in the United States, conducted in 1964 (N = 1,975) by Charles Glock and his associates at the University of California, Berkley. The 1984 data come from the 1984 National Election Study conducted at the University of Michigan (N = 2,257); the 2004 data come from the Fourth National Survey of Religion and Politics (N = 6,000) conducted at the University of Akron. The religious categories used in this analysis are based on denominational affiliation (see Green, *The Faith Factor*, chapter 2; and appendix 6A). Although the religious affiliation questions were not asked the same way, each survey produced a detailed list of specific denominations, which were coded so as to be as consistent as possible across the four surveys. The surveys also did not ask worship attendance in the same way, but for these purposes the measures were recoded to be as consistent as possible. For details, please contact the authors.

17. The classic description is Dean Kelley, *Why Conservative Churches are Growing* (San Francisco: Harper and Row, 1972).

18. On the postwar attendance increase, see Martin E. Marty, *A Nation of Behavers* (University of Chicago Press, 1976); on the post-1960s decline in attendance, see Robert D. Putnam, *Bowling Alone: The Collapse and Revival of American Community* (New York: Simon and Schuster, 2000); on the recent stability of worship attendance, see Stanley Presser and Mark Chaves, "Is Religious Service Attendance Declining?" *Journal for the Scientific Study of Religion* 46 (2007): 417–23. On measurement problems related to worship attendance, see Green, *The Faith Factor*, chap. 3.

19. For an overview of these issues, see Roger Finke and Rodney Stark, *The Churching of America, 1776–1990: Winners and Losers in Our Religious Economy* (Rutgers University Press, 2005). Also see Robert Wuthnow, *The Restructuring of American Religion* (Princeton University Press, 1988).

20. For a fuller discussion of these possibilities, see Green, *The Faith Factor*, chap. 8.

21. James D. Hunter, *Culture Wars: The Struggle to Define America* (New York: Basic Books, 1991).

22. For a fuller discussion of these issues, see E. J. Dionne, *Souled Out* (Princeton University Press, 2008).

23. Robert Wuthnow, *After Heaven: Spirituality in America after the 1950s* (University of California Press, 1998).

24. See Daniel Cox and Gregory Smith, "A Portrait of Republican Social Issue Voters," Pew Forum on Religion and Public Life (http://pewforum.org/docs/?docid+253).

25. See John C. Green, "The Faith-based Vote in the United States: A Look to the Future," in *Religion and the American Future,* edited by Christopher DeMuth and Yuval Levin (Washington: American Enterprise Institute, 2008).

26. For more on these developments, see Dionne, *Souled Out.*

seven

The Aging of the Boomers and the Rise of the Millennials

Scott Keeter

Generational forces played an important role in the polarized politics of 2008. Yet these forces may, in time, lead the nation away from the intense divisions of today. Younger Americans, reflecting continuity with the past as well as potential for change, are not yet an important political force but will gradually become one.

The vast social and political changes of the 1960s are reflected in the polarized attitudes of the people who came of age during that tumultuous period and who now occupy positions of power in government, business, the non-profit world, and academia: the baby boomers. Although clearly reflecting the more liberal social and economic values that marked that period in our history, this generation is hardly monolithic. Bill Clinton and George W. Bush epitomize the strongly held and widely divergent views of this cohort. Like them, younger voting-age Americans reflect the imprint of their own turbulent times. Those socialized to politics during the 1990s and in the present decade—the so-called millennial generation—reflect not only the values of their parents, most of whom are baby boomers, but also the particular political climate of this contentious period in American politics.[1]

The generation that lies between these two, famously named Generation X for its lack of a defining characteristic, plays its part as well, sharing more of its political values with its older brothers and sisters in the latter part of the baby boom generation than with its younger siblings. Indeed, Generation X and late boomers are treated as a single cohort in many of the analyses in this chapter.

And while a few of America's so-called greatest generation of World War II heroes and their counterparts on the home front remain, most older Americans came of age in the 1950s and early 1960s, a time of great economic change but—apart from the tensions of the cold war—relative international peace and domestic tranquility. (For an overview of the generations of 2008, see table 7-1.)

The story of generational change in the United States and its implications for politics is hardly clear-cut. The U.S. population is composed of not only those who have lived its recent history but also their offspring and a large number of recent immigrants. This latter group brings its own concerns and interests, and though for now they are less consequential politically than their raw numbers would suggest, they nonetheless have an important voice in ongoing debates and will grow in influence over the coming years.

Today's Generations

A person's political identity is the product of many influences. These include the age-related exigencies of the person's life (life-cycle effects) and the influences that are generational (cohort effects). A generation usually becomes a

Table 7-1. The Generations of 2008

Cohort	Birth years	Ages now	Size	Events, late adolescence and early adulthood
Millennials	1977–90	18–31	About 58 million	Late 1990s economic boom, Clinton presidency, G. W. Bush presidency, 9/11, Iraq War, Hurricane Katrina
Gen X	1965–76	32–43	About 50 million	Reagan presidency, fall of Berlin Wall, AIDS, GHWB election, low inflation, Gulf War, first years of Clinton presidency
Late boomers	1956–64	44–52	About 41 million	Iran hostage crisis, high inflation, Reagan election
Early boomers	1946–55	53–62	About 37 million	Vietnam War, late period of civil rights movement, assassinations of John Kennedy, Martin Luther King, and Robert Kennedy, Nixon presidency, low inflation, Watergate, women's rights movement
World War II	1945 and earlier	63+	About 48 million	World War II, cold war, start of civil rights movement, economic boom of 1950s

generation because its members experience events or circumstances in a very different way than those who are just older and just younger. These influences reflect the Zeitgeist, or the spirit of the time.

The generational impact of the Great Depression and World War II probably dwarfs anything that has happened since then, but the political influence of those who experienced these events during adolescence and early adulthood is limited now that most of this age cohort is no longer with us. So more recent history helps to explain why Americans hold the views that they do. For example, the first wave of the baby boom generation formed its political consciousness during the Vietnam War, the civil rights movement, the women's liberation movement, and other manifestations of countercultural reaction.

Richard Nixon's election as president in 1968, in part a reaction against the rapid cultural change of the 1960s, was followed by his reelection in 1972, in one of the largest Republican landslides in the nation's history. But the Watergate affair brought an early end to Nixon's presidency, and the Democrats consolidated their political gains in 1974 and retook the White House in the 1976 election. The Zeitgeist of this period strongly favored the Democratic Party.

Subsequently, the nation experienced a period of political retrenchment in reaction to energy costs, inflation, and the foreign policy fiasco in Iran. This retrenchment ushered in the administration of Ronald Reagan and a Republican majority in the U.S. Senate. After a rocky start, Reagan won reelection by a landslide and achieved a relatively high level of popularity, which persisted— with ups and downs—until he left office. Following many years of favorable circumstances for the Democrats, the Reagan era was a good one for the GOP in its impact on young people forming their political identities.

The presidency of George H. W. Bush, the father of George W. Bush, saw remarkable extremes of public reaction. In the aftermath of the Persian Gulf War, Bush's job approval rating soared to nearly unprecedented levels. But a sharp recession in 1991 and 1992, coupled with disgruntlement among Republican conservatives over his fiscal policy, doomed his reelection prospects and left him with dismal ratings in his final months in office. Bush's presidency marked the start of a very favorable period for the Democratic Party in its impact on younger Americans.

Bill Clinton's presidency was also marked by significant shifts in public reaction, including those during the midterm elections of 1994, which were catastrophic for the Democratic Party. In part because this election represented the consolidation of changes in the leadership of both parties (changes that had been building for many years), the impact of the election on government was longer lived than the impact on public opinion. The Republican Party maintained its control of the U.S. Senate until 2001 and the U.S. House until 2007. But while the party experienced gains in public support from 1993 to 1995, these were quickly reversed. The economic boom of the late 1990s, and the negative reaction of the public to the impeachment of President Clinton, damaged the GOP's image and helped sway Americans toward the Democrats.

The next President Bush also saw great swings in public reaction to his administration. After a desultory start in 2001, Bush's ratings spiked after 9/11, reflecting a very positive public reaction to his handling of the terrorist attacks. But these high ratings steadily fell throughout 2002, and despite a temporary uptick at the start of the war in Iraq continued to decline. Following the government's handling of the Hurricane Katrina disaster along the Gulf Coast, both Bush and the GOP experienced sharp declines in public regard.

Against this backdrop of recent history, we consider the values, attitudes, and habits of the several age cohorts, with a special focus on the youngest adults.

The Millennials

The millennial cohort stands out as distinctive from previous generations on several social and demographic dimensions that have political relevance. The tumultuous social changes of the 1960s and 1970s are now largely woven into the fabric of everyday life and form the context for the millennial generation's life. In pragmatic terms, this has meant that far more of these young people have grown up in what were once called nontraditional households. Fewer millennials grew up in two-parent households (61 percent) than other age cohorts overall (74 percent) and had two married parents (64 percent compared to 78 percent); and many more had a mother who worked full time outside of the home (57 percent, compared to 39 percent). Yet this shift away from the traditional notion of the nuclear family was not accompanied by higher levels of social dysfunction, as many feared would be the case. Millennials, coming of age in the 1990s and early in the present decade, experienced lower levels of teenage pregnancy than their immediate predecessors, equal or lower levels of substance abuse, and lower rates of violent crime.

The economic backdrop of their time of socialization is marked by increasing national wealth coupled with growing economic inequality and insecurity. Lifelong employment with a single employer became a thing of the past during their coming of age, and a more dynamic and risky job market arose. This transformation of work has had a profound impact on the expectations of young workers regarding their careers. Related to this (but important in other ways) is that this cohort experienced technological change rooted in electronic innovation that arguably exceeds that of the era of industrialization and mechanization or even the early years of electronics, including the birth of radio and television.

Following the lead of preceding age cohorts, young people are taking advantage of America's expanding opportunities for postsecondary education and promise to achieve ever higher levels of formal schooling. About one-third of those ages eighteen through twenty-four (the millennial cohort) are enrolled in college, and nearly four in ten (including those with and without college experience) intend to enroll in the future. In sharp contrast to earlier generations, women are at the forefront of this push for higher education, comprising a growing majority of the college student population.

In part because of high levels of immigration in the past decades, not only from Latin America but also from all over the world, the millennial cohort is racially and ethnically diverse. In 1972, 87 percent of young adults ages eighteen through twenty-four were non-Hispanic whites; now non-Hispanic whites are only 60 percent of the cohort. Latinos make up nearly 20 percent, while African Americans remain at about the percentage they were in the 1970s (12–13 percent). Asian Americans now constitute nearly 5 percent. Even among relatively small immigrant populations, younger people have a predominant share.

Geography

The millennial generation is found in especially high concentrations in western and southwestern states and in major cities. The presence of large Hispanic populations in states such as California, Texas, Arizona, and New Mexico and the large Mormon populations in the mountain states of Utah, Idaho, and Nevada contribute to the large percentage of millennial residents in these places.

Democrats outnumber Republicans among millennials in every region of the country, but the margin is especially large in the Northeast (56 percent Democratic, 29 percent Republican). The margin is narrowest in the South (46 percent Democratic, 38 percent Republican). Even among whites, millennials are more Democratic than Gen X and the late baby boomers in every region except the South.

One striking aspect of states and regions experiencing rapid growth of minorities is the presence of what the demographer William Frey calls a racial generation gap—a situation in which the young population is highly diverse ethnically and racially, while the older population is overwhelmingly white.[2] It is apparent in states such as California, where a substantial majority of millennials are members of racial and ethnic minority groups and an equally large majority of preboomers are white. It is also evident in fast-growing states such as Georgia, where an already substantial young black population is being expanded by an in-migration of African Americans (there also is growth in the Hispanic and Asian populations). This racial generation gap is magnified in urban areas, adding the element of cultural conflict to the already significant potential for competition between older and younger people for public resources.

While young people have long found urban areas attractive, this gravitational pull has been accelerated as rising educational levels, cultural changes, and the growth of the "knowledge economy" have increased the mobility of the young. Joseph Cortright observes that "the growth in the number of college-educated young adults is fueling prosperity in places like Austin, Charlotte, Atlanta, Portland and Phoenix."[3] Even within destination cities, younger residents choose to live in different places than their predecessors did, preferring close-in neighborhoods. Such choices have implications for the economic vitality of urban areas, bringing new life to locations that may have even lost residents. Locational decisions also have political implications, creating concentrations of more socially liberal voters. Many magnet cities are in conservative states like Texas, North Carolina, and Virginia and may contribute to a political shift in these states.

Other demographic shifts with implications for politics include new patterns of migration among African Americans. In addition to no longer leaving the South and in fact returning to the South, they also are moving to fast-growing cities in the interior West, the South, and the Southwest (Atlanta, Dallas, Tampa, Las Vegas, Phoenix, Sacramento). In so doing, they add to the already sizable minority populations in these locations. The political clout of these newcomers will depend on black-Hispanic relations, among other factors.

Technology

It is not the least bit hyperbolic to describe the innovation in digital technology since the 1990s as a revolution, with far-reaching economic, social, and political implications. Millennials came of age during this revolution. If most of the rest of us are merely profoundly affected by it, millennials have lived and absorbed it. No one yet knows how these changes will affect the politics of the country. Howard Dean's campaign in 2004 was made possible in large part by the ability of his supporters to organize from the bottom up, using the Internet. It turned out that most of these activists were not in fact young but were baby boomers.[4] Yet it is a good bet that young people will have the last word, or laugh, on how technology changes the country's politics.

The numbers make this clear (table 7-2): 90 percent of millennials interviewed in the fall of 2007 were Internet users; 69 percent had e-mailed, sent an instant message, or sent a cell phone text message in the past day. In an earlier survey 13 percent of millennials and 9 percent of the Gen X and younger boomer cohort said they get news by way of their cell phone, PDA, or podcast; hardly anyone in older groups was doing this.

Perhaps the most significant innovation is the growth of social networking sites, such as MySpace, Facebook, and LinkedIn. These sites have attracted enormous numbers of members, not to mention large sums of capital. A late December 2007 Pew poll found that 62 percent of millennials used one of these sites, and 25 percent said they had gotten information about presidential candidates or their campaigns on the site. Nearly 8 percent had "friended" a candidate (publicly endorsing him or her and encouraging others to do so).

Table 7-2. The Generations and Technology

Percent

Technology use	Total	Millennials	Late boomers/ Gen X	Early boomers	Preboomers
Internet user	73	90	78	76	36
Cell phone only	13	30	12	6	2
Cell + landline	62	53	71	65	50
Landline only	25	17	17	29	48
Yesterday sent or received					
Text message	19	43	20	7	4
E-mail message	65	56	70	69	63
Instant message	21	29	22	15	14
Any of these three	56	69	63	50	37
Personal letter	20	18	22	19	18
Uses social network sites	22	62	14	7	1
Received campaign info from social network sites	7	25	2	1	0
"Friended" a candidate	2	8	1	1	0
Get news from					
Cell phone	5	8	6	1	1
Blackberry or Palm Pilot	2	4	3	1	0
Podcast	2	4	3	1	0
Any of these three	7	13	9	3	1

Source: Pew Research Center; National Health Interview surveys.

The full implications of social networking technology for politics will not be known for some time, and it is unclear that it is having a concrete impact on the political process, but there certainly is a lot of political activity and communication associated with it. Networking technology is inherently decentralizing, which shifts control from leaders to motivated followers and to those who best understand how the technology can be used in a variety of settings. Thus young people who have employed social networking technology to organize social activity, find common-interest groups, and establish personal identities may be better able to guide the application of these technologies for political uses. In turn this will give millennials influence that might not have come their way through conventional political channels.

Family and Work

Most millennials are very satisfied with their work and family lives. A very high percentage of them maintain regular contact with their parents, and the vast majority say that their parents spent an adequate amount of time with them while they were growing up. While not fully satisfied with their economic situation, young people are little different from older cohorts in their assessment of their finances (table 7-3).

Two-thirds of millennials say that their parents spent about the right amount of time with them while they were growing up, the same percentage

Table 7-3. The Generations and Their Characteristics and Views
Percent

Characteristics and views	Total	Millennials	Late boomers/ Gen X	Early boomers	Preboomers
Very happy with life	34	28	36	33	37
Very satisfied with					
Standard of living	42	39	38	41	52
Family life	72	73	73	73	70
Housing situation	63	52	63	66	72
Always feel rushed	24	25	29	22	12
Parental attention to you					
Too little	26	22	31	23	22
About right	69	66	67	74	73
Too much	4	11	2	2	3
If parents are living					
Talk with them daily	32	42	29	24	32
Talk with them weekly	46	43	50	48	26
Low social trust	38	48	39	37	26

Source: Pew Research Center.

as the Gen X and late baby boomer cohort. One in five say they did not receive enough parental attention, comparable to older baby boomers and preboomers but lower than the 31 percent of Generation X, who complain that they did not get enough time with their parents. One in ten millennials say that their parents spent too much time with them.

Millennials appear to be keeping in remarkably close touch with their parents: 42 percent say they talk with their parents every day, and a comparable number do so at least weekly. Gen X and younger boomers are less likely to talk with parents daily, but overall they match the millennials in at least weekly contact.

Social values regarding family and marriage are undergoing substantial change. Fewer millennials than other age cohorts say that sex between unmarried adults is always or almost always wrong: just 26 percent believe this, compared with 37 percent of the Gen X and late boomer cohort, 40 percent of early boomers, and 54 percent of the World War II generation.

Most millennials (62 percent) do say that marriage is important when a man and a woman plan to spend the rest of their lives together as a couple, but this percentage is considerably lower than among other cohorts (68 percent of Gen X and late boomers, 74 percent of early boomers, and 81 percent of the World War II generation). Similar percentages of each cohort say that marriage is important when a couple has a child together. As a corollary, just 51 percent describe the growing number of children born to unmarried mothers as a "big problem." At least 72 percent of all other age groups see this as a big problem.

If hair ("shoulder length or longer") was a distinguishing characteristic of the youthful early boomer generation, tattoos, body piercing, and hair color are the distinguishing characteristics of young people today (table 7-4). Four in ten millennials report that they have or have had a tattoo. One-third say that they have a piercing somewhere other than their ear. And a quarter report having had their hair dyed in an untraditional color. Older generations—even the Gen X and late boomer cohort—are much less likely to report these kinds of personal adornment.

Young people have complex reactions to work. The vast majority of millennials who are employed express satisfaction with most aspects of their jobs (table 7-5). Surveys have long found high levels of job satisfaction generally (people tend not to stay in jobs in which they are very unhappy), but what is notable is that young people do not differ from others despite the fact that fewer of them work in career-oriented positions than is true for older cohorts and a majority say they have no retirement plan other than Social Security.

Table 7-4. The Generations and Body Art

Percent

Body art	Total	Millennials	Late boomers/ Gen X	Early boomers
A tattoo	24	41	23	8
Men	25	37	24	9
Women	23	44	22	8
Hair dyed an untraditional color	17	26	17	10
Men	15	21	17	4
Women	20	31	18	14
Piercing somewhere other than the ear	15	33	11	4
Men	13	23	12	4
Women	17	43	11	5

Source: Pew Research Center.

About nine in ten express satisfaction with the kind of work they do and with their job security. Fewer say they are "completely satisfied" with these things (42 percent are completely satisfied with their job security), but this is comparable across all cohorts.

There is no evidence that young people are slackers. According to government surveys they work fewer mean hours per week than older cohorts, but their working hours are little different from their age counterparts of thirty years ago. Most of the age-related difference is a result of high levels of enrollment in college.

Table 7-5. The Generations and Work

Percent

Work	Total	Millennials	Late boomers/ Gen X	Early boomers	Preboomers
Current job					
Satisfied	90	88	90	90	95
Completely satisfied	28	30	27	27	43
Kind of work					
Satisfied	92	89	92	96	99
Completely satisfied	44	45	41	47	56
Job security					
Satisfied	84	88	83	85	81
Completely satisfied	39	42	37	39	48
Job gives sense of identity	51	50	53	53	46
Very likely to switch careers	28	49	25	12	14
Very likely to stay with current job	42	21	39	64	79
Has no retirement plan	38	62	30	26	39

Source: Pew Research Center.

One aspect of today's employment situation is quite different however: a much higher percentage of millennials (70 percent) than their age counterparts in 1977 (52 percent) say they are likely to leave their jobs in the next twelve months. Increased options for further education combined with a more dynamic job market likely account for this shift. It is interesting to note, however, that the percentage of Generation X saying they are likely to leave their current employer is about the same as their age counterparts in 1977, suggesting that the high level of job churn seen among the young is most characteristic of entry-level jobs.

Party Affiliation

The distinctive imprint of the 1960s and early 1970s is seen in the partisan identities of those who came of age during that period. Baby boomers born in the first ten years after World War II ended are much more likely than other adults (with the exception of the youngest cohort) to identify with the Democratic Party or to say they "lean" Democratic. According to Pew polling, 51 percent of those who turned eighteen between 1969 and 1972 are Democrats, compared with about 36 percent who are Republican (figure 7-1). Young people who have come of age since 1997 divide 51 percent Democratic to 33 percent Republican.

Figure 7-1. Party Affiliation, by Age, 2007

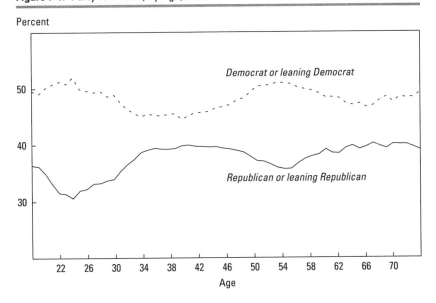

Percent

Democrat or leaning Democrat

Republican or leaning Republican

Age

In the age cohorts between the early segment of the baby boom generation and the millennials, party affiliation is more balanced. The Democratic Party still has an advantage, but it is much more modest. And it is also more modest among those who came of age before the baby boom generation.

While partisanship tends to be relatively stable throughout the life cycle, it does shift in response to events. In the past several years the Democrats have been advantaged among young people who are forming their political identities. In the 1980s the Republican Party finally achieved parity with Democrats after enduring decades of large Democratic advantages. Following a surge in Democratic support in the early 1990s, the GOP took a modest lead in party affiliation during 1994 and 1995, a change reflected in the election tsunami that washed away the Democratic Party's long-standing congressional majority. In the aftermath of 9/11, the GOP once again pulled even with the Democrats, but the advantage was fleeting. For most of the period from the mid-1990s to the present, an array of troubles for the party and for President Bush created a hospitable political climate for the Democrats as young people were forming their political identities. In particular, disillusionment with the Iraq War, the botched handling of Hurricane Katrina and its aftermath, economic problems, and the concomitant unpopularity of the president have significantly damaged the image of the Republican Party. This is seen most clearly in the fact that only 37 percent of adult registered voters affiliate or lean toward the party, the lowest number since before Ronald Reagan came into office (figure 7-2).

Figure 7-2. Party Identification, 2000–08

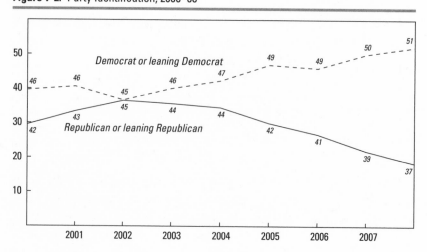

The shift is a product of two distinct forces. The recent decline in Republican identification is coming largely from a drop in the number of people who describe themselves as Republican in response to a question about their basic party affiliation. It is notable that the Democratic Party has not gained adherents, according to this indicator. The second source of change is that the balance of affiliation among leaners has shifted in favor of the Democratic Party. Young people are playing an important role in this movement because they are a disproportionate share of those who initially decline to affiliate with a party.

Society, Culture, and Religion

Across a range of measures, young people express more liberal or tolerant attitudes. And to the extent that we have longitudinal data on these issues, it is apparent that the age differences are not a function of life cycle but are generational.

One of the most divisive issues in recent U.S. politics is the question of homosexual rights. This took tangible political form in the 2004 election over whether gays and lesbians should be allowed to marry and was elevated on the political agenda by reaction to a Massachusetts Supreme Court decision in 2003 requiring the state to accommodate gay marriage. Young people are substantially more likely than older ones to favor gay marriage (figure 7-3).

Figure 7-3. Support for Gay and Lesbian Marriage, by Age, 2007

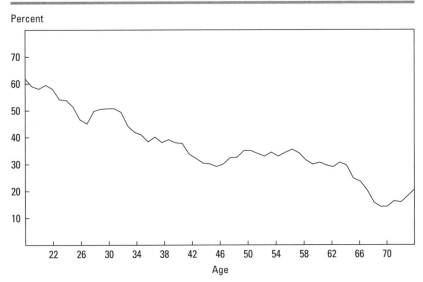

Percent

Age

Among millennials 58 percent favor gay marriage and 35 percent are opposed; the younger members of the cohort are the most supportive. Among older cohorts, 60 percent are opposed, with only 31 percent in favor.

Opinions on the issue of homosexuality are shifting. There is greater acceptance of homosexual teachers now than there was even ten years ago. And the portion who believe that homosexuality is innate rose from 20 percent in 1985 to 36 percent in 2006. Young people are actually more likely than others to believe that homosexuality is a lifestyle choice, though they also are more likely than other groups (except the early boomers) to believe that homosexuality cannot be changed.

Gay marriage and other policy questions related to homosexuality do not appear likely to play as large a role in the 2008 presidential election as they did in 2004, given the importance of the economy and the war in Iraq to voters. But the intensity of feeling on the gay marriage question, especially among those opposed to homosexual rights, guarantees that the issue will continue to be a polarizing one for some time to come. The generational change in acceptance of homosexuality as well as the slow shift in attitudes overall perhaps portend that the issue will eventually become less divisive in the long run. But in the next few years opinion shifts may simply lead to a more even division of opinion, which may lead to greater conflicts.

The same pattern of generational difference is seen on other social issues, including support for women's rights, the rights of African Americans, and acceptance of immigration and immigrants. Attitudes about race, in particular, have undergone tremendous change since the 1950s and 1960s (table 7-6). This change is seen in a variety of ways, including generally favorable views of blacks among whites, broad opposition to segregation, large increases in the percentage of people expressing willingness to vote for an African American candidate, and wide acceptance of interracial dating and marriage. Regarding the latter, millennials express near-universal acceptance of black-white dat-

Table 7-6. The Generations and Acceptance of Interracial Dating, 1987–88, 1997, 2007

Percent

Generation	1987–88	1997	2007	Change 1987–2007
Preboomers (born before 1946)	36	58	65	29
Early boomers (1946–55)	59	67	86	27
Late boomers/Gen X (1956–76)	n.a.	83	85	n.a.
Millennials (1977 on)	n.a.	n.a.	94	n.a.
Total	49	70	83	+34

Source: Pew Research Center.

ing, with boomers and Gen Xers not far behind. Those born before the baby boom are somewhat less supportive, but both they and the early boomers have become more accepting over the past twenty years.

On the issue of immigration, young people (who include a larger percentage of recent immigrants than other age cohorts do) express less concern than their elders about either the economic or cultural impact of immigration and are more supportive of a so-called path to citizenship for illegal immigrants already in the country (figure 7-4).

One important social issue is an exception to the pattern: abortion. Young people are not more accepting of abortion than most older people (figure 7-5); in fact, the youngest members of the millennial cohort are slightly more conservative on the issue (those in their mid-to-late seventies also tend to be less accepting of abortion than other age groups).

The greater liberalism of the millennial generation on most social issues is undoubtedly a product of many forces, but one in particular is related to religion. There are significant cohort differences in religiosity. Younger cohorts are less likely to be affiliated with a religious tradition and to agree with traditional beliefs about Judgment Day, prayer, and God. This is true in spite of the fact that the millennial cohort includes relatively larger numbers of recent immigrants, who tend to be more religious and to hold traditional religious beliefs.

Figure 7-4. Support for Illegal Immigrants' Path to Citizenship, by Age, 2007

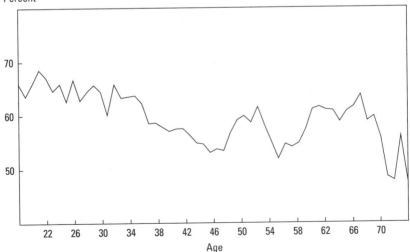

Figure 7-5. Support for Legal Abortion, by Age, 2007

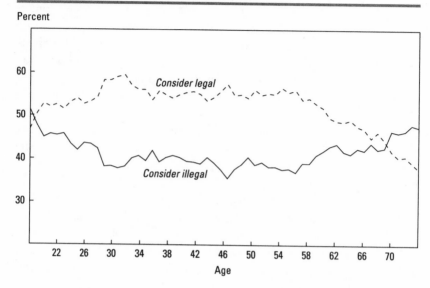

Religious affiliation among young people is a generational rather than a life-cycle phenomenon. Consider the percentage of people who reported being secular or unaffiliated during 2006–07 (figure 7-6). The strong relationship with age is apparent, which could be a product either of affiliation growing with age or of a generational difference. But the dotted line shows the percentage of unaffiliated among respondents in the same age cohorts interviewed early in the 1990s. It is clear that as these individuals aged their level of religious affiliation changed very little. Another way to see this is to group respondents into age cohorts and compare them at different points in time (table 7-7). The percentage of unaffiliated in each cohort has not changed over time, and a higher percentage of each new cohort is unaffiliated, compared with its predecessor.

One other important facet of generational shifts in religion is the growing number of non-Christians. While they remain a very small minority overall (about 5 percent), non-Christians (a group that includes Jews, Muslims, Hindus, Buddhists, and many others) are more numerous among younger cohorts.

Government and Business

The millennial generation also differs substantially from older ones on questions regarding the scope and performance of the national government,

Figure 7-6. No Religious Affiliation, by Age, 2007

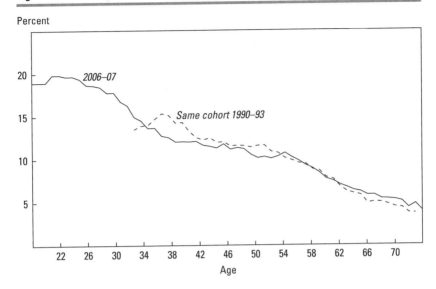

Percent

expressing greater support for active government and greater approval for the job that the government does. But there is good reason to doubt that this age-related difference is predominantly generational.

Young people, when asked to choose between a "bigger government providing more services or a smaller government providing fewer services," are much more likely than older people to opt for bigger government (figure 7-7). But this pattern is not new. In survey questions over the past several decades of polling, young people have consistently expressed greater support for activist government than have their elders, and as they age this distinctiveness is lost. The trend toward a preference for smaller government as one ages, if

Table 7-7. The Generations and Atheism, Agnosticism, or No Religion, 1987, 1997, and 2006–07

Percent

Generation	1987	1997	2006–07	Change 1987–2007
Preboomers (born before 1946)	5	4	5	0
Early boomers (1946–55)	10	9	11	+1
Late boomers/Gen X (1956–76)	n.a.	14	14	n.a.
Millennials (1977 on)	n.a.	n.a.	19	n.a.
Total	8	9	12	+4

Source: Pew Research Center.

Figure 7-7. Support for Big Government, by Age, 2007

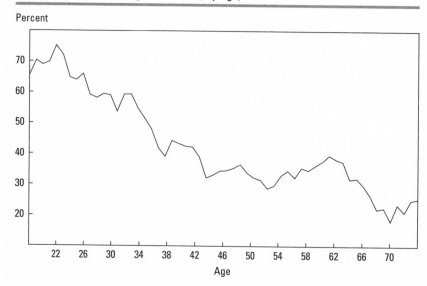

Percent

truly universal, may have occasioned Aristide Briand to remark (in one of many variations on the sentiment), "The man who is not a socialist at twenty has no heart, but if he is still a socialist at forty he has no head."

One issue of note does not fit this pattern: entitlement reform. President Bush's effort to persuade Congress to add private investment accounts to the Social Security system was met with skepticism and eventual resistance from most of the public. But young people reacted differently: they were substantially more open to the idea of having the ability to invest in the stock market and more supportive of the president's plan (figure 7-8). Part of the reason for this is that they are more likely than older people to believe they can make wise decisions about investments. And part of the reason may be skepticism about the solvency of the system. The possibility of an intergenerational clash over entitlement spending has been raised by many observers but has yet to materialize.

Support for bigger government is typically accompanied by skepticism about the power of business, but this pattern is weaker for young people (table 7-8). Indeed, young people are significantly more pro-business than other age groups. In Pew's 2007 values survey, 81 percent of millennials agreed that "the strength of this country is mostly based on the success of American business." In the sample as a whole 72 percent agreed with the statement.

Figure 7-8. Support for Private Social Security Accounts, by Age, 2007

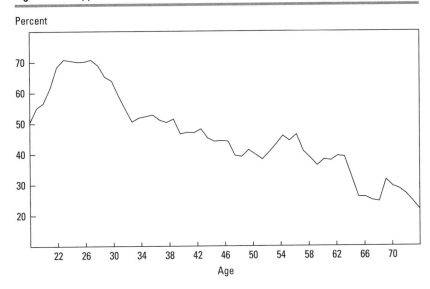

Percent

Age

Similarly, millennials are somewhat more likely than other age groups to say that business usually strikes a fair balance between making profits and serving the public interest. The youngest cohort was roughly divided on this question (45 percent agree, 52 percent disagree), but other cohorts tilted much more in an antibusiness direction (among the early boomers, 62 percent disagreed, 33 percent agreed). The more positive views of young people are manifested despite the fact that overall opinion on this question has become more negative in recent years.

The age pattern of responses on questions regarding government and business suggests that young people are less polarized on what is perhaps the cen-

Table 7-8. The Generations and Belief in Fairness of Business, 1987, 1997, 2007

Percent

Generation	1987	1997	2007	Change 1997–2007
Preboomers (born before 1946)	44	47	32	−15
Early boomer (1946–55)	38	32	33	1
Late boomers/Gen X (1956–76)	n.a.	47	37	−10
Millennials (1977 on)	n.a.	n.a.	45	n.a.
Total	42	45	38	−7

Source: Pew Research Center.

tral fault line of the national political alignment in place since the time of the New Deal. But whether this portends a significant change in U.S. politics is not clear. Given the evidence that progovernment views are at least partially related to life cycle, it is entirely reasonable to conclude that less polarization among young people means that they are simply less judgmental than older people about these institutions. Whether this is a result of a lack of knowledge or of youthful idealism is not known. It is intriguing that young people express significantly greater satisfaction with national conditions than older age groups do (figure 7-9).

Priorities

Despite the fact that young people have been in the vanguard of antiwar protests, it is not the case that youth in general are typically more opposed to the use of military force when faced with a decision about a specific conflict. A case in point is that during the mid-1960s older baby boomers were actually more supportive of the Vietnam War than older people were (table 7-9). In 1966 people ages twenty-one through twenty-nine overwhelmingly said that the war was not a mistake (71 percent versus 21 percent). Opinion was more divided, as well as uncertain, among those fifty years old and older

Figure 7-9. Satisfaction with the Way Things Are Going in the United States, by Age, 2007

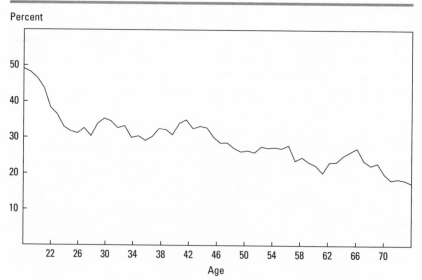

Table 7-9. Age Cohorts and Belief that the United States Made a Mistake in Going to War in Vietnam, March 1966 and May 1970

Percent

Opinion	Total	21–29	30–49	50+
March 1966				
Made a mistake	25	21	23	30
Did not make a mistake	59	71	63	48
Don't know	16	8	14	22
May 1970				
Made a mistake	56	49	53	61
Did not make a mistake	36	48	41	26
Don't know	8	3	6	13

Source: Gallup polls.

(30 percent said it was a mistake, 48 percent said it was not, and 22 percent had no opinion). Even in 1970, as protests were occurring on college campuses around the country, younger people remained less likely to say that the war was a mistake.

Pew Research Center polling before the start of the war in Iraq found a similar pattern, with young people more likely to say that they favored military action (table 7-10). Even as discontent about the war grew in the spring of 2004, young people continued to express greater certainty that the United States would achieve its goals in Iraq (62 percent of those ages eighteen through twenty-nine said this, compared with about 50 percent of those older than twenty-nine).

Current polling finds a somewhat different pattern about the war. In no age group does a majority believe that the United States made the right decision in using military force, and the millennial cohort is slightly less likely than Gen X or late boomers to say the war was right (figure 7-10). Millennials are more likely than other groups to say that this country should remove its troops from Iraq "as soon as possible" (figure 7-11), but these differences are relatively modest.

Table 7-10. Age Cohorts and Belief in Military Force against Iraq, Fall 2002

Percent

Opinion	21–29	30–49	50–64	65+
Favor	69	66	61	51
Oppose	23	24	26	31
Don't know	8	10	13	18

Source: Pew Research Center.

Figure 7-10. Support for Iraq Invasion, by Age, 2007

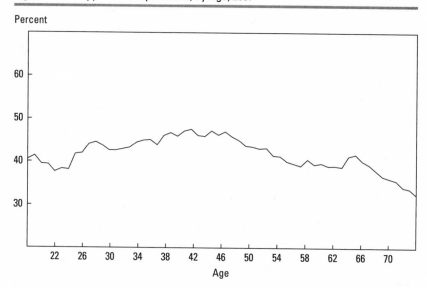

Figure 7-11. Support for Bringing the Troops Home from Iraq, by Age, 2007

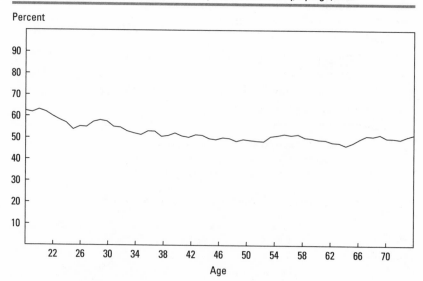

Apart from specific instances of military conflict, there are broader questions about the role of the United States in the world, including but not limited to the use of force. Following the election of 2004, the Pew Research Center found that the strongest predictor of the presidential vote was a question asking respondents about the use of military force in achieving peace. A version of this question has been asked since 1987. In general, younger cohorts have been less likely to say that force is the key to peace, and the millennials are no exception to this pattern (table 7-11). In 2007 the percentage of Americans taking this view was somewhat lower than it was in the 1980s and 1990s (and even lower than it was in 2002, in the aftermath of 9/11). In each sampling of the public, younger people have been less supportive of military force, and millennials (at 43 percent agreement) fall 6 points below the national average.

One conclusion from this review of attitudes about war is that young people tend to be more skeptical of the use of military force in principle than in practice, at least when facing a new conflict. Young people have shifted more in an antiwar direction over the course of the conflict in Iraq, but before its start and in its early months they were somewhat more supportive than other age groups.

One of the most important facets of political power is the ability to set the agenda—to determine what issues will be dealt with by the legislature and the executive. The political agenda is influenced by many forces, but one of them is what the citizenry considers to be priorities. This leads to an obvious question: Are the issue priorities of different age cohorts similar or different? As table 7-12 shows—somewhat surprisingly—on many issues there is little difference in the priority that older and younger people assign to them.

However, a few exceptions are revealing. More young people rate education as a high priority, and fewer are concerned about Social Security. They

Table 7-11. The Generations on Achieving Peace through Military Strength, 1987, 1997, and 2007

Percent

Generation	1987	1997	2007
Preboomers	64	73	56
Early boomers	51	59	54
Late boomers/Gen X	n.a.	48	48
Millennials	n.a.	n.a.	43
Total	56	57	49

Source: Pew Research Center.

Table 7-12. Priorities of the Cohorts

Percent

Priority	Total	Millennials	Late boomers/ Gen X	Early boomers	Preboomers
Strengthening economy	75	75	78	73	75
Defending against terrorism	74	70	75	74	76
Reducing health care costs	69	69	67	77	65
Improving education	66	79	68	60	52
Securing Social Security	64	57	59	75	73
Creating jobs	61	65	59	62	64
Securing Medicare	60	57	55	66	68
Resolving energy problems	59	51	62	63	60
Reducing budget deficit	58	56	55	61	63
Protecting environment	56	61	54	59	55
Reducing crime	55	59	52	54	60
Providing health insurance	54	62	54	58	42
Dealing with problems of poor	51	53	53	53	47
Dealing with illegal immigration	51	43	49	54	67
Reducing middle-class taxes	46	46	45	45	51
Dealing with moral breakdown	44	38	41	46	53
Strengthening the military	42	27	44	41	51
Reducing influence of lobbyists	39	21	35	57	52
Dealing with global trade	37	35	37	39	40
Dealing with global warming	35	39	34	39	31
Making income tax cuts permanent	29	37	34	44	36

Source: Pew Research Center.

are also less likely to say that dealing with illegal immigration is a high priority, and there is an even bigger gap between them and other age groups—especially preboomers—on the need to strengthen the military. Compared with older people, they are somewhat less likely to place a high priority on dealing with energy problems and only slightly more likely to say that the environment and global warming should be top priorities. (The environment barely makes the top third of the list for young people, and global warming falls into the bottom third of the list.) Similar patterns are seen when the questions are posed in terms of importance of each issue area to prospective presidential votes.

Older Americans, understandably, place a higher priority on securing Social Security and Medicare, concerns that are matched by the early boomers. The latter group is especially concerned about reducing health care costs, perhaps because most of them are not yet eligible for government-sponsored insurance, are encountering more health problems, and may be dealing with the health care expenses of older children and elderly parents as well. Early boomers also place great emphasis on reducing the influence of lobbyists, a problem of little concern to millennials. Early boomers and millennials express similar levels of concern about the environment and global warming.

Political and Civic Engagement

The question of whether the millennial generation helps to mitigate or exacerbate political polarization depends not only on the nature of their opinions but also on the degree to which they are politically engaged and the form their participation takes. Many observers lament the low levels of engagement among younger generations.[5] Young people have long lagged behind their elders in political participation. Typical of current indicators is a question asked periodically by the Pew Research Center about following government and public affairs (figure 7-12). Only about 30 percent of young respondents follow public affairs "most of the time," compared to about 70 percent of older respondents.

There are many good reasons for this gap in engagement. Young people lack motivation, resources, and opportunities to follow the conventional political discourse. Many of these deficiencies will correct themselves as they become settled in a community, have children, pay taxes, accumulate knowledge about the political world, and build social networks that include politi-

Figure 7-12. Followers of Public Affairs, by Age, 2007

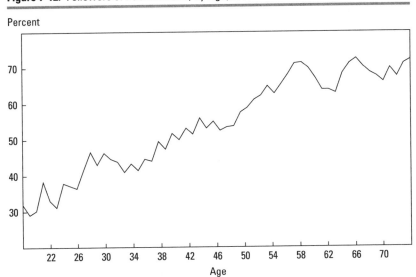

Percent

Age

cally active people. The more important question is whether the gap is growing, shrinking, or staying about the same. It is also important to know the nature and extent of the gap; that is, are some forms of participation more difficult or more amenable for young people? And it is important to know what the political impact of the gap is: How would our politics be different if younger people participated at rates similar to that of older Americans?

These questions are at the heart of a lively debate among scholars and practitioners. One assessment of the state of civic and political engagement places much of the blame for a decline in social capital and civic engagement on generational change (perhaps aided and abetted by television). Others argue that a revival in some types of engagement may be under way.[6] In research conducted with Cliff Zukin, Molly Andolina, Krista Jenkins, and Michael X. Delli Carpini, I found that millennials come much closer to older cohorts in some forms of civic engagement, particularly regular volunteer activity, and in the expression of certain types of political voice.[7] Russell J. Dalton goes further, arguing that social and political changes in the past few decades have brought about a shift in the very definition of good citizenship, from a duty-based notion to what he calls engaged citizenship.[8] These changes, he argues, are not limited to the United States but can be seen in many Western democracies. Martin P. Wattenberg notes the evidence for gains in some forms of participation but concludes that the age gaps remain very substantial.[9]

The most significant gap in participation is in voter turnout. Despite the fact that voting is considered by many to be an easy form of participation, young people fall far below older ones in rates of voter registration and turnout. The median reported rate of turnout among voting age (and eligible) adults ages eighteen through twenty-four over the past five presidential elections is 40 percent; among those ages twenty-five and older, the median turnout rate is 63 percent. The gap is even larger in off-year congressional elections.[10]

Though characterized by ups and downs, especially a spike in 1992, voter turnout has slowly trended downward among young people in the elections following the adoption of the Twenty-Sixth Amendment in 1971, which lowered the national voting age to eighteen. At the same time, the trend among those twenty-five and older was relatively flat, with the effect that the turnout gap between older and younger Americans was growing (figure 7-13).

Owing in part to the intensely polarized political climate of the time and partly to vigorous efforts by political parties, political campaigns, and mobilization efforts by other kinds of organizations, young people voted at substantially higher rates in the 2004 presidential election than in the two previous contests, closing the turnout gap with older Americans to its small-

Figure 7-13. Voter Turnout, by Age Group, 1972–2004

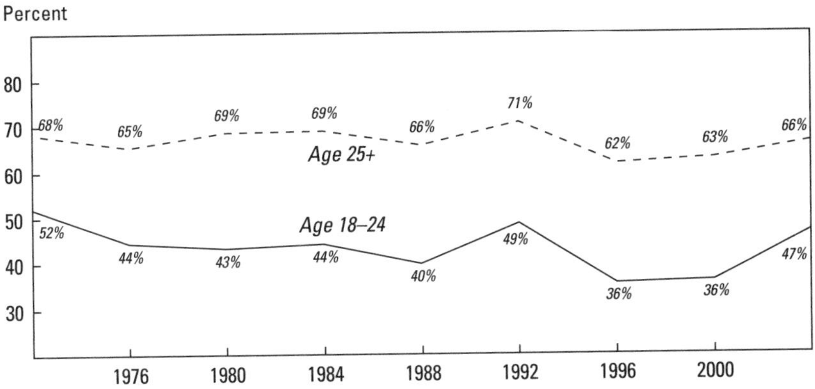

Percent

Source: U.S. Census surveys analyzed by CIRCLE.

est point since 1972 and contributing much of the overall spike in turnout observed that year. Indeed, focusing only on the highly contested states where the bulk of mobilizing activity took place, the surge in youth turnout was even greater than that observed nationally. And in 2006, in similarly charged circumstances, the turnout gap also shrank compared with previous elections (though the size of the spike in youth turnout was understandably more modest).

In addition to showing a smaller turnout gap, young people were also catching up with older people in other forms of electoral engagement. In presidential elections through much of the 1980s and 1990s, young people lagged behind in the number who tried to influence the vote of other people, who attended a campaign event, or who exhibited their candidate allegiance by displaying a sticker, button, or sign. In 2004 younger people reported that they did these activities at slightly higher rates than older people.

The evidence from these elections suggests that the forces acting upon young people were different from those in the past, perhaps a reflection of the particular and unique circumstances of the times. The terrorist attacks of 9/11, the intense reactions to George W. Bush, and the war in Iraq all may have contributed to these changes. And young Americans may also be reflecting other positive aspects of their socialization during the 1990s.

The UCLA survey of college freshmen also reflects an uptick in political interest, with the number of freshmen saying that it is very important to keep up to date with political affairs rising in the past few years, after nearly a decade of decline. Newspaper readership among young people, while very low, appears to have stabilized after a long period of decline. Data from the General Social Survey indicate that the rate of newspaper reading among the millennial generation is about the same as it has been over the past decade and a half among Generation X. The Gen X rate is lower than the boomer rate, which in turn is lower than the rate for the oldest cohort.

In other ways as well, there are positive signs regarding the engagement of the millennial generation. Rates of civic activity such as volunteering, community problem solving, and charitable fundraising among millennials are comparable to those of older cohorts. A 2006 survey by CIRCLE, assessing engagement in the three dimensions of civic, electoral, and political voice, found that young people (ages fifteen to twenty-five) participated at rates comparable to, or only modestly behind, older adults on most measures (table 7-13).[11]

While Dalton—and to a lesser degree Zukin and others—argues that the patterns of civic engagement among the young are signaling a possible trans-

Table 7-13. Civic and Electoral Activity, Two Age Groups, 2006
Percent

Activity	15–25	26 and older
Civic		
Volunteered in last year	36	34
Raised money for charity in last year	24	29
Active member of at least one group	20	26
Regular volunteer for nonpolitical group	19	24
Community problem solving in last year	19	20
Ran/walked/biked for charity in last year	18	15
Electoral		
Tried to persuade others in an election	35	40
Is regular voter	26	56
Displayed campaign button or sign	23	28
Member of group involved in politics	16	26
Donated money to a candidate or party	7	14
Regular volunteer for political candidates or groups	2	3
Political voice		
Engaged in boycott in last year	30	38
Engaged in buycott in last year	29	33
Signed a paper petition in last year	18	26
Signed an e-mail petition in last year	16	21
Contacted an official in last year	11	22
Protested in last year	11	5
Contacted print media in last year	7	11
Contacted broadcast media in last year	9	8
Canvassed in last year	3	2

Source: Center for Information and Research on Civic Learning and Engagement (CIRCLE).

formation in styles of citizenship, Wattenberg offers important caveats.[12] In addition to noting the relatively modest size of the differences between younger and older adults on many of these indicators, increased volunteer activity among the young may be tied more to high school requirements and resume buffing by college-bound young people than by a revival of civic virtue. While these cautions are well-taken, it seems clear that many positive changes are occurring, even if the trends are weak and the causes ambiguous.

The Future, Near and Far

The present is only partially a prologue to the future. The wide partisan skew now seen among young people does not portend that Republicans can never win among this age group. From watching previous cohorts of young people we can reasonably predict that this one will become more skeptical of government and perhaps more economically conservative. Less likely is the possibility that it will become more socially conservative and—relevant to the Democratic Party's nomination contest in 2008—unaccepting of black or female political candidates.

Despite the shifts in party affiliation in the past few years, decades of political science research demonstrate the fundamental durability of party affiliation once it has been assumed in adolescence. The sizable swings in Democratic and Republican identification seen in the past several years suggest that movement in response to events is still possible, but the persistence of a Democratic advantage among older baby boomers shows why early impressions matter: they provide an attachment to a party that endures during harder times. Popular presidencies attract young people to a party, and unpopular ones repel them, and no one can predict how successful a McCain or Obama presidency will be.

The 2008 Election

In the short run, the Democratic tilt of young voters is potentially bad news for the GOP. In the primary elections in 2008, voter turnout was up very sharply, especially among young people. They are a larger share of the expanded electorates in most states where good comparisons to previous primaries exist (table 7-14). Turnout in Republican primaries has also been up (compared with 2000, the last time the party had a competitive race), but the increase among young people has been more modest than in Democratic contests.

Table 7-14. Democratic Primary and Caucus Voters, Ages Seventeen through Twenty-Nine as Share of Total Voting, by State, 2008 and 2004

Percent

Primary or caucus	2008	2004
Iowa caucus	22	17
Georgia	18	11
New Hampshire	18	14
Utah	17	n.a.
Ohio	16	9
Texas	16	10
Wisconsin	16	n.a.
California	16	11
Illinois	15	n.a.
New York	15	8
Maryland	14	8
Virginia	14	n.a.
Massachusetts	14	9
Missouri	14	9
South Carolina	14	9
Mississippi	14	n.a.
Rhode Island	13	n.a.
Alabama	13	n.a.
Tennessee	13	7
Pennsylvania	12	n.a.
Vermont	11	n.a.
Connecticut	10	5
Arkansas	9	n.a.
Oklahoma	9	6
New Mexico	8	n.a.
Arizona	8	7
Total	14	9

Source: NEP exit polls.

Younger voters are strongly supportive of the candidacy of Barack Obama, the youngest candidate in the race. His multicultural background and campaign message of a break with the past—even the relatively well-regarded recent past of Bill Clinton's administration—resonate with millennial voters (table 7-15). Hillary Clinton remained generally popular with those eighteen through twenty-nine, even if they have not chosen her in the primaries. (It is useful to keep in mind that younger members of the millennial generation would not have adult memories of the Clinton presidency: eighteen-year-old voters in 2008 were eleven years old when Bill Clinton left office.) Young voters strongly supported John Kerry and turned out in record numbers for him in the 2004 general election contest, despite giving him relatively modest personal ratings. This suggests that the main thing many Democratic members of this cohort want to change is the Bush administration.

Table 7-15. Democratic Primary Support among Voters Ages Seventeen through
Twenty-Nine, by State

Percent

State	Obama	Clinton
Virginia	78	22
Georgia	77	20
Mississippi	73	25
Illinois	69	29
South Carolina	67	23
Missouri	65	30
Maryland	64	34
Vermont	64	31
Alabama	64	32
Wisconsin	64	33
Ohio	61	35
Pennsylvania	60	40
Texas	59	40
New Jersey	59	39
Arizona	59	37
Connecticut	58	39
Iowa	57	11
New York	56	43
New Mexico	55	42
Rhode Island	53	47
Tennessee	53	44
New Hampshire	51	28
California	49	49
Massachusetts	48	49
Arkansas	43	56
Total	59	35

Source: NEP exit polls.

On the Republican side, younger voters are somewhat less supportive of
the presumptive nominee, John McCain, who does best among the oldest
of GOP primary voters.

But the potential for the Democratic tilt among the young to do immediate harm to the Republican Party continues to be mitigated by the low
levels of conventional political activity in this age group. Although their
turnout is up, young cohorts still fall well below older cohorts in their rate
of participation. This will change in time. Young people were John Kerry's
best age group in 2004 and probably will be the Democratic candidate's best
group in 2008—and there likely will be more of these voters this time
around. But they remain a minority, and their clout is further diminished by
their low turnout.

Nevertheless, it is important to remember that the political views of much
of the American public have relatively shallow roots and, at least in the short

run, can be shifted by events. The attitudinal roots among the young are especially shallow. Moreover, politics today are marked by an exceedingly close balance between the parties, in which even modest shifts among small groups can change the outcome of elections. What young people do—or do not do—politically matters a great deal.

Also relevant to a consideration of the future is the fact that the early baby boom generation—a key part of the Democratic constituency—is getting older. The more conservative and Republican-leaning late boomer and Gen X cohort will soon be taking over, as early boomers move into retirement. That demographic fact does not ensure that the GOP will stage a rally, but given the partisan leanings of the age group immediately on deck, it will make life easier for the Republican Party.

The Generations and Polarization

How will generational change affect the level of polarization in American politics? At least three cohort differences could shape the degree to which America is a purple nation as opposed to a red or blue nation.

One: religion, one source of political polarization, is undergoing significant change. Growth in the secular, religiously unaffiliated population, for example, could lessen political polarization. Further, religious diversity is growing. James Madison, in *Federalist* No. 51, discusses how religious diversity could reduce the potential for tyranny by a majority. He is not talking about polarization per se, but a similar logic might explain why religious conflict has been more muted in the United States than in some other countries. Religiously mixed marriages are not unusual in this country, and interactions in school, work settings, and social life tend to bring us into contact with people from a wide range of religious backgrounds. Even within large religious groups such as Protestants, the diversity in beliefs and practices is very great. The absence of sizable blocs of intensely committed followers of particular religions reduces the potential for conflict.

Two: the political views of millennials do not fit together in quite the same way as those of earlier generations. To some extent, this is a pattern seen in the past as younger people take their time to learn politics. But millennials may be more likely than their predecessors to reject the connectedness of certain issues. It is clear that the alignment of social and economic conservatism (and its counterpart on the left) underlying today's partisan system is not necessarily a natural or logical one and may be undermined by generational changes in social and cultural values. Political scientists long ago wrote about the role of cross-cutting cleavages in reducing or mitigating political conflict.

While the term often referred to the patchwork of political interests and social factors that apply to individuals, it also can refer to the alignment of opinions. A dealignment of cleavages could contribute to a reduction in polarization.

Three: generational changes in the style and nature of political engagement—as yet only tantalizing and suggestive—could lead to lower levels of polarization. Even if the underlying values of citizens—values that will remain in conflict—do not change, the ways that citizens bring these values to political expression is one factor in the intensity of political dispute. Dalton's notion of engaged citizenship, involving as it does a more personal and communal style, may be less amenable to the harsh rhetoric and tactics characteristic of our polarized politics.

Notes

1. Neil Howe and William Strauss, *Millennials Rising: The Next Great Generation* (New York: Random House, 2000).

2. William H. Frey, "America's Regional Demographics in the 00's Decade: The Role of Seniors, Boomers, and New Minorities," special report (Research Institute for Housing America and Brookings, 2006).

3. Joseph Cortright, "The Young and Restless in a Knowledge Economy" (Chicago: CEOs for Cities, 2005), p. 5.

4. Scott Keeter, Courtney Kennedy, and Cary Funk, "Deaniacs and Democrats," in *The State of the Parties: The Changing Role of Contemporary American Politics,* edited by John C. Green and Daniel J. Coffey (Lanham, Md.: Rowman and Littlefield, 2005).

5. See, for example, Robert D. Putnam, *Bowling Alone: The Collapse and Revival of American Community* (New York: Simon and Schuster, 2000).

6. Ibid.

7. Cliff Zukin and others, *A New Engagement? Political Participation, Civic Life, and the Changing American Citizen* (Oxford University Press, 2006).

8. Russell J. Dalton, *The Good Citizen: How a Younger Generation Is Reshaping American Politics* (Washington: CQ Press, 2008).

9. Martin P. Wattenberg, *Is Voting for Young People?* (New York: Pearson Longman, 2008).

10. Tabulations by Center for Information and Research on Civic Learning and Engagement (CIRCLE), University of Maryland (www.civicyouth.org/popups/factsheets/FS_youth_voting_72-04.pdf [January 13, 2008]).

11. Center for Information and Research on Civic Learning and Engagement (CIRCLE), "Census Data Shows Youth Voter Turnout Surged More than among Any Other Age Group (http://civicyouth.org/popups/releasecps04_youth.pdf).

12. Dalton, *The Good Citizen;* Zukin and others, *A New Engagement?;* Wattenberg, *Is Voting for Young People?*

Contributors

Alan Abramowitz
Emory University

Alan Berube
Brookings Institution

Bill Bishop
Austin American-Statesman

Robert Cushing
University of Texas–Austin

E. J. Dionne Jr.
Brookings Institution

William Frey
Brookings Institution

John Green
Pew Forum on Religion
    and Public Life
University of Akron

Scott Keeter
Pew Research Center

Robert Lang
Virginia Tech

Thomas Sanchez
University of Utah

Tom W. Smith
University of Chicago

Ruy Teixeira
Brookings Institution
Center for American Progress
Century Foundation

Index

Figures and tables are denoted by f and t following page numbers.

196, 209; and postwar period, 206–07, 211, 213; as Republicans, 70, 209, 212, 217; support for Bush (G. W.), 201–03, 218; support for Kerry, 204; as trend in American society, 195–96, 198, 199–200, 214, 221; white, 6, 194, 197, 200. *See also* Protestants; Religion

Exurbs: classification of, 28, 30; and commuting patterns, 28; and emerging suburbs, 7–8; and House vote, 33; Huckabee's success in, 70; population growth in, 1, 7, 31; Republican support in, 26, 35, 36; support for Kerry in, 32; support for Obama in, 38–39; in 2000–06 national elections, 34; voters from, 5. *See also* Counties; Suburban politics

Fairfax County (Virginia), 27, 28, 29, 36
Faith and faith-based politics. *See* Evangelicals; Religion
Falwell, Jerry, 220
Families and family values, 147–93; attitudes toward, 35, 147, 151–57, 162, 164; and cohabitation, 152, 164, 169*t*, 180*t*; and divorce, 152, 163, 180*t*; future trends, 15, 160–61, 162, 164, 193*t*; and gender roles, 150–51, 153–55, 162, 164, 178*t*–179*t*; and generational forces, 232–35; and labor-force participation, 150–51, 161, 172*t*, 178*t*–179*t*; and marriage, 14, 148, 152, 164, 168*t*, 171*t*–172*t*, 180*t*; and millennials, 232–35, 232*t*; and neighborhoods, 156, 186*t*; nuclear, 228; and politics, 157–59, 163, 188*t*–191*t*; and sexual mores and practices, 14, 155–56, 162, 184*t*–185*t*; and socioeconomic status, 159–60, 191*t*, 192*t*; structure of, 1, 15, 147, 157–60,

161–64, 187*t*, 183*t*, 188*t*. *See also* Children
Federalist No. 51 (Madison), 256
Fenton, John, 67–68
Fertility rates. *See* Birth rates and fertility
Fishman, Robert, 26
Fitzgerald, Thomas, 216–17, 218, 219
Florida, 80, 95
Ford, Gerald, 50–51, 118
Foreign-born residents, 63, 63*f*
Frank, Thomas, 68, 120, 123, 127, 129
Franklin County (Ohio), 29
Frey, William H., 10–11, 79, 229–30

Gaps. *See* Affiliation gap; Attendance gap; God gap; Translation gap
Gays and gay marriage. *See* Homosexuals and homosexuality
Gender roles, 14, 150–51, 153–55, 162, 164, 178*t*, 179*t*. *See also* Men; Women
General Social Survey (GSS), 14, 87, 89, 252
Generational effects. *See* Cohort differences and effects
Generational forces, 225–57; family and work, 17, 232–35, 232*t*; future trends, 253–57; and geography, 229–30; government and business, 19, 240–44, 242*f*, 243*t*; and millennials, 17, 228–53; and party affiliation, 235–37, 235*f*, 236*f*, 254*t*, 255*t*; and polarization, 256–57; political and civic engagement, 19, 249–53, 251*f*, 257; and priorities, 19, 244–49, 244*t*–245*t*, 246*f*, 247*t*–248*t*; society, culture, and religion, 20, 237–40, 237*f*, 238*t*, 239*f*, 240*f*, 241*f*, 241*t*; and technology, 18, 230–32, 231*t*; in today's society, 226–28, 226*t*; and 2008 presidential election,